D1082594

How Ottawa Spends
2003–2004

*Regime Change
and Policy Shift*

EDITED BY
G. BRUCE DOERN

OXFORD
UNIVERSITY PRESS

OXFORD

UNIVERSITY PRESS

70 Wynford Drive, Don Mills, Ontario M3C 1J9
www.oup.com/ca

Oxford University Press is a department of the University of Oxford.
It furthers the University's objective of excellence in research, scholarship,
and education by publishing worldwide in

Oxford New York
Auckland Bangkok Buenos Aires Cape Town Chennai
Dar es Salaam Delhi Hong Kong Istanbul Karachi Kolkata
Kuala Lumpur Madrid Melbourne Mexico City Mumbai Nairobi
São Paulo Shanghai Taipei Tokyo Toronto

Oxford is a trade mark of Oxford University Press
in the UK and in certain other countries

Published in Canada
by Oxford University Press

The National Library of Canada has catalogued this publication as follows:
How Ottawa spends
1983-
Prepared at the School of Public Administration, Carleton University.
Publisher varies.
Continues: How Ottawa spends your tax dollars, ISSN 0711-4990.
Includes bibliographical references.
ISSN 0822-6482
ISBN 0-19-541917-0 (2003-2004 edition)

1. Canada—Appropriations and expenditures—Periodicals.
I. Carleton University. School of Public Administration

HJ7663.S6   354.710072'2   C84-030303-3

1 2 3 4 – 06 05 04 03

This book is printed on permanent (acid-free) paper ♾.

Printed in Canada

Contents

Preface

Special thanks are owed to our contributing authors, drawn from several universities across Canada and internationally. Their willingness to contribute their time and analytical effort is crucial to providing a high-quality publication. The contributions and professionalism of Michele Morrison, Donna Malone, Rachel Laforest, and Karine Levasseur in the School of Public Policy and Administration have been crucial not only technically but also in the provision of the two appendices. The excellent editorial work of Douglas Campbell is also gratefully acknowledged, as is the support of Laura McLeod and Mark Piel at Oxford University Press.

My personal thanks are also extended to my colleagues and to the secretarial staff in the School of Public Policy and Public Administration at Carleton University, and in the Politics Department at the University of Exeter.

G. Bruce Doern
Ottawa
February 2003

The opinions expressed by the contributors to this volume are the personal views of the authors of individual chapters and do not necessarily reflect the view of the Editor or the School of Public Policy and Administration at Carleton University.

1

Governing Unnaturally: The Liberals, Regime Change, and Policy Shift

G. BRUCE DOERN

This year's How Ottawa Spends covers a period of Canadian politics that historians are bound to view as unique. We examine how Canada's natural governing party, the Liberal Party of Canada, is governing 'unnaturally'. Prime Minister Jean Chrétien, relatively fresh from a third straight majority government mandate, conferred by Canadian voters in 2000, is ousted by his party at the instigation of the heir apparent, Paul Martin, and apparently also with the implicit support of the Canadian electorate, as gauged by opinion polls. The net result in the 2002 to 2004 period is 'regime change' and policy shift, with the real and imagined legacies of the departing leader clashing with the hoped-for policies of the imagined new regime. And the old and new regimes are caught up in a House of Commons that is also displaying an unaccustomed assertiveness against its leaders on both the government and opposition sides of the partisan divide, but in a situation where the opposition parties are weak and in disarray. As a direct result, the Martin 'government-in-waiting' sits inside the divided Liberal Party of Canada.

The unusual regime change period also coincides with complex relations with the United States, in the context of not only a probable US-led war with Iraq but also continuing border issues and larger security issues related to global terrorism. These include genuine Canadian concerns about the Bush administration's conception of an 'axis of evil', and its adoption of a policy of pre-emptive strikes in foreign military and security policy relations. The Chrétien government's handling of the Iraq issue has been criticized in some quarters, but its cautious approach undoubtedly enjoys broad support among a Canadian electorate that is not anti-American, but is very doubtful about the intentions and capacities of the Bush administration.

The 2003–2004 edition examines the dynamics of national priority-setting and public spending in this context, and provides an informed look at many of the key policy issues caught up in the new realities and in the longer track record of the Chrétien years since 1993. These include policies and spending in the following areas: the Kyoto Protocol and climate change, health care in the wake of the Kirby and Romanow reports, the new national security agenda, North American integration, higher education, the innovation agenda, government S&T, connectedness and Internet broadband access, the new governance of pensions, and student financial aid. A key chapter also looks at the way the House of Commons—the ultimate crucible of Canada's democratic politics—has changed in the Chrétien era.

The account in the present chapter of the nature and causes of political regime change and policy shift proceeds in three steps. First, the core politics of regime change are examined, including early signs of conflict between the two Liberal camps in the January 2001 Throne Speech and the December 2001 Budget. Second, we look at the nature of the policy shifts produced during the strange legacy politics of the Chrétien 'long goodbye', a period that includes both the 30 September 2002 final Chrétien Speech from the Throne and the February 2003 Budget, the first one forged by Finance Minister John Manley, but with Paul Martin looking closely over his shoulder. Third, we examine key aspects of the Paul Martin 'preview', an account that necessarily includes Martin as minister of finance, Martin as political predator, and Martin as 'imagined' prime minister. A preview of the following chapters is then presented. Finally, conclusions on key themes complete the analysis.

THE POLITICS OF REGIME CHANGE

The nature of the regime change underway in the 2002–2004 period is quite remarkable. Prime Minister Jean Chrétien had, after all, won a solid third consecutive majority in the December 2000 election, a political achievement few prime ministers have accomplished. Presumably the overall view of voters was that even if this was Chrétien's last term, he would serve out most of it and carry out his basic election agenda. Retirement would be graceful, and an electorate that had basically liked and supported Chrétien would applaud his leaving and thank him not only for his considerable, albeit imperfect efforts in office over a difficult but increasingly prosperous decade, but also for a long and recognized political career in which he had held virtually every cabinet job.

The January 2001 Throne Speech had captured some of the sense of the Chrétien confidence. It said that the Liberals would focus on

- building a world-leading economy driven by innovation, ideas and talent;

- creating a more inclusive society where children get the right start in life, where quality health services are available to all, and where Canadians enjoy strong and safe communities;
- ensuring a clean, healthy environment for Canadians and the preservation of our natural resources;
- and enhancing our Canadian voice in the world and our shared sense of citizenship.[1]

The fact that the innovation agenda made it to the top of the Liberal priority list was itself an indicator of relative political serenity, because ordinarily such science and technology-oriented realms of policy simply do not pass the test of what will appeal to ordinary Canadians.

And then came 11 September 2001, in the aftermath of which the Liberals had little choice but to cobble together a security package in response not only to US pressure but also to domestic support and sympathy for Canada's closest neighbour and ally.[2] As Reg Whitaker's analysis in Chapter 3 shows, the security package was complex and mixed. It consisted of several measures: anti-terrorism legislation with new, quite draconian powers; changes in immigration law; new budgetary and personnel resources for the Department of National Defence, CSIS, and national police and border control capacities; heightened attention at Health Canada regarding Canada's readiness to deal with the anthrax threat and other forms of bio-terrorism; and airport safety and the related precarious state of Canada's airline industry—the collapse of the airline Canada 3000, and Air Canada's demands for federal bail-out funds.

Finance Minister Paul Martin's Budget Speech of 10 December 2001, his last as finance minister, was crafted as a de facto second Throne Speech, and as a budget for 'securing progress in an uncertain world'.[3] In the speech itself, Martin argued that his budget does four things:

- First, it provides the necessary funding for the security measures to deal with the threats we face.
- Second, it recognizes the vital importance of an open Canada–US border to our continuing economic security.
- Third, it supports Canadians through difficult times while continuing our long-term plan to build for the future.
- And fourth, it provides Canadians with a full and open accounting of the nation's finances.[4]

In the larger Budget Plan documents, where the focus was even more explicitly fiscal and economic, the budget message was reworked into a slightly different ordering, but it was still couched in double-edged notions of security—physical security and economic security. The security package included new money for intelligence and policing, $1.6 billion; screening of entrants to Canada, $1 billion; emergency preparedness and military deployment, $1.6 billion; a new approach to air security,

$2.2 billion (including a new federal air security authority), funded by a new Air Travellers Security Charge; and border security and facilitation, $1.2 billion.

Chrétien had been criticized by the media and by the opposition parties, particularly the Canadian Alliance, for his slow and sluggish response to the security agenda, but basically Canadian public opinion polls kept confirming that Chrétien had got the response about right. Nonetheless, by early 2002, a sense of leadership malaise seemed to be taking hold. Chrétien himself was giving confusing signals about his own intentions. Initially he appeared to signal to possible leadership contenders in his own Liberal party that it would be all right if quiet 'behind the scenes' campaign preparations began. One minister who quickly took up the invitation was the then Industry Minister, Brian Tobin. But by mid-January 2002, Tobin had resigned from Cabinet and from politics after losing a bruising pre-budget battle with Finance Minister Paul Martin, largely over the issue of broadband Internet technology and access policy (see Richard Schultz's analysis in Chapter 12).

However, at other times Chrétien indicated that he might stay on, and that, in any event, ministers should stick to their knitting and deal with their jobs as ministers. The one minister who was most inclined to campaign and knit at the same time was Paul Martin. Martin and his supporters inside and outside the parliamentary Liberal party caucus were campaigning and fund-raising and beginning to advance openly some elements of an alternative Martin policy agenda. Public opinion polls began backing Martin as the overwhelming heir apparent to succeed Chrétien. The Martin versus Chrétien battle reached its first moment of truth on 2 June 2002, when Martin resigned from Cabinet, or was forced out by Chrétien. Free then to campaign from a backbench seat as a far from ordinary member of parliament, Martin, with the backing of his supporters, then pushed for the ouster of Chrétien. Aware of the writing on the political wall, Chrétien announced on 21 August 2002 that he would be stepping down as leader . . . but not until February 2004. Compared to any other previous period of leadership change, such as in the post-Pearson, post-Trudeau, post-Turner, and post-Mulroney eras, this would be the longest of political goodbyes . . . an 18-month divisive interregnum.

Both the 30 September 2002 Throne Speech and the February 2003 Budget had to be forged in unnatural ways, with a government-in-waiting functioning within a government in nominal power, but with a prime minister who indicated that he would be taking initiatives, and that he would regard a defeat of any of these initiatives as a vote of non-confidence, which would lead to an election that no one wanted.

If there is a leadership race underway for the Liberal party crown, it is a decidedly gangly one-legged race. Paul Martin is far and away the leading candidate and has virtually been conceded victory. Other nominal contenders from within the Liberal Cabinet are certainly interested, but early in 2003 their prospects are severely limited. Finance Minister John Manley has had to steer a budget through (see below) that will meet the needs of the new halfway world of interregnum politics and policy, but his operative political spectrum is very similar to Martin's, on the centre-right of the Liberal party. Allan Rock, the Industry Minister, is arguably more

left-of-centre, but he trailed Martin badly both among Liberals and in public opinion, and therefore withdrew from the race in January 2003. The Minister of Canadian Heritage, Sheila Copps, a more populist left-of-centre candidate, is in the race,
but she has little chance of winning.

The period of the long goodbye is thus a period in which the Chrétien government is governing in unnatural ways. And, of course, the ultimate further circum-
stance that makes all of this unnatural governing possible is the divided state of the
opposition parties. The Canadian Alliance survived its brief Stockwell Day leadership debacle, but under its relatively new leader, Stephen Harper, it remains very
much a right-wing regional party centred in Western Canada and with few prospects
of gaining ground in Ontario or Quebec, all the more so if Paul Martin becomes
Canada's de facto 'conservative' prime minister. The Progressive Conservative party
and the New Democratic party meanwhile were both going through their own leadership races in 2003, each playing for a niche slice of the political marketplace. The
election of Jack Layton, a radical politician straight out of Toronto city politics, as
leader of the NDP will make national politics more interesting, but the odds are that
it will not help the NDP at the polls nationally. Meanwhile, the Bloc Québécois
remained ensconced in its regional Quebec base, hunkered down while it waits to
see what happens to the separatist Parti Québécois government of Quebec, which is
struggling to stay in power. The PQ is governing in a changed Quebec political scene,
in which a new third party challenge is emerging in the form of Mario Dumas's
Action Démocratique du Québec (ADQ),[5] and the PQ government has withdrawn
from its referendum commitment.[6]

PRIORITIES, LEGACIES, AND POLICY SHIFT
IN THE CHRÉTIEN 'LONG GOODBYE'

The Chrétien era's final Speech from the Throne, presented on 30 September 2002,
is entitled 'The Canada We Want'. It reflected Jean Chrétien's final effort to sum up
key aspects of his legacy, interspersed with some new and recent initiatives whose
route into the Throne Speech, and their higher ranking in virtue of their presence
there, could not have been easily predicted from the previous Throne Speech, the
initial 'third mandate' Speech of January 2001. These newer entrants included a
considerable focus on cities and on smart regulation, as well as the ratification of
the Kyoto Protocol (which Chrétien had announced in Johannesberg in August at
the Summit on Sustainable Development). Table 1 captures the main themes and
priorities of the final Chrétien Throne Speech, along with a sample of particular initiatives promised.

The 18 February 2003 Budget, tabled by Finance Minister John Manley, brought
more financial flesh to the bones of the Chrétien agenda. Its spending increase of 20
per cent over three fiscal years was the largest in a single budget since the early
1980s, and it was clearly cast and seen as a 'people's budget', and as a $25-billion
Chrétien legacy.[7] However, any notion that this was a spending spree must be set

Table 1.1

Main Throne Speech Themes and Priorities

Canada and the World
- Safety and security for Canadians in the post-11 September context
- A doubling of Canada's development assistance by 2010, with at least half of the increase earmarked for Canada's support for the New Partnership for Africa's Development

Health Care in the Twenty-First Century
- An early 2003 commitment to put in place by the next budget a comprehensive plan for health care reform, including enhanced accountability to Canadians, and the necessary federal long-term investments
- Steps to strengthen the security of Canada's food system
- A First Nations Health Promotion and Disease Prevention Strategy

Children and Families
- Another significant increase in the National Child Benefit for poor families
- Early childhood development programs for First Nations
- A reform of the Criminal Code to increase the penalties for abuse and neglect

Climate Change and the Environment
- A resolution to Parliament on the issue of ratifying the Kyoto Protocol on Climate Change
- The creation of ten new national parks and five new National Marine Conservation Areas over the next five years

Talent and Investment
- Skills, learning, and research
- Smart regulation
- Competitive cities and healthy communities

Government and Citizens
- A new institution that brings together the National Archives of Canada and the National Library of Canada
- A commitment to the goal of doubling within ten years the number of high school students with a working knowledge of both English and French
- The provision of clear guidance and better enforcement with respect to the ethical standards expected of elected officials and senior public servants

---

against the fact that federal spending as a percentage of GDP is projected to be 12.2 per cent for 2003–4, compared to 16.5 per cent in 1993–4, 19.2 per cent in 1983–4, and 15.2 per cent in 1963–4. Manley closely and immediately linked the Budget Speech to the Throne Speech theme, 'the Canada that Canadians want'. He presented a budget that would be balanced in the current and following two years, and declared that the new spending was both needed and affordable, in the context not only of past surpluses, but also of projected economic growth of 3.2 per cent in 2003 and 3.5 per cent in 2004. Despite the huge spending initiatives, the budget was also cast against an implicit comparison with the US Bush administration budget, which had centred on large deficits and deficit projections, and whose central tax-cut provisions were largely pro-rich in scope and nature.[8] The key budgetary initiatives of the Manley budget are these:

- $17.3 billion more for health care over three years; $34.8 billion over five years.
- An increase in the National Child Benefit to a maximum for the first child of $2,632 in 2003 and $3,243 by 2007.
- An annual increase of $800 million for the military, plus $150 million in each of next two years.
- $3 billion over five years for the environment, including $2 billion to help implement the Kyoto Protocol, and $600 million for water and sewers on First Nations reserves.
- $3 billion over ten years for infrastructure, such as roads.
- A rise in RRSP and RRP contribution limits to $18,000 from $13,500 over four years.
- A reduction in the air travellers security charge to $14 for round-trip domestic flights, down from $24.
- An increase in foreign aid of $1.4 billion over three years.
- $935 million over five years for affordable day care.
- $135 million a year over three years to fight homelessness.
- A reduction in EI contributions by just over 5 per cent next January.
- The elimination of the federal capital tax over the next five years.
- An increase of 50 per cent (to $300,000) over four years in the small business tax deduction limit.
- An increase in total spending by 20 per cent over three years; up by $14.3 billion, or 11.5 per cent, in 2002–3.
- A reduction in the debt to $507.7 billion this year, 44.5 per cent of the economy.[9]

The Budget Speech referred to the large tax reduction program still underway, and added the tax and revenue reduction measures from the above list, such as the measures on RRSPs, the federal capital tax, the small business tax deduction, and the EI contribution reductions. However, there is little doubt that the Budget Speech and its spending provisions were intended to position John Manley as a candidate to succeed Jean Chrétien. Its social focus is intended to broaden Manley's constituency from its right-of-centre core, where it is similar to Paul Martin's, so as to include those on the centre-left of the Liberal party. But Manley has also presented the economic aspects of the budget in terms that he had used in earlier economic speeches, casting Canada as a 'Northern Tiger'. This was a metaphorical reference to the Asian 'tiger economies', which had developed policies centred on lower taxes, high innovation, and a willingness to attract and welcome foreign investment. It was also Manley's way of building on his own record on the innovation and university funding front at Industry Canada. Key provisions in his budget are very favourable to the small business sector of the Canadian economy, to which Manley has listened quite attentively.

While the budget's heavy social spending focus loses Manley some of his support from the right wing and perhaps from the big business community, he stoutly defended its overall fiscal prudence. The Budget Speech also included a commitment to accountable government, one feature of which is to be an implementation plan to 'reallocate spending from lower to higher needs and from less effective to more effective approaches', such that 'beginning in 2003-2004 the Government will allocate an ongoing $1 billion per year from existing spending to fund higher priorities of Canadians'.[10] The analysis by Joanne Kelly in Chapter 8 indicates clearly how difficult this 'reallocation' challenge is likely to be in an age of budgetary surpluses.

A consideration of the regime-change era of 2002-4 inevitably requires a discussion of Prime Minister Chrétien's real legacies over the ten years of his regime, his last-minute legacies, and his unfinished business. The main legacy from the ten-year period as a whole is undoubtedly the tackling and defeat of the federal budget deficit. The second legacy is the perilously narrow victory over the Parti Québécois in the 1995 Quebec referendum. The third legacy, perhaps surprisingly and less well known, is the Chrétien-era support for higher education policy, under the rubric of science and technology and innovation policy.

When Chrétien took office, it was not at all clear that he would be a deficit-fighter. It is undoubtedly the case that the steel in the deficit-fighting backbone of the government came more from Finance Minister Paul Martin, but, equally, Martin would not have succeeded had it not been for the steady backing of the Prime Minister. The 1995 Quebec Referendum was a near debacle, and could have ended Chrétien's political career, but he slipped through unscathed more as the result of good luck than of good leadership or management. The decision to take a tougher line on post-referendum Quebec, as articulated in the Clarity Act, was important, but even this was attributed more to other key ministers, such as Stéphane Dion, than to Chrétien himself. Nonetheless, over his whole decade in power, extending to the early 2000s, Chrétien's luck held out, and he will get some of the political credit for the Parti Québécois's relative demise, and the achievement of the significant majority view in Quebec that another referendum on sovereignty makes little sense.

The Chrétien record on higher education and on related science and technology and innovation policy is also a significant genuine legacy. Allan Tupper's account in Chapter 7 shows that this is a considerable achievement, which began to take shape as the first budgetary surpluses appeared in 1997. Again, Chrétien backed these changes and spending programs, but many of the key initiatives came out of Paul Martin's Department of Finance and were backed by Industry Canada's minister, John Manley. It is of some importance to note that Chrétien had the good sense to leave good ministers in their portfolios. Martin was Minister of Finance for nine years as was Manley in the Industry portfolio. Manley's tenure in the Industry portfolio, which in earlier eras had been an arena of proverbial ministerial musical chairs, was the longest since that of the legendary C.D. Howe in the 1950s. This is one of the reasons that the Chrétien government's innovation policies took shape and held. John de la Mothe's assessment in Chapter 11 of the 2002 'Innovation Strategy' is very critical, precisely because that strategy paper seemed to lose its connection with the longer-term innovation frameworks that had been advanced during the nine-year Manley tenure as a whole. The return to the old-style quasi-pork-barrel industrial policy is evident in the analysis by Richard Schultz in Chapter 12. Schultz is rightly critical of the way the federal broadband access policy was handled, not only in the brief Brian Tobin period at Industry Canada, but also earlier.

With regard to the last-minute legacies of the Chrétien long goodbye period, three have become focal points of Chrétien's last months in office: the Kyoto Protocol decision, renewed health care funding, and, surprisingly, the effort to reform party finance laws. Each decision is potentially significant, but each of course may also be seen not only as very belated but as opportunistic as well, given Chrétien's decision to leave office.

Chrétien's announcement in Johannesberg in August 2002 that Canada would ratify the Kyoto Protocol undoubtedly threw the proverbial cat among the energy and environmental policy pigeons. As a result, as the account in Chapter 5 by Debora VanNijnatten and Douglas MacDonald shows, the larger politics, symbolism, and practical realities of Kyoto Protocol commitments became more starkly revealed. The Chrétien government and the provinces then faced the looming deadline for Canada to actually ratify the Kyoto Protocol to reduce greenhouse gas emissions. Several past and current positions converged and collided.

The first of these was that Canada's initial Kyoto commitments had always been partly the expression of political symbolism at a high, Chrétien-led level: the desire to simply *look* better than the United States and thus to radiate green foreign policy virtue to the rest of the world. When the Bush administration abandoned Kyoto in June 2001 and announced its own largely market- and incentive-based alternatives in February 2002, the Chrétien government was in a sense hoist with its own petard.[11] Not only was the Bush administration saying that it did not really care much about how it *appeared* to the rest of the world, but also, Canada's Kyoto position now had to be crafted in the light of the fact that its oil and gas industry (mainly Alberta's oil and gas exports, but also new Atlantic Canada sources of supply) and Canadian industry in general (mainly in central Canada) could be put at a comparative disadvantage in its main market, the United States, in that they would have to pay higher energy costs than their US competitors. Moreover, the United States was now keenly interested in longer-term Canadian oil and gas supplies. Hence, selling oil and natural gas, especially the latter, was a key imperative, all the more so because Chrétien was also determined, in early 2001, to woo Alberta for the next political-electoral round of Canadian politics in the context of the weakened political standing of the Canadian Alliance, particularly during the brief Stockwell Day era.[12] Thus, at this time Chrétien went to Alberta and pledged himself to be an ardent energy salesman for Alberta oil and gas.

The other imperative was that as real decisions were needed in 2002 and 2003, the exact specifics with respect to the kinds of reductions in emissions or the arrangement of credits had to be determined through a more focused cost-benefit analysis of regulatory, tax, and other policy alternatives and instruments. During 2002 this resulted in a flurry of studies and leaked reports of what the costs and benefits—but mainly the costs—of action and inaction would be. Competing studies and projections by business (both general and petroleum) lobby groups and by Alberta and other producing provinces showed such costs to be very high, with Alberta claiming at times that ratification of the Protocol would decimate the Alberta economy. The federal government and some NGOs claimed that these and earlier cost projections were highly exaggerated, and often ignored the costs of not taking action.

These dynamics, coupled with the availability and demonstrated effect of the Bush administration's alternative to Kyoto, helped sow the seeds of a 'made-in-Canada' alternative to Kyoto as well. The Alberta Conservative government began seeking support among the provinces and in Ottawa for a package of initiatives: it would focus on energy efficiency, and partly reduce emissions, but at a slower pace, until 2020; it would rely more on the development of alternative technologies; and it would be calibrated to keep Canadian energy competitive in US markets.

It is not unreasonable to offer a kind of 'plague on both your houses' critique of both the pro- and anti-Kyoto forces, whether these are described as the Chrétien-led federal government versus Alberta, or the oil and gas and business lobby versus environmental NGOs. The devil indeed is in the details of any Canadian (largely post-Chrétien) plan to deal with the Kyoto Protocol commitments. But the devil is also in the double denial that both sides have exhibited. Both sides knew what was coming in a fundamental way and yet both fudged, avoiding key analytical and policy issues. Both sides knew in a fundamental way, but usually could not admit, that the other side was half right with respect to the issues that had, and still have, to be resolved. The Kyoto Protocol debate is an example of the Prime Minister's habitual tactic of delay: he eventually and belatedly made the crucial decision to ratify, but in a way that left the pieces to be picked up by his successor, and by Canadians as a whole.

Health care funding and policy is a second key legacy issue for the Chrétien regime-change period. In Chapter 6, Gerard Boychuk examines the key dimensions of the debate, noting the centrality of the issue in public opinion and its status as a high national priority. He demonstrates how the Kirby Report and the Romanow Commission encapsulated the key issues and the different perspectives regarding costs, methods of financing, and the relative roles of public sector delivery on the one hand and some possible private care supplements to the system on the other. From the perspective of the Chrétien legacy, the health care issue had undoubtedly to be dealt with as a game of political catch-up. It was the Chrétien (and Martin) government that, in the name of deficit-fighting, had cut the federal share of health care spending. Chrétien wanted to remedy this blot on his political legacy. He first appointed former Saskatchewan NDP Premier Roy Romanow to head up a Royal Commission, knowing that in him he had someone who would back the public system and who had sufficient political prestige to influence the national debate. But Chrétien did not want to simply put the previously reduced health care money back into the provincial coffers. He also wanted any package of funding to cover some newer program areas, in which Ottawa could claim and hopefully receive political credit, much as Ottawa did in the early medicare debate of the 1960s. Not for the first time was the federal spending power being used, and not for the first time did the provinces mightily object—but then quite gladly take whatever money they could get.

Thus, Chrétien's meetings with the provincial premiers on 6 February secured a $27 billion infusion of funds over a five-year period.[13] The larger portion of it was for new programs such as home care and protection against onerous drug costs, but there was also replenished funding for the provinces' existing basic health care components. The larger parts of the funding were skewed toward the latter part of the five-year period, in part to allow Ottawa to satisfy itself that appropriate accountability systems are in place regarding the efficiency and effectiveness of the health care funding. Parts of the funding package were also directed at ways of ensuring the reshaping of the health care system. Both the Romanow and the Kirby studies had stressed that money alone would not solve Canada's health care problems. In health care, then, Chrétien appears to have secured a recovered 'half-loaf' legacy, made possible by the surpluses that arose from the successful deficit battle and from a growing late 1990s and early 2000s economy.

The third hoped-for belated legacy for Prime Minister Chrétien that has surfaced in the interregnum period is a surprising one: the reform of political party financing. Buoyed by his new-found political freedom to take risks, Chrétien introduced a bill into the House of Commons in January 2003 whose central features are to severely limit (to $1000) how much corporations and unions can contribute to individual politicians or constituency associations, and to prohibit them from contributing to political parties.[14] Individuals could make contributions up to a total of $10,000 to a political party, an individual politician, or a constituency association. The proposal caught Chrétien's own Liberal caucus by surprise, but the Prime Minister announced that he was serious, and that the legislation would be a matter of confidence in the House of Commons. If it were to be defeated in the Commons, an election would follow.

At time of writing the fate of this initiative is still to be determined. Not surprisingly, many saw it as a cynical ploy to make life difficult for his successor (assumed to be Paul Martin). Chrétien retorted that he was doing this because he thought the initiative would help in the longer run to reduce the cynicism of Canadians about politics and about the role of money in influencing political decisions and processes.

PRIORITIES AND POLICY HINTS
IN THE PAUL MARTIN 'PREVIEW'

There is little doubt that Paul Martin is the overwhelming favourite to succeed Jean Chrétien as leader of the Liberal party and as prime minister. If he does not win the leadership contest it will be one of the biggest political upsets in Canadian political history. Thus the Chrétien 'long goodbye' period is also the Martin 'preview' or 'short hello'. But of course Canadians already know a fair amount about Martin.[15] They know about Martin as minister of finance. They know more now about Martin as de facto leader of the opposition and determined political predator. And they are receiving hints and some previews of Martin as imagined prime minister.

Paul Martin as finance minister is essentially Paul Martin as deficit slayer and pro- ducer of budgetary surpluses. His continuous high standing in the opinion polls is undoubtedly due to this achievement, but, as we have seen, this is an achievement he shares with Jean Chrétien. He has also been a consistent supporter of the educa- tion and innovation agendas referred to above. His overall policy achievements and core interests place him solidly in the centre-right of the Liberal party. Indeed, as Alberta's Premier Ralph Klein has publicly and candidly acknowledged, Martin is the closest thing to a national conservative leader that Canadian conservatives can find.[16]

While there is undoubtedly considerable personal animosity between Chrétien and Martin, there is also a long set of real or perceived differences. Chrétien's core political instincts are more left-of-centre, and this is what is belatedly coming to the fore in his final 18 months in office. Martin's political roots within the Liberal party, dating back to both the 1983–4 and the 1990–1 Liberal leadership races, are much more in the conservative John Turner and earlier Robert Winters wing.

In 2002 and 2003, Canadians have been witnessing Martin in the role of political predator and instigator of regime change. This performance is undoubtedly fuelled by an 'It's my turn and I deserve it' view of political leadership, which, in Martin's case, Canadian public opinion largely seems to support. But Martin's ability to be a regime-change instigator is still overwhelmingly attributable to the continuing weakness of Canada's conservative opposition parties, the Canadian Alliance and the Progressive Conservative party. They too are behaving 'unnaturally'—in the role of opposition—and this state of affairs is undoubtedly due to the formation of Preston Manning's Reform party, since transformed into the Canadian Alliance, which decided that it would prefer to be a debating society that occasionally influ- ences the national agenda than a party groomed and built to actually govern Canada.

As for the hints of Paul Martin as future prime minister, Canadians have been given several indicators of policy shift or possible policy shift. The extent to which these indicators are substantive as opposed to tactical remains to be seen. But sev- eral can be highlighted, including parliamentary reform; Kyoto Protocol commit- ments; the cities agenda; defence policy; and relations with the United States, or North America more generally.

Parliamentary reform has been a Martin theme for some time, but he made a par- ticular issue of it as soon as he resigned from or was pushed out of the Finance port- folio and became a not so ordinary 'ordinary' MP. The decision late in 2002 to allow parliamentary committee members to elect their own chairpersons was seen as a first indicator of the strength of the Martin agenda and the Martin forces in the Lib- eral caucus. Martin's apparent motivation for parliamentary reform was to respond to the argument that the Chrétien era had been dominated by an unprecedented centralization of power in the prime minister's office and realm.[17] But this is an argument that Martin can afford to take only so far, because if there was increased centralization during the Chrétien era, large chunks of it were in fact centralization in Martin's Department of Finance. Finance departments are always a form of 'government within a government', but this may have been especially true for most of the 1990s, when the deficit battle was waged, and then also when the early 'budgetary surplus' years took hold.

The Kyoto Protocol debate has already been discussed, in the context of the Chrétien legacy, but there is plenty left for Martin to do in the way of crafting plans for action in the longer run. During the Kyoto debate in late 2002 Martin supported ratification, but intimated strongly that he would take another hard look at the important details. Martin already enjoys considerable support in Alberta, and thus, if his own eventual electoral strategy is fashioned around an energy-centred Alberta or Western Canada approach, then Kyoto Protocol details and other energy issues, such as the Alberta oil sands, will loom large.

Another issue that arises when we review Martin's agenda as he positions himself for leadership is federal policy with respect to Canada's major cities, and its financing. This issue surfaced immediately after the 2000 election and then gained a following in the Liberal caucus, although it did not loom large in the Manley budget of 18 February 2003. Martin appears to be quite attuned to these urban forces, especially in the context of the politics of greater Toronto, but also that of other large cities, which are facing genuine socio-economic and infrastructure problems. Since cities are an area of provincial jurisdiction, Martin or any new prime minister will have to tread carefully. But it must be remembered that Martin as finance minister had no compunctions about using the federal spending power to pour money into universities, even though these are also provincial creatures. To a set of now grateful universities Martin may wish to add a set of grateful cities. Indeed, the two are in some respects joined, in that federal innovation policy speaks increasingly of bottom-up clusters of innovation, centred in cities and in communities linked to research universities and educational institutions.

Defence policy and funding is another realm of priorities in which the Martin agenda is likely to be different. As we have seen, the 2003 budget, the final one of the Chrétien era, did boost the defence budget, but overall defence spending was not a high priority during the Chrétien era, with the result that the capacities of the armed forces have been seriously weakened in the face of new and greater demands, including the looming possibility of war with Iraq. But defence policy is ever more entwined in the larger dilemmas regarding Canada's relations with the United States and with North America in general. Early indications are that Martin, in alliance with John Manley, is likely to want to fashion closer relations with the Bush administration. Both see the anti-Bush and even anti-American feelings and rhetoric of many Liberal MPs, coupled with the slow and cautious Chrétien approach to relations with the United States, as often not being in Canada's best interests.

Geoffrey Hale's analysis of Canada's approach to North American relations shows that there is indeed much unfinished business in the Chrétien legacy, but it is also evident that dealing with it will be a risky business for his successor as well. The key question here is under what policy premises these relations might be crafted and driven in the coming few years. One approach, as Hale suggests, is to continue to use the problem-solving incremental approach. But part of the broader context is the upcoming tenth anniversary of NAFTA. This is triggering review discussions within and among the three NAFTA countries,[18] and these discussions in turn are linked to the eventual negotiation by 2005 of a Free Trade of the Americas Agreement (FTAA).

But a formal NAFTA 2 round is not necessarily in the cards, in part because there are advocates of an alternative model of Canada–US and North American relations centred on the perimeter-security agenda. This links border measures, overall security, and defence policy in a way that would produce a North America quite different from that governed by a more traditional, trade regime focus. This emerged in the months after the 11 September crisis, but it has resurfaced in a major way in 2003. This broadly security-driven agenda has considerable currency in the United States,[19] and has been explicitly advocated in Canada by bodies such as the influential Canadian Council of Chief Executives.[20] It is also a part of the change examined in the recent report of the House of Commons Standing Committee on Foreign Affairs and International Trade.[21] If adopted, a model of this kind would likely move like a juggernaut as the dominant motivation for North American reform or reform of Canada-US relations, while Mexico is shunted to the sidelines, at least in terms of Canadian strategy.

AN OVERVIEW OF THE VOLUME

- **Geoffrey Hale** assesses the Chrétien legacy in Canada–US relations, contrasting its relatively coherent approach to many domestic priorities with its drifting, reactive responses to developments on cross-border policy issues. Hale argues that the federal government's traditional balancing act between the accommodation of closer economic relations with the United States and the pursuit of a 'distinctly Canadian' foreign policy has become increasingly tenuous since 11 September 2001. He shows that this challenge is reinforced by the segmentation and decentralization of policy development on cross-border issues. It arises also from the traditional federal desire to avoid linkage between the management of cross-border disputes and internal debates over the most effective means of promoting Canadian sovereignty and identity. The chapter reviews tentative efforts by federal politicians to frame the continuing debate over Canada–US relations in ways that balance different concepts of sovereignty and political choice, efforts that will set the terms for debate during the upcoming Liberal leadership contest. Hale's overall view is that Canada-US relations are very much an unfinished legacy of the Chrétien era.

- **Reg Whitaker** examines the national security agenda. He argues that the terrorist attacks on the United States on 11 September 2001 were a relatively rare example of an external event's suddenly reprioritizing the policy agenda in Ottawa. Although domestic concerns about security (supported by particular interests and advocates) were important, the most pressing factor in shaping the new agenda was the expectations of the United States with regard, first, to common standards and practices among coalition participants in the US-declared war on terrorism, and second, to the implications for Canadian economic security of Canada–US border restrictions, post-11 September. The Canadian response with respect to administrative arrangements, and civil liberties and due process, is contrasted in this chapter to the US response. Attention is paid to the legal response (The Anti-Terrorism act, the Public Safety bill); the budgetary reallocations to security; the reorganization of security and intelligence functions; the military contributions to the war on terrorism; the initiatives on border security and refugee policy; and the management of the impact of ethnic risk profiling on multicultural relations. Canada's responses are assessed as more damage limitation in relation to Canadian economic security than as positive anti-terrorist initiatives. Nor is the impact very durable: within less than a year, priorities had largely reverted to the old, pre-11 September policy agenda.

- **Jonathan Malloy** sheds important light on the status of the House of Commons under the Chrétien government, particularly since the 2000 election, but also over the whole Chrétien era. He argues that the House of Commons has seen significant but not transformative changes under Jean Chrétien. Looking at four different dimensions of parliamentary activity—policy ideas, accountability, the passage of bills, and leadership struggles—Malloy's analysis shows that MPs have become more assertive and influential, even undermining their own party leaders. Malloy suggests that a major reason for Members' assertiveness is the unusually high number of seasoned MPs in the current 37th Parliament. The relatively low turnover of MPs in the 1990s compared to earlier periods means that the large group of government backbenchers elected in 1993 have become thoroughly familiar with parliamentary institutions and policy issues. They also realize that their hopes of cabinet promotion are increasingly slim, and these factors have prompted them to develop more assertive and influential identities as backbench MPs. However, conflicting expectations and assumptions remain about the role of Members in a parliamentary system of government such as Canada's.

- **Debora VanNijnatten** and **Douglas MacDonald** focus on the three policy options currently being considered by the Chrétien government as it attempts to both meet an international Kyoto commitment and continue to use energy policy as a major element of economic development. These options are: a) moving to a lower-carbon economy; b) developing technology to reduce the carbon intensity of manufacturing and transport; and c) gaining credit for carbon sinks and clean energy exports. The chapter shows that the contradiction between the Chrétien government's energy objectives and its climate objectives could be resolved by a combination of these three measures, but only if the Prime Minister and cabinet provide leadership far more clear and consistent than any seen to date. Moreover, the lack of a coherent strategy at the political level is replicated at the administrative level. Although there has been greater coordination of energy and climate policy objectives and programs over the past few years, the development of climate policy continues to rest with Environment Canada, whose raison d'être is environmental protection, while implementation rests largely with Natural Resources Canada, the premier energy department. This division of responsibilities, the authors argue, must give way to far better organizational and program coherence.

- **Gerard W. Boychuk** examines federal health care policy in the wake of the Kirby and Romanow reports. He shows that the federal political context has shifted dramatically and that the challenges to the successful achievement of major health care reform now seem significantly more daunting. Internal leadership challenges have undermined the Chrétien government's ability to deal forcefully with the provinces, and the latter appear well positioned to demand large financial concessions from the federal government. At the same time, internal leadership politics are likely to constrain the commitment of federal funds. In the wake of the Kirby Committee and Romanow Commission reports, the federal government will undoubtedly undertake a major health care reform initiative. However, given these changing political dynamics, it will take considerable skill for the Prime Minister to successfully deliver major health care reform. In examining these issues, this chapter first provides an overview of the main substantive issues confronting the federal government in health care. It then considers how the federal role in health care reform has been affected by the politics of both the Chrétien legacy agenda and the federal Liberal leadership. Finally, it briefly examines the Kirby Committee and Romanow Commission reports and considers whether they seem likely to provide a promising blueprint for federal health care reform in the final period of Jean Chrétien's tenure as prime minister.

- **Allan Tupper** takes a focused look at the Chrétien government's approaches to higher education, and argues that they have produced a quiet revolution in Canadian public policy. He notes that major programs for research at Canadian universities have been launched and argues that such programs have substantially strengthened the research capacity of universities. Major federal initiatives include the Canada Foundation for Innovation, the Canada Research Chairs, the Canadian Institutes for Health Research, and the Millennium Scholarship Foundation. These programs are the driving forces in Canadian universities. They are strongly supported by universities, even though they have altered university priorities. The government of Canada sees university

research as a crucial determinant of Canada's economic future. Its overall program for universities is designed to attract outstanding researchers to Canada,
to promote greater commercialization of university research, and to provide
incentives for interdisciplinary research. These themes are emphasized in the
Innovation Strategy, unveiled in 2002 by Industry Canada and Human
Resources Development Canada. Another major federal program for universities—this time for the 'indirect costs' of federal research—is likely to be funded
very soon. Tupper concludes that Canadian universities look to Ottawa, not to
provincial capitals, for leadership. He notes that anxiety has been expressed
about the possibility that the role of smaller universities, where research is a
lesser priority, will be diminished, and about the impact of federal policy
on humanities and social science. A major question is whether universities
can meet Ottawa's high expectations for substantial economic payoffs from
university research.

- **Joanne Kelly** takes us behind the scenes of public spending by probing a
  crucial but elusive puzzle, which all governments face, namely, to what extent
  they can review programs and reallocate budgets rather than rely on new
  spending. Kelly shows that the Chrétien government's efforts to reform the
  expenditure management system in Ottawa provides some important lessons
  about the usefulness of review and reallocation in public expenditure management. Firstly, review and reallocation have been used on various occasions by
  the government, but to pursue three distinct budgetary objectives: fiscal
  restraint, reprioritization, and the encouragement of better program management. As the budgetary environment shifted—deficit turned to surplus, or the
  government moved to implement new policy initiatives—new budget tools
  were developed that adapted the practices of review and reallocation to
  address specific budgetary problems. Kelly shows that no single model was
  able to achieve all three goals equally well. This reminds us that review and
  reallocation are useful tools in expenditure management but are not ends in
  themselves. A second and related point is that any view or assumption that
  review and reallocation are inextricably linked is not supported by recent experience. Reviewing government programs can provide useful information for
  budget decision-makers, but it will not necessarily provide evidence that leads
  incontrovertibly to support for reallocation. Nor will it replace the need for the
  government to make political choices. Finally, review and reallocation will
  often undermine one of the fundamental—if oft forgotten—objectives of government budgeting: conflict resolution. Incorporating reallocation and review
  into the expenditure management system is politically and technically
  difficult. Kelly concludes that governments will only tolerate the political
  turmoil associated with review and reallocation if they believe the pain is
  unavoidable, or that it will be counterbalanced by rewards in other areas.
  Under these circumstances it is difficult to envisage any technical solution that

would provide the 'best way' to encourage review and achieve reallocation, despite the rhetoric of some.

- **Michael Prince** looks closely at a lesser-known but highly important institution, the Canada Pension Plan (CPP) Investment Board. A Chrétien-era creature, the Board was established in 1998 by the federal government and participating provincial governments, as a Crown corporation with a mandate to invest CPP savings in capital markets. Prince examines the political origins of the Board, its corporate governance, its organizational culture, its investment policy framework, and the performance of the assets it manages. He argues that the Board has governance requirements and ethical practices that are exemplary for pension plans and for government organizations. While definitely an instrument of federal and provincial policy, on matters of management or investment the Board is largely independent of governments. The Board strives to be a virtual corporation, maintaining a small-sized staff by relying on the contracting of investment, legal, and other services with external partners. The Board is also guided by policies of transparency to the public and strong policies on conflict of interest. Prince concludes that with the Board's assets likely to approach $150 billion within a decade, its long-term achievements may facilitate the expansion of CPP retirement benefits. Whereas executive federalism in the past may have restrained the liberalization of pension benefits, the equity capitalism of the Investment Board may well give confidence in the future and promote the expansion of CPP benefits.

- **Ross Finnie, Saul Schwartz,** and **Eric Lascelles** provide an in-depth look at the changing state of student financial aid programs in Canada. They show that the last decade was a tumultuous one for these programs. With tuition fees rising substantially, provincial governments replaced many of their grant programs with loans; loan remission programs were then introduced a few years later. The structure of the Canada Student Loans Program (CSLP) changed twice. Loan limits and other program parameters were adjusted, and interest relief programs for those experiencing repayment difficulties were expanded. Education-related tax credits were ramped up and a new credit for interest on student loans was put in place. The Canada Millennium Scholarship Foundation was created and began disbursing funds. The chapter estimates the amount of government spending on the various student financial aid programs in the 2000-1 fiscal year. It includes not only the standard types of aid, such as loans and grants, but also some less obvious ones, such as tax credits. The results are interesting and in some cases surprising, including a finding that spending is increasingly geared to supporting the middle classes rather than low-income students and families. These estimates create an empirical basis for future discussions regarding such matters as the structure of government spending on student financial assistance; how resources could perhaps be spent differently; and whether overall spending levels should be adjusted.

- **John de la Mothe** examines the Chrétien Liberals' February 2002 Innovation Strategy against the backdrop of both leadership politics and the longer track record of the government since 1993. He argues that innovation is centrally important to the future of Canada, and that many parts of the government are attentive to what has been done (and why). However, de la Mothe argues that the Liberals' 2002 Innovation Strategy lacks content, and as a policy exercise was fraught with confusion. He shows that the strategy demonstrated remarkable discontinuity with more progressive science and technology and innovation policy documents produced by Chrétien governments between 1993 and 2000. To a much greater extent, these earlier documents were informed by a framework. He concludes that the entire 2002 Innovation Strategy process has resulted in nothing resembling a strategy, an agenda, or a consultation.

- **Richard Schultz** probes the politics and the spending choices associated with the recent federal fight for a federal policy on broadband access—an initiative that is linked to the longer-term Chrétien-era policies devoted to the development of Internet connectedness and to the debate about the so-called 'digital divide'. Shultz shows that ever since the 2000 election and the subsequent 2001 Speech from the Throne, the federal government has placed a high priority on a program to provide all Canadian communities with high-speed broadband access to the Internet. He analyses the political, bureaucratic, and interest group processes that resulted in a very different program—a much more modest one in terms of both funds and focus. The chapter begins with a discussion of two of the most important background issues that should have informed the policy development process, but for the most part did not, namely, the perils of designing policy at a time of technological turmoil, and the confusion that exists over the very concept of a 'digital divide'. It then reviews the National Broadband Task Force, and assesses its results and the reactions to it. The Task Force was dominated by corporate and bureaucratic interests, which would be among the primary beneficiaries of a generous, largely federally-funded broadband 'pipeline' policy. The analysis shows how the proposed policy became caught up in political competition, not only between the then ministers of Finance and Industry, but between their departments as well. The chapter concludes with a commentary on the more limited program that was announced in September 2002.

- **Jeff Kinder** examines a further, more particular, but key aspect of Canada's Innovation Strategy, namely the Chrétien government's announced intention to double the federal investment in research and development by 2010. Much of this investment, if it materializes, will likely pass through the federal government to universities and the private sector. But supporters of science performed within the federal government are hopeful that, after sustaining tight budgets and in some cases deep cuts during the 1990s, government laboratories and research institutes will receive new investments to deal with the diverse and complex challenges they are expected to address. Kinder shows that while new investment may be tied to the promotion of an 'innovation agenda', there are other 'public good' roles supported by government science that make calls for new funding compelling. Kinder argues, however, that any such reinvestment will likely come through new funding models that stress national priority issues, horizontal collaboration, and competitive selection. This chapter traces the historical evolution of government science, and its diverse roles within the national innovation system. It then explores recent initiatives, including the proposed Federal Innovation Networks of Excellence (FINE), intended to reform the governance of government science. Finally, the chapter offers some conclusions as to the future direction of government science and its role in the overall innovation agenda of Canada.

CONCLUSIONS

It is important to see the 2002–4 period of regime change and policy shift as being historically unique. The political forces of change and continuity are being played out largely within the contours of the Liberal party, with Canadians seemingly supportive in one sense, but also feeling increasingly like spectators peering through the Liberal looking glass. In the long run, this is powerfully unhealthy for Canadian democracy. It is to be hoped that the Chrétien-Martin interregnum movie has no sequels.

In the full context of the Chrétien era decade and legacy, several things are clear. First, the Chrétien era was largely dominated by economic policy, primarily because the main policy challenge was the deficit. In the long economic day of the Chrétien decade, the 2003 Budget Speech constituted the main and perhaps only social policy 'hour'. The triumph over the deficit can also be seen in relation to the relative power of the federal government and the provinces. One of its key consequences is that it has transformed the federal government from its state in the early 1990s, when it was cast as an enfeebled entity unable to act in the face of global forces and provincial aggressiveness, to that in the early 2000s, when it enjoys renewed power and room for initiatives, albeit always constrained by the complexities of the globalized policy and political-economic world, and by the nature of Canadian federal-provincial and interregional politics and economics.

But, as always, the questions will be 'initiatives for whom?' and 'over what time frame of relevance and considered thinking and action?' The analysis of the Martin preview has indicated that a Martin era may have greater room for initiatives related to Canadian cities and defence policy, and perhaps a more focused approach to dealing with the United States both in the context of NAFTA and in a larger security context. But the curious regime change period of 2002–4 has provided only a glimpse of future possibilities. The chapters in this volume have indicated that there is much to do—that many agendas are unfinished, while others are not even imagined.

NOTES

Special thanks are owed to my colleague, Michael Prince, for helpful and constructive comments on an earlier draft of this chapter.

1　Canada, Speech from the Throne to Open the First Session of the 37th Parliament of Canada, 2.
2　See Michael Hart and Brian Tomlin, 'Inside the Perimeter: The US Policy Agenda and Its Implications for Canada', in Bruce Doern, ed., *How Ottawa Spends 2002–2003: The Security Aftermath and National Priorities* (Don Mills: Oxford University Press, 2002), 48–68.
3　www.fin.gc.ca/budget01/speech/speeche.htm.
4　Ibid., 2.
5　Philip Authier, 'Dumont Mirrors Quebec's Mood', *The Globe and Mail* [Toronto], 15 Nov. 2002, A12.
6　Rhéal Seguin, 'PQ Withdraws Referendum Commitment', *The Globe and Mail* [Toronto], 9 Sept. 2002, A4.
7　Department of Finance, *The Budget Speech 2003* (Ottawa: Department of Finance, 18 Feb. 2003). See also Shawn McCarthy, 'The $25 Billion Legacy', *The Globe and Mail* [Toronto], 19 Feb. 2003, 1.
8　See Deborah McGregor, 'Bush Takes the Initiative on Economic Agenda', *The Financial Times*, 8 Jan. 2003, 10.
9　'Budget Highlights', *The Globe and Mail* [Toronto], 19 Feb. 2003, 1.
10　Department of Finance, *Budget Speech 2003*, 12.
11　See Bruce Doern and Monica Gattinger, *Power Switch: Energy Regulatory Governance in the 21st Century* (Toronto: University of Toronto Press, 2003).
12　See Allan Tupper, 'Toward a New Beginning? The Chrétien Liberals and Western Canada', in Bruce Doern, ed., *How Ottawa Spends 2002–2003*, 88–101.
13　See Brian Laghi and Shawn McCarthy, 'Premiers Grumble but PM Gets Deal on Health', *The Globe and Mail* [Toronto], 6 Feb. 2003, 1.
14　Shawn McCarthy, 'PM's Donation Ban to Cost $110 million', *The Globe and Mail* [Toronto], 30 Jan. 2003, 1.
15　See 'Paul Martin's Legacy', three articles in *Policy Options* (Oct. 2002), 6–18.
16　See Patrick Brethour, 'Klein Sees Martin as Best Hope for PM', *The Globe and Mail* [Toronto], 31 Jan. 2003, 1.
17　See 'The Chrétien Legacy', several articles in *Policy Options* (Nov. 2000), 6–43.
18　See John Cavanagh and Sarah Anderson, 'Happily Ever NAFTA?' *Foreign Policy* (Sept./Oct. 2002), 58–65, and Michael Hart, 'NAFTA at Ten: Yesterday, Today and Tomorrow', paper presented at the NAFTA at Ten Conference, Woodrow Wilson Center, 9 Dec. 2002.
19　See Gary C. Hufbauer and Vega Canovas, 'Whither NAFTA: A Common Frontier?' in Peter Andreas and Thomas J. Biersteker, eds, *The Rebordering of North America? Integration and Exclusion in a Security Context* (London: Routledge, 2003), 38–55.

20 Canadian Council of Chief Executives, *Security and Prosperity: The Dynamics of a New Canada–United States Partnership in North America* (Ottawa: Canadian Council of Chief Executives, 14 Jan. 2003).

21 Standing Committee on Foreign Affairs and International Trade, *Partners in North America: Advancing Canada's Relations with the United States and Mexico* (Ottawa: House of Commons, Standing Committee on Foreign Affairs and International Trade, Dec. 2002).

2

The Unfinished Legacy:
Liberal Policy on North America

GEOFFREY E. HALE

The approach of the end of the Chrétien era has not only triggered a search for a Prime Ministerial 'legacy', it has also created opportunities for the renewal of Canada's political leadership. Jean Chrétien's decade in office may have resulted in a Mackenzie King-like redefinition of Canadian Liberalism as it applies to domestic politics—the renewal of the federal government's solvency, and with it its capacity for policy leadership and selective social activism.[1] However, his Kingly ambivalence with respect to Canada's growing economic and security integration in North America reflects some of the biggest challenges facing his prospective successors.

Central to this ambivalence is the paradox of linkage. Canadian politicians and diplomats have traditionally sought to avoid linkages between competing economic interests when managing cross-border disputes related to trade or investment. In their dealings with foreign powers they have also attempted to separate economic and diplomatic initiatives—accommodating both Canada's growing economic interdependence with the United States, on the one hand, and its efforts to maintain an independent decision-making capacity in other areas of foreign policy on the other, and attempting to balance the two.

However, the inexorable growth of North American economic integration—and of regional trading blocs in general—is blurring the distinctions between domestic and international issues in politics and economics.[2] Economic and trade issues vital to

Canada's prosperity and to the fiscal capacity of its governments to maintain and enhance key social policies and public services are becoming increasingly intertwined with concerns over security and environmental issues. As a result, the federal Liberals are facing growing pressures to redefine their Chrétien-era balancing act in Canada-US relations. A growing number of policy observers and policy-makers are suggesting that the exercise of political discretion in domestic politics, which is a major element of political sovereignty, is increasingly dependent on effective—not merely symbolic—engagement with North American, hemispheric, and global issues.[3]

This chapter assesses the legacy of the Chrétien government with respect to Canada-US relations, contrasting its relatively coherent approach to domestic priorities with its drifting, reactive responses to developments on cross-border policy issues—particularly as they relate to major domestic policies and federal-provincial relations. It examines the federal government's balancing act during the past decade between the accommodation of closer economic relations with the United States on the one hand and the pursuit of a 'distinctly Canadian' foreign policy on the other—and the increasingly tenuous character of this balancing act since September 2001. It summarizes the political, economic, and institutional factors that have contributed to the segmentation and decentralization of policy development on cross-border issues, and that have limited the government's willingness to pursue systematic policy coordination—even before recent distractions over leadership and legacies. It notes the growing challenges of coordinating federal and provincial policies and priorities in these areas, and the tentative efforts by federal politicians to frame the continuing debate over Canada–US relations in ways that balance different concepts of sovereignty and political choice.

It also analyses growing pressures for a more strategic approach to North American and cross-border issues that clearly articulates Canada's national interests and priorities, as distinctions between domestic, hemispheric, and global policy issues become increasingly blurred. Finally, it analyses the challenges that face potential leadership candidates in addressing these issues in a post-Chrétien era.

THE CHRÉTIEN LEGACIES: CONTRASTING DOMESTIC AND INTERNATIONAL BALANCING ACTS

Jean Chrétien's political style has occasionally been compared with that of William Lyon Mackenzie King, a canny survivor whose mastery of political ambiguity enabled him to become Canada's longest-serving prime minister.[4] Cautious, pragmatic, wary of grand visions, Chrétien has tended to approach politics as a balancing act among competing interests and political goals, moving incrementally to deal with specific problems, until a political opportunity or an opponent's misstep creates an opening for decisive action—described by one student of his leadership style as 'governing by bolts of electricity'.[5]

The political mantra of 'balance' shaped the Liberal Red Book of 1993, with its gradualist approach to deficit reduction and its apparently grudging acceptance of

Canada–US free trade, camouflaged behind a nominal commitment to make NAFTA more responsive to a shopping list of Liberal concerns.[6] Chrétien's domestic balancing act between social and business Liberals during his second term was epitomized by his commitment to divide prospective surpluses '50–50' between tax and debt reduction on the one hand and new spending on the other.[7] Behind the Prime Minister's smokescreen of rhetorical ambiguity, his government's key economic ministries—Finance, Foreign Affairs and International Trade, and Industry—gradually evolved an overarching strategy intended to integrate fiscal, economic, and social policy objectives. Fiscal discipline, supplemented with the 'big bang' tax cuts of Paul Martin's pre-election budget of October 2000, would permit gradual reductions in key tax rates and in the ratio of federal debt to GDP. A series of incremental initiatives targeted increased federal spending and tax support to innovation, research, and post-secondary education—policy areas vital to Canada's competitiveness and the growth of its skilled work force. A series of social policy initiatives sought to reinforce 'active labour market' policies intended to foster skills acquisition, reduce barriers to employment, reduce poverty, and encourage labour mobility. Periodic increases in (or restorations of) federal-provincial transfers were targeted primarily at politically sensitive health care budgets.[8]

In federal-provincial relations, Chrétien made a virtue of necessity during his first term—decentralizing power to the provinces in several areas and collaborating in the development of the National Child Benefit while reducing federal transfers, as part of Martin's broader strategy of deficit reduction.[9] Since 1997, Chrétien has tended to act from a position of strength in federal-provincial relations, whether in the negotiation of 'collaborative' agreements on tax collection and social policy or in the unilateral assertion of federal power—as in its passage of the Clarity Act or Chrétien's decision to ratify the Kyoto Protocol over the objections of several provinces.[10]

Most of these initiatives lend credence to Alain Noel's contention that 'the new policies and instruments preferred by the federal government all have in common that they preserve its flexibility and control'.[11] This approach allows Ottawa to function independently of the provinces within its own jurisdiction, and thus enables it to maintain policy discretion and maximize political credit in areas traditionally addressed through intergovernmental transfers or shared-cost programs.

Officials at both levels may be able to negotiate policy initiatives that complement one another, as with proposals for regulatory coordination, trade promotion, infrastructure projects, or the coordination of new initiatives in support of research and innovation. However, these initiatives toward 'complementary' or 'parallel' federalism tend to reflect ad hoc, informal, or micro-level policy coordination rather than a broader strategic approach to the management of public policies and programs.[12] This tendency toward policy fragmentation and 'ad hockery' has been even more visible in the handling of a wide range of cross-border issues—as will be discussed later in this chapter.

The restoration of fiscal flexibility and discretion, if not necessarily control, may be considered the greatest domestic policy legacy of the Chrétien-Martin era after the marginalization of Quebec separatism. The centralization of power in the offices of the Prime Minister and the Minister of Finance, while disparaged by some as a key element of Canada's democratic deficit, has permitted the federal government to impose a degree of consistency and coherence on economic and social policies for the first time in many years—despite periodic lapses into blatant pork-barrelling and 'politics as usual'.[13] Sustainable fiscal policies based on modest surpluses and consistent debt repayment, combined with mutually reinforcing tax and social policy initiatives, have contributed to steady economic growth and improved living standards—after a decade of declining or stagnant incomes for Canadians.[14]

The same techniques of political balancing and rhetorical ambiguity used by the Chrétien government in domestic politics can be seen in its handling of foreign policy in general and Canada–US relations in particular. However, in sharp contrast with its gradual development of a relatively coherent, disciplined strategy for managing fiscal, economic, and social policy renewal in domestic politics, the Chrétien government has tended to pursue a more reactive policy in its dealings with the United States.

The Chrétien Legacy in Foreign Policy and Canada–US Relations

Chrétien's legacy in foreign economic, diplomatic, and security policies is harder to discern—especially as these policies intersect with major aspects of Canada–US relations. Liberal foreign policy has consistently sought to accommodate and balance continental and global economic integration with selective liberal idealism in the diplomatic and security aspects of foreign policy. In foreign economic policies, Chrétien Liberalism has been largely indistinguishable from Mulroney Conservatism—overseeing the progressive economic integration of North America while pursuing a wide range of bilateral and multilateral initiatives intended to complement and balance Canada's overwhelming dependence on US markets for its exports. The economic benefits of continuing North American economic integration are acknowledged, and sometimes even welcomed, while Ottawa attempts to encourage the diversification of Canada's export markets and political relationships.[15]

Ministers responsible for foreign economic relations, from Paul Martin and Roy McLaren during Chrétien's first term to John Manley and Pierre Pettigrew since Martin's enforced exit from cabinet in June 2002, have pursued a relatively consistent line in linking domestic and foreign economic policies—supporting framework policies, political initiatives, and trade promotion initiatives that reinforce market access and, at least notionally, the competitiveness of Canadian industries in global markets.[16] The fiscal and economic gains resulting from Canada's growing economic integration with the United States have enabled the Liberals to take political credit for growing prosperity while attempting to preserve a cautious political distance between the two countries.

Economic integration under NAFTA has become sufficiently embedded in the Canadian political consensus that even traditional spokesmen for the government's nationalist wing such as Industry Minister Allan Rock could dismiss the notion that economic liberalization is a 'golden straitjacket', and argue that the increases in two-way trade and investment have allowed Canadians to become 'more relaxed . . . about our own identity', 'more pragmatic about our interaction with the United States', and 'more confident in our ability to make our own choices' in 'balancing national identity and globalization'.[17] Repeated opinion surveys suggest that while a majority of Canadians want to be different from Americans, they also acknowledge that they benefit from living beside the world's largest economy, and profit from close relations with it.[18]

The public face of the Prime Minister's engagement in foreign economic policy has involved a strong emphasis upon multilateralism: trade promotion through Team Canada trade missions, participation in international economic summitry, and, more recently, efforts to promote the NEPAD process for promoting greater economic development, democratization, and transparency in governance in Africa. Some observers, inspired by British efforts in the same direction, have suggested that these initiatives are, or should be, part of a larger 'branding' effort to establish a more distinctive international identity for Canada, its policies, and its products.[19]

At a bureaucratic level, Chrétien has accommodated DFAIT initiatives toward Latin America as Canada's underdeveloped trade and investment frontier—both as a source of new market opportunities and as a potential counterweight to American power. Despite (or, perhaps, because of) periodic disputes with Brazil and Argentina, Canada has consistently pursued a two-track strategy: negotiating incrementally toward a possible Free Trade Agreement of the Americas while negotiating bilateral free trade agreements with Chile, Costa Rica, and, prospectively, several other Central and South American countries, particularly members of the Andean Community.[20] However, the glacial pace of international trade talks and the intermittent and largely symbolic character of Chrétien's visible involvement make it harder to discern the substance of the Prime Minister's legacy in these areas.

Canada's diplomatic activity during the Chrétien era, sometimes characterized as 'building coalitions of the willing',[21] has reflected traditional themes of Canadian foreign policy, particularly in its attempts to foster problem-solving and conflict management through multilateral institutions. However, its emphasis on 'soft power, human security, peacebuilding', and co-operation with international NGOs in the selective pursuit of a reformist agenda often appears to have been directed as much to the goal of distancing Canada from the United States as to that of 'democratizing foreign policy'.[22] Canadian support for closer economic ties with Cuba, an international landmines treaty, and multilateralism on security issues, and Canada's one-upmanship of the United States on the Kyoto Protocol, have all owed as much to the conscious pursuit of 'difference' as to the policy merits of each position. Other elements of the human security policy—advocating protection of children in areas of conflict, circumpolar affairs, efforts at international conflict resolution— have been described as 'emotionally appealing, media-friendly, and inexpensive'; they develop a positive media image and some goodwill for Canada, but they lead to little substantial commitment of resources or effective follow-through.[23]

However, while Chrétien has indulged in rhetorical nationalism, invoking 'Canadian values' as a club with which to belabour his domestic political opponents and shore up Liberal support within the third of the Canadian electorate that consistently responds to such appeals, these tactics could be dismissed by a recent American ambassador as the kind of political expediency necessary to win elections and protect the government against media accusations of selling Canadian interests short.[24]

The 'Axworthy Doctrine' of emphasizing soft power and human security also provided Canada with the cover to take advantage of the 'peace dividend' of the early 1990s—pursuing a rhetorically ambitious policy of collective security on the cheap, while allowing Canada's seemingly superfluous military capacity to decline to near irrelevance.[25] Ironically, during this period Canada's armed forces became progressively more integrated with those of the United States, not only in traditional areas such as North American air defence but in the growing interoperability of naval and air forces—even before the events of September 2001 and the subsequent Afghan War.[26]

At a bureaucratic level, these discrete strategies have reinforced Ottawa's tendency to compartmentalize the management of Canada–US relations by sector or clusters of issues. Policy functions are increasingly compartmentalized by department—and even within the Department of Foreign Affairs and International Trade—and thus reflect significant differences of attitude and emphasis within the federal cabinet. Interdepartmental coordination tends to be ad hoc, as with Ottawa's hurried response to issues related to trade and security after the terrorist bombings of September 2001.[27] The effects of compartmentalization are visible in the very different approaches to interdepartmental and federal-provincial coordination taken by individual ministers and departments in response to the ongoing softwood lumber dispute, post-September 11 issues of cross-border security, transportation policies and related infrastructure initiatives, energy and environmental policies, and a wide range of other issues.[28] This decentralized approach to policy-making stands in sharp contrast to federal efforts in recent years to coordinate economic and social policies as part of a broader strategy to promote Canada's economic competitiveness, social cohesion, and fiscal sustainability.

However, the ambivalence and contradictions inherent in Canada's policies toward the United States were brought into glaring relief by the September 2001 bombings. The Chrétien government's initially hesitant response to the bombings was followed by its belated recognition of the threat to Canadian economic security that would result from an American border clampdown. An ad hoc cabinet committee on security, led by Deputy Prime Minister John Manley, brought together senior officials in the foreign affairs, law enforcement, customs, immigration, and transportation bureaucracies to engage the new American Office for Homeland Security. The outcome was the 30-point 'Smart Border Action Plan' announced in December 2001, most of whose components were implemented during 2002.[29]

Although it actively sought the inclusion of Canadian troops and ships in the Americans' Afghan strike force, the Chrétien government's transparent efforts to avoid discussion of a North American security perimeter or closer defence coordination revealed significant divisions within cabinet and the Liberal caucus over basic issues of policy coordination. Subsequent efforts to make Canadian support for American action against Iraq conditional on prior United Nations approval have barely papered over the divisions between those Liberals who view Canada's national interests as broadly aligned with the United States and those who emphasize the fundamental differences between Canadian and American values.

These divisions tend to reinforce the deeply institutionalized reluctance of Canadian governments to engage in strategic 'linkage' between 'unrelated issues' in managing periodic disputes between the two countries. They also reflect the growing challenges of policy coordination and 'multi-level governance' in cross-border relationships that touch upon virtually every major area of Canadian political and economic life. The following section examines the main principles and factors that have shaped Ottawa's management of Canada–US relations, and the pressures that are emerging to take a more strategic approach to this multidimensional relationship.

CANADA IN NORTH AMERICA: CROSS-CUTTING PRESSURES

The dynamic of economic growth . . . is more and more a cross-border phenomenon. To encourage investment, to attract and foster innovation, and to create jobs, the single-playing-field context demands, as never before, coherence in the choice and use of economic instruments. Policy-makers (both federal and provincial) responsible for domestic transportation, telecommunications, labour, environmental and taxation laws and regulations must review their bailiwicks with a wider, more competitive eye.

Keith H. Christie[30]

The United States is our region. That is the reality.

Allan Gotlieb[31]

Veteran diplomat and business executive Allan Gotlieb has described 'Canada's vulnerability to US power and influence' as the dominant problem in Canada's foreign and economic policies since the 1960s—if not long before. During the 1970s and 1980s, federal cabinet policy mandated centralized control over political and bureaucratic dealings with the United States in the then Department of External Affairs and, frequently, in the Prime Minister's Office, to enable the effective coordination of Canadian strategies and responses. The apogee of policy coordination was the creation of the centralized process for the negotiation of the Canada–US Free Trade Agreement in 1985–8.[32] However, a number of factors—institutional, economic, and political—have contributed to the *dis*integration of intergovernmental relations in Canada since the late 1980s, despite Ottawa's clear constitutional jurisdiction over foreign policy and the negotiation of international agreements.

Institutional Factors

National governments' efforts to coordinate policies and manage conflicts in many different sectors have contributed to the proliferation of functionally specialized international organizations in largely uncoordinated systems of 'multilevel governance'—'the condition wherein power and institutionalized decision-making authority is distributed among national, sub-national and supra-national bodies'.[33] These separate policy regimes, addressing different aspects of security, trade, environmental, human rights, fisheries, transportation, cultural, and other issues, have contributed to the emergence of systems of multiple accountability in which 'public policy and regulation are taken out of the control of constitutional government and given over to a complex of agencies answering to multiple constituencies.'[34]

The practical effect of these arrangements on Canadian policy-makers has been the emergence of numerous specialized, quasi-autonomous international relations functions at the departmental level, combined with independent ministerial-level consultations on issues as various as agriculture, consumer affairs, education, natural resources, and immigration.[35] Before the events of September 2001 prompted a new spasm of cross-border initiatives, Foreign Affairs listed on its website 190 Treaties and Agreements, affecting most major federal departments, between Canada and the United States alone.

While usually seeking to engage provinces in the negotiation and implementation of treaties affecting areas of provincial jurisdiction, as required by the Supreme Court's 1937 ruling in the Labour Conventions case, Ottawa has historically enforced its monopoly over international treaty negotiations.[36] However, the recent

Table 2.1

Treaties and Agreements in Force Between Canada and the United States (Updated to 1997)

Defence	34
Boundary Waters	21
Navigation	15
Boundaries	12
Commerce	9
Radio and Television	8
Fisheries	7
Air	6
Environment	6
Law Enforcement	6
Science	6
Other	70

Source: Foreign Affairs and International Trade Canada, January 2002.

application of this principle has varied from federal quasi-unilateralism, as in the negotiation of Canada's commitments under the Kyoto Protocol, to close federal-provincial co-operation in recent softwood lumber negotiations with the United States—reflecting the very different political styles and cultures of the individual ministers and departments responsible for each file. Discussions with a wide range of federal officials suggests the absence of any coordinated strategy for managing Canada–US relations, of the institutional capacity to develop such a strategy, given the number of cabinet and departmental players involved in major issues, and of the political will to create such a capacity.[37]

Economic Factors

Canada's growing economic integration within North America has vastly complicated strategic policy coordination on cross-border economic issues, both within the federal government and in federal-provincial relations. Provincial governments have been generally deferential to federal government on international and cross-border issues, except when core provincial interests have been seen to be at risk. However, in the absence of a clear strategic agenda capable of bringing together diverse federal, provincial, and private sector interests, the growth in the scale and scope of cross-border trade and investment has increased the difficulty of comprehensive policy coordination.

Since the mid-1980s, Canada's international exports, particularly those to the United States, have grown far more rapidly than interprovincial exports. By 2001, every single province exported more to other countries than to other provinces.[38] Pastor and others suggest that this process is part of a broader pattern: in Europe, East Asia, and North America, intra-regional trade is growing more rapidly than 'global' trade (see Table 2.2).[39]

While the real value of foreign direct investment (FDI) in Canada doubled between 1989 and 2001, foreign investments by Canadian companies grew even faster, reaching a record $389 billion at the end of 2001, 21 per cent more than the total volume of FDI in Canada. Investment by US firms in Canada accounted for two-thirds of FDI in Canada, while Canadian investments in US operations totalled 51 per cent of Canadian investments abroad.[40]

Table 2.2

Intraregional Trade as a Share of Total Two-Way Trade (per cent)

	European Union	*North America*	*East Asia*
1980	53.2	32.6	28.8
1990	60.6	42.8	35.0
1999	61.7	54.6	39.1

Source: Robert A. Pastor, *Toward a North American Community* (Washington, DC: Institute for International Economics, 2001).

The trend toward a greater degree of integration of Canada's economy with that of the United States, and the differing provincial responses to it, have contributed to an increase in regional diversity in fiscal and economic policies, as a consequence of differences in provincial economic structures, political priorities, and policy capacities.[41] However, Helliwell and others have noted that while globalization and continental economic integration may have reduced the importance of national borders, shared legal, cultural, and other locational factors play a significant role in the persistence of national trade links and capital markets, and in the continued relevance of national and provincial policies for economic competitiveness and social cohesion.[42]

While heightened American security concerns, the threat of gridlock at major border points, and business pressure forced the federal government to organize a concerted effort to address border security issues after the events of September 2001,[43] there appears to be little political appetite within the government to come to grips with broader issues of Canada–US relations in the waning months of Chrétien's leadership.

Political Factors

Chrétien Liberalism's cautious, managerial pragmatism has been built on an aversion to the politics of vision or large-scale change—except perhaps as a last resort. This aversion has been reinforced by the disparate character of the present Liberal coalition, particularly as Chrétien drifts toward his enforced retirement. As previously noted, Liberal party elites are deeply divided over Canada's capacity to maintain its decision-making autonomy as it becomes more deeply integrated in the North American and global economies. Central to these divisions are contending views of the degree of linkage that should be accommodated or sought between cross-border security issues, defence policy coordination, and Canada's fundamental interests in the security and ease of access of Canadian exports to US markets and Canadian travellers to US destinations.

Leading Liberals such as Finance Minister John Manley, Trade Minister Pierre Pettigrew, and former Trudeau chief-of-staff Tom Axworthy clearly view Canada's close economic relationship with the United States, complemented by other trade relationships, as an advantage that provides Canadian governments with the financial resources to maintain and enhance social programs and social cohesion. Axworthy also argues that Canadian foreign policy should be aimed at 'tip[ping] the balance in the internal US debate towards liberal internationalism' rather than pursuing policy differences largely to reinforce appearances of foreign policy independence. In this view, some combination of increased defence spending and security coordination is critical to Canada's capacity to engage US domestic and foreign policies.[44]

Others, such as former Foreign Minister Lloyd Axworthy and, less vocally, several current cabinet members and a significant segment of the Liberal caucus, emphasize the need for Canada to distance itself from American policies or dependence on the

United States. While increased defence spending may be entertained, it should be targeted primarily toward peacekeeping and multilateral security initiatives such as an independent United Nations rapid response force independent of American control.[45] Chrétien and Foreign Minister Bill Graham have appeared to oscillate between the two poles of the debate, depending on the specific issues at stake.

Liberal pollsters and academic analysts note the ambivalence among traditional Liberal constituencies over growing economic interdependence with the United States. NAFTA is broadly perceived as providing an economic benefit to Canada—if marginally less than to the United States or Mexico. However, most Liberals (and a strong plurality of Canadians) would prefer Canada to be less like the United States and to diversify Canada's trade relationships. On balance, public opinion appears to be broadly supportive of the status quo in Canadian foreign and trade policies, while viewing 'globalization' as a somewhat more benign force than increased North American integration (see Table 2.3).[46]

This 'permissive consensus' may be conducive to incremental changes and extensions of Canadian policies—as long as Canada maintains its capacity to maintain independent cultural and social policies.[47] However, it provides little incentive for Mr Chrétien to pursue major new policy initiatives toward the United States as long as President Bush and his senior advisors are engaged elsewhere, particularly with political attention shifting to the looming Liberal leadership contest. However, the growing leadership vacuum is contributing to pressures from both inside and outside Liberal government circles for a more coherent strategy not only to address Canada–US relations, but to permit the more consistent integration of Canada's major domestic and foreign policy objectives.

Table 2.3

Perceived impact of Globalization on:	Positive %	No Impact %	Negative %
Canada's economic well-being	**59**	16	24
Canada's social well-being	**44**	24	31
Canada's environment	37	24	38
Canadian culture	**40**	28	31
Perceived impact of North American Integration on:			
Canada's economic well-being	**55**	18	24
Canada's social well-being	34	24	**39**
Canada's environment	29	22	**46**
Canadian culture	31	26	**42**

Source: Ekos Research Associates (2002d), 9.

Pressures for Strategic Policy Change

No state is fully autonomous . . . (but) the promotion of choice or enhanced autonomy in an admittedly interdependent world should be a preeminent goal for Canada in the 21st century.

Thomas S. Axworthy[48]

Even before the events of September 2001, several major factors were leading influential economic interests and policy experts to explore new strategies for strengthening Canada's competitive position in North American and global markets. While Canada ranked third overall in the World Economic Forum's 'Global Competitiveness Index' for medium-term growth prospects in 2001,[49] both government officials and industry leaders have expressed concern over the productivity of Canadian industries relative to that of their competitors, and other micro-economic factors that influence competitiveness and standards of living.

A growing literature suggests that 'increased economic integration at the international level implies that Canada will need strategies that maximize economic opportunities'[50] without sacrificing its capacity to make independent social and economic policy choices. Policy flexibility is seen to depend in large measure on the achievement of rates of investment and economic growth above those of the United States, and on the wise investment of those surpluses in economic and social policy initiatives that reinforce higher living standards, greater social cohesion, and increased fiscal capacity.[51] For example, the Conference Board of Canada has noted that despite economic growth and rising incomes during the late 1990s, the average Canadian still earns substantially less than his US counterpart, and this 'income gap', measured as per capita GDP, at PPP-adjusted exchange rates, grew from $3,400 in 1989 to $7,600 in 2000, while Canada's share of incoming foreign investment had declined relative to *both* the United States and Mexico during the 1990s.[52] Some observers argued that the decline in the value of the Canadian dollar was increasing the vulnerability of Canadian companies to foreign takeovers, while reducing pressures on Canadian businesses to engage in the research and innovation necessary to compete internationally.[53]

These analyses, echoing concerns raised by officials (and occasionally ministers) of Industry and Finance, emphasized the dynamic nature of international economic competition and the need for continuous adaptation and improvement in order to preserve the competitiveness and relative living standards of Canadian businesses and workers.[54] While not directly challenging government policies, they noted that in the absence of direct political leadership, Canadian policies and standards in many areas would be likely to converge with American ones by default rather than as the result of a considered process that carefully defined and advanced Canadian interests.[55] As an alternative to 'harmonization by default', some observers have argued for the development of a coherent strategy to achieve 'functional' integration by negotiating different levels of 'interoperability', 'mutual recognition', and 'coordination' of standards, in order to accommodate both similarities and differences in policy goals among Canada, the United States, and Mexico.[56]

Business groups and trade policy experts have also expressed concern over the slowing of the momentum of international trade negotiations, the rise of protectionist sentiments in the United States, the apparent preoccupation of powerful American politicians with Mexico and the Hispanic vote, and the large number of cross-border trade and regulatory issues that have created both obstacles to and opportunities for increased trade and competitiveness.[57] The terrorist attacks of September 2001 changed the context of the debate, if not its underlying terms. The threat of continued and increased American restrictions on cross-border trade and travel, as well as ongong protectionist pressures on the softwood lumber issue, raised apprehensions about the exclusion of Canadian goods and the harassment of Canadian travellers at the border. Many policy observers expressed concern over the apparent aimlessness of Canadian government policies and Canada's virtual invisibility in Washington. Several argued that if Canada wished to influence an American political system preoccupied with US global interests and the regular business of interest group politics, the federal government would have to take a more proactive, coherent, and focused approach to defining and promoting Canada's interests within North America.[58]

Some policy experts and business leaders, including Wendy Dobson and Allan Gotlieb, have called for a 'grand bargain' between Canada and the United States, which would exchange more secure market access and increased labour mobility for closer security and defence coordination, and possibly a common external trade policy.[59] However, most recognize that asymmetries in size and power between the two countries, along with the much 'harder' view of national sovereignty that exists in the United States, are major obstacles to the creation of shared political institutions—even if Canadians were willing to sacrifice that degree of political discretion.[60] American domestic political realities and foreign policy interests may well require parallel US–Mexican negotiations on issues of common concern.[61]

As a result, attention has shifted to the possibility of extending existing cross-border agreements such as NAFTA and NORAD to address issues such as

- 'greater ease of travel for those working between the two countries;
- 'a reduction in the regulations that hinder the flow of goods, services, capital and people;
- 'an integrated energy market, including the development of northern sources of gas in Alaska and the Mackenzie Valley;
- 'cooperation in defence, such as in strengthening Northern security;
- 'elimination of subsidies that distort trade patterns and reduce economic gains from trade'.[62]

These pressures have gradually, if slowly, begun to engage the attention of the Chrétien government's leading economic ministers and those who provide them with polling and strategic advice. The tenth anniversary of the signing of NAFTA in October 2002 was marked by a series of speeches by key economic ministers emphasizing the benefits of economic integration, the importance to Canada's national identity and political sovereignty of both prosperity and the capacity to make 'independent policy choices', and possible initiatives for future action.[63] Liberal-friendly pollsters such as Frank Graves of Ekos, who currently surveys public opinion for both Environment Canada and Foreign Affairs and International Trade Canada, echoes these themes, noting that value differences between the two countries 'seem to permit both common economic space and separate moral communities'.[64]

The most coherent expression of a possible road toward NAFTA extension as the preferred option for dealing with cross-border concerns came from International Trade Minister Pierre Pettigrew in mid-October 2002. While suggesting that talk of a 'grand bargain' was premature, Pettigrew outlined six policy priorities that could shape the evolution of federal policies. These included promotion of an increase in export penetration of American markets and an expansion of two-way investment within North America, and a review of cross-border regulatory initiatives to increase cooperation and accommodate differences arising from different market conditions or policy priorities. Pettigrew also called for 'removing the border as an impediment to trade' through the application of new technologies, customs screening procedures, and provisions for increased labour mobility; 'smarter representation and advocacy in the United States', including the building of coalitions with compatible US domestic interests; and—Canada's perennial demand—the reform of US trade remedy laws, including anti-dumping and countervailing duty rules.[65]

While most of these proposals are logical extensions of existing government policies and programs, in the absence of cabinet approval they appear to reflect efforts by Pettigrew (and other ministers) to begin defining an agenda for the post-Chrétien era, rather than a concerted effort to define a prime ministerial legacy. The possible exception is the so-called 'smart regulation' initiative mentioned in the September 2002 Throne Speech, in which the Privy Council Office was assigned responsibility for actively encouraging and coordinating departmental initiatives.

THE CHRÉTIEN LEGACY: OPTIONS FOR THE FUTURE?

The federal government has yet to evolve a coherent strategy for engaging the Americans, and its capacity to engage either the Bush administration or Congress will be diminished until concerns over Middle East politics relinquish centre stage. However, Republican gains in the 2002 congressional elections, which provided President Bush with a narrow majority in both houses of Congress and removed protectionist senators such as Montana's Max Baucus from key congressional leadership positions, may have provided Mr Bush with enough political capital to enable him to take the initiative in international trade negotiations—if he can prevent it from being consumed in the quicksands of the Middle East.

Just before the November 2002 congressional elections, the Chrétien government tabled with the White House a proposal entitled 'Securing Growth', which reportedly attempts to build on the December 2001 'Smart Border Agreement' by easing restrictions on cross-border travel, by initiating a process for enhancing the compat-ibility or mutual accommodation of regulatory processes across NAFTA countries, and by exploring processes for improved environmental coordination. President Bush's response to these proposals and the Prime Minister's willingness to invest his dwindling political capital in pursuing these initiatives will determine whether the political will to address these issues coherently exists on either side of the border.

These concerns are likely to be reinforced by the narrow division of both houses of a Congress many of whose members, in order to ensure their own political sur-vival, tend to be largely focused on parochial issues, and by the shallow support of American public opinion for closer trade links and increased labour mobility with Mexico. The elimination of US anti-dumping and countervailing duties is privately admitted to be a political non-starter in Congress in the absence of a far broader agenda for trade policy coordination.

These issues—and the underlying economic forces that drive them—are unlikely to go away in the foreseeable future; a legacy of unfinished business will be left for the new Liberal leader to be elected in November 2004. As candidates for the Prime Minister's chair rush to claim the broad centre of the political spectrum that is likely to define the future of Canadian Liberalism, they will be challenged to articulate a persuasive vision of Canada's national interest—one that balances prosperity, social cohesion, and a distinct Canadian identity as it steers through the shoals of increas-ing North American integration.

The Chrétien legacy with respect to Canada's place in North America remains to be written. It may be a government and a party deeply at odds with itself in its efforts to define Canada's place in the world and its relationship with the United States—or one capable of balancing and integrating these two critical dimensions of Canadian public policy in a coherent whole. It may be a fragmented approach to Canada–US and North American relations that muddles through from crisis to crisis or one that succeeds in engaging the Bush administration and Mexico's President Fox in negotiations over an NAFTA-plus agenda that deal effectively with hemi-spheric security and concerns about energy and the environment.

Ironically, the emerging Liberal leadership race may help to clarify this legacy, whether by design or default. Prospective candidates hoping to challenge Paul Mar-tin's substantial head start in winning the hearts and minds of Liberal delegates—and his grip on the wallets of party contributors—will be forced to define their vision of Canada's future in an increasingly integrated North America. Their ability to do so, or to elicit a clearer sense of direction from the Prime Minister-in-waiting, may well determine whether the next Liberal government can translate its rhetoric on 'a new Canadian confidence' into a coherent and constructive reality.

NOTES

1 Geoffrey E. Hale, 'Managing the Fiscal Dividend: The Politics of Selective Activism', in Leslie A. Pal, ed., *How Ottawa Spends 2000–2001* (Toronto: Oxford University

Press, 2000), 59–94; Geoffrey E. Hale, 'Innovation and Inclusion: Budgetary Policy, the Skills Agenda, and the Politics of the New Economy', in G. Bruce Doern, ed., *How Ottawa Spends 2002–2003* (Toronto: Oxford University Press, 2002), 20–47.

2   Jeffrey A. Frankel, *Regional Trading Blocs in the World Economic System* (Washington, DC: Institute for International Economics, Oct. 1997); Alan G. Rugman, *The End of Globalization: Why Global Strategy Is a Myth and How to Profit from the Realities of Regional Markets* (New York: Amacom, 2000); Robert Pastor, *Toward a North American Community* (Washington, DC: Institute for International Economics, 2001).

3   Jack M. Mintz, 'Smart Sovereignty: Canadian Prosperity in an Integrating World Economy' (Toronto: C.D. Howe Institute, 2 Apr. 2001); Daniel Schwanen, 'After Sept. 11: Interoperability with the U.S., not Convergence', *Policy Options* (Nov. 2001), 46–9; Perrin Beatty, 'Isolation or Integration: Canada in North America' (Ottawa: Canadian Manufacturers and Exporters, Feb. 2002), photocopy; Michael Hart and Brian Tomlin, 'Inside the Perimeter: The US Policy Agenda and Its Implications for Canada', in G. Bruce Doern, ed., *How Ottawa Spends 2002–2003* (Toronto: Oxford University Press, 2002), 48–68; Wendy Dobson, 'Shaping the Future of the North American Economic Space', Commentary # 162 (Toronto: C.D. Howe Institute, Apr. 2002); John Manley, 'My Vision for the Canada–US Relationship' (Halifax: AIMS, 15 May 2002); Ekos Research Associates, 'Conclusions: A Way Forward', presentation to Ekos/Public Policy Forum Symposium, Toronto, 18 June 2002; Allan Gotlieb, 'Why Not a Grand Bargain with the U.S.?', *The National Post*, 11 Sept. 2002, A16; Thomas S. Axworthy, 'A Choice not an Echo: Sharing North America with the Hyperpower', paper presented to a conference on 'Searching for a New Liberalism', 27–9 Sept. 2002, photocopy.

4   Edward Greenspon and Anthony Wilson-Smith, *Double Vision* (Toronto: Doubleday Canada, 1996) 26, 51–2;

5   Hale, 'Managing the Fiscal Dividend'; Geoffrey E. Hale, 'Priming the Electoral Pump: Framing Budgets for a Renewed Mandate', in Pal, *How Ottawa Spends 2000–2001*, 29–60; Donald A. Savoie, *Governing from the Centre* (Toronto: University of Toronto Press, 1999), 313ff.

6   Greenspon and Wilson-Smith, *Double Vision*; James J. Blanchard, *Behind the Embassy Door* (Toronto: McClelland and Stewart, 1998), 79–83.

7   Liberal Party of Canada, *Securing Our Future Together [Red Book II]* (Ottawa, 1997); Hale, 'Priming the Electoral Pump', 34–5.

8   Ibid.; Hale, 'Innovation and Inclusion'; Canada. Department of Finance, *The Budget Plan: 1998*; *The Budget Plan: 2000*; *The Budget Plan: 2001* (Ottawa, annual).

9   Paul Barker, 'Disentangling the Federation: Social Policy and Fiscal Federalism', in Martin Westmacott and Hugh Mellon, eds, *Challenges to Canadian Federalism* (Toronto: Prentice Hall, 1998), 144–54.

10 Heather Smith, 'Canadian Federalism and International Environmental Policy Making: The Case of Climate Change', working paper, Institute for Intergovernmental Relations, Queen's University, 1998, 10–13.

11 Alain Noel, 'Power and Purpose in Intergovernmental Relations', *Policy Matters* 2, 6 (Montreal: IRPP, Nov. 2001).

12 Interview, senior federal government officials.

13 Geoffrey Hale, *The Politics of Taxation in Canada* (Peterborough: Broadview Press, 2001); Jeffrey Simpson, *The Friendly Dictatorship* (Toronto: McClelland and Stewart, 2001); Kenneth J. McKenzie, 'A Tragedy of the House of Commons: Political Institu-

tions and Fiscal Policy Outcomes from a Canadian Perspective' (Toronto: C.D. Howe Institute, 8 Nov. 2001).

14 Keith Banting, Andrew Sharpe, and France St.Hilaire, *The Longest Decade: Canada in the 1990s. The Review of Economic Performance and Social Progress* (Montreal: IRPP/CSLS, 2001).

15 Manley, 'My Vision'; Pierre Pettigrew, 'The Canada We Want in the North America We Are Building' (Ottawa: Foreign Affairs and International Trade Canada, 16 Oct. 2002); Allan Rock, 'A New Canadian Confidence', speech to the Canadian–American Business Council, Toronto (Ottawa: Industry Canada, 16 Oct. 2002); Brian J.R. Stevenson, 'Too Close to the Americans, Too Far from the Americas: A Liberal Policy Towards the Hemisphere', in M.A. Molot and F.O. Hampson, eds, *Vanishing Borders: Canada Among Nations 2000* (Toronto: Oxford University Press, 2000), 223–45.

16 The analysis contained in a 1993 DFAIT policy paper suggests a remarkable degree of coherence and continuity in Canada's international economic policies since then. Keith H. Christie, 'Different Strokes: Regionalism and Canada's Economic Diplomacy', *Policy Staff Paper* 93/08 (Ottawa: Foreign Affairs and International Trade Canada, May 1993).

17 Rock, 'A New Canadian Confidence,' 2–3.

18 Matthew Mendelsohn, Robert Wolfe, and Andrew Parkin, 'Globalization, Trade Policy and the Permissive Consensus in Canada', *Canadian Public Policy* 28, 3 (Sept. 2002), 351-71; Ekos Research Associates, 'Canadian Attitudes Toward International Trade', prepared for Department of Foreign Affairs and International Trade (Ottawa, 15 Apr. 2002); Ekos Research Associates, 'North American Economic Dimensions', presentation to Ekos/Public Policy Forum Symposium, Toronto, 18 June 2002; Ekos, 'Conclusions: A Way Forward', Centre for Research and Information on Canada, *BorderLines Survey*, 28 Oct. 2002; on the Internet at www.cric.ca

19 Andrew F. Cooper, 'Coalitions of the Willing: The Search for Like-Minded Partners in Canadian Diplomacy', in Leslie A. Pal, ed., *How Ottawa Spends 1999–2000* (Toronto: Oxford University Press, 1999), 221–47; Andrew F. Cooper, 'Vertical Limits: A Foreign Ministry of the Future', *Journal of Canadian Studies* 35 (Winter 2001), 111–29; Susan Delacourt, 'Updating P.E.T. Theories', *The National Post*, 5 Oct. 2002, A10; Wayne Hunt, 'A Brand Canada for a Connected World', paper presented to the 'Searching for a New Liberalism' conference, Toronto, Sept. 2002.

20 Christie, 'Different Strokes'; Stevenson, 'Too Close to the Americans'; Canada. Standing Committee on Foreign Affairs and International Trade, 'Strengthening Canada's Economic Links with the Americas', *Report # 22* (Ottawa: House of Commons, 14 June 2002); Louise Elliott, 'Canada Seeks New Bilateral Trade Deals', *The Financial Post*, 4 Nov. 2002, FP5. The United States initiated free trade negotiations with five Central American countries under its 'fast track' legislation in October 2002. Max Baucus, 'Statement for the Record on Congressional–Executive Consultations on Trade' (Washington, DC: Senate Committee on Finance, 17 Oct. 2002); on the Internet at: http://finance.senate.gov/press/pr101702.pdf

21 Cooper, 'Coalitions of the Willing'.

22 Yvon Grenier, 'Our Dictatorship: Canada's Trilateral Relations with Castro's Cuba', in Molot and Hampson, *Vanishing Borders*, 247–73; Denis Stairs, 'Canada in the 1990s: Talk Loudly and Carry a Bent Twig', *Policy Options* (Jan.-Feb. 2001), 43–9. Allan Gotlieb has made similar observations about Canadian foreign policy during the Trudeau era: *The United States in Canadian Foreign Policy*, O.D. Skelton Memorial Lecture (Ottawa: DFAIT, 10 Dec. 1991), 12.

23 Daryl Copeland, 'The Axworthy Years: Canada's Foreign Policy in an Era of Diminished Capacity', in *The Axworthy Legacy: Canada Among Nations 2001* (Toronto: Oxford University Press, 2001), 161-5.

24 Michael Marzolini, 'The Politics of Values', *Liberal Times* (Mar. 2001); Blanchard, *Behind the Embassy Door*, 79-83, 128-59.

25 Stairs, 'Canada in the 1990s'; Copeland, 'The Axworthy Years', 152-72; Brian MacDonald, 'Will Canada's Forces Have What They Need When They Need It?' *Policy Options* (Mar. 2001), 32-8; Canadian Council for Canadian Security in the 21st Century, 'People's Defense Review' (Calgary, 11 Sept. 2002), 11-15; T.S. Axworthy, 'A Choice not an Echo,' 7-9; Norman Spector, 'Nix the Toys for the Boys,' *The Globe and Mail* [Toronto], 10 Oct. 2002, A19.

26 J.L. Granatstein, 'A Friendly Agreement in Advance', Commentary # 166 (Toronto: C.D. Howe Institute, June 2002), 7; Andrew Richter, 'Strategic Ambitions and Fiscal Realities: Give the Navy Priority', *Policy Options* (Apr. 2002), 27-31.

27 Andrew F. Cooper, 'Vertical Limits'; Douglas M. Brown, 'Aspects of Multilateral Governance in Australia and Canada' (Institute of Intergovernmental Relations, Queen's University, 2002), photocopy; interviews, Foreign Affairs and International Trade Canada, Industry Canada, and Privy Council Office.

28 Brown, 'Aspects of Multilateral Governance', 11-18; G. Bruce Doern, 'Seven Key Policy Issues and Challenges: Canadian Energy Policy in the Sustainable Development Era', CRUISE Conference on Canadian Energy Policy in the Sustainable Development Era, 18 Oct. 2002, photocopy; interviews, Foreign Affairs and International Trade Canada, Industry Canada, and Privy Council Office.

29 Canada. Department of Foreign Affairs and International Trade, 'The Smart Border Declaration' (Ottawa, 12 Dec. 2001); United States of America. White House, 'Gov Ridge, Deputy PM of Canada Discuss Smart Border Plan' (Washington: Office of Press Secretary, 8 Apr. 2002); John Manley, 'Notes for Address to Can-Am Border Trade Alliance' (Ottawa: Department of Foreign Affairs and International Trade, 6 May 2002).

30 Christie, 'Different Strokes', 7.2.

31 Gotlieb, *The United States in Canadian Foreign Policy*, 7.

32 Ibid., 11, 14-15; G. Bruce Doern and Brian Tomlin, *Faith and Fear: The Free Trade Story* (Toronto: Stoddart, 1991), 108-25, 130-3; 163-7.

33 Michael Hart, 'The Trade Model of Multi-Level Governance: Lessons from Fifty Years of Cautious Pragmatism', paper presented to a Conference on 'Globalization, Multi-Level Governance and Democracy', Institute for Intergovernmental Relations, Queen's University, May 2002, 2.

34 Michael Keating, 'Challenges to Federalism: Territory, Function, and Power in a Globalizing World', in Robert Young, ed., *Stretching the Federation: The Art of the State in Canada* (Kingston: Institute for Intergovernmental Relations, Queen's University, 1999), 21. For a partial discussion of the sectoral effects of this phenomenon, see papers presented at a conference on 'Globalization, Multilevel Governance and Democracy: Continental, Comparative and Global Perspectives', Institute for Intergovernmental Relations, Queen's University, May 2002; on the Internet at: http://qsilver.queensu.ca/iigr/conferences/globalization/presentations.html

35 Interviews, Foreign Affairs and International Trade Canada; Brown, 'Aspects of Multilateral Governance', 12-15; see also Conference Board of Canada, *Canada 2010: Challenges and Choices at Home and Abroad: Performance and Potential: 2002-2003* (Ottawa, Sept. 2002), 95-8.

36 Brown, 'Aspects of Multilevel Governance', 11–12; *A.G. Can. V. A.G. Ont. (Labour Conventions)* [1937] A.C. 354; interviews, Department of Foreign Affairs and International Trade.

37 See also Cooper, 'Vertical Limits'.

38 Statistics Canada, *Provincial Economic Accounts*, Cat. # 13–213 (Ottawa, Apr. 2002), 311, 314.

39 Frankel, *Regional Trading Blocs*; Rugman, *The End of Globalization*; Pastor, *Toward a North American Community*.

40 Statistics Canada, *Canada's International Investment Position*, Cat. 67–202 (Ottawa, annual); Canada. Department of Foreign Affairs and International Trade, *Third Annual Report on Canada's State of Trade* (Ottawa, May 2002), 35.

41 Geoffrey Hale, 'Balancing Autonomy and Responsibility: The Politics of Provincial Fiscal and Tax Policies', in Christopher Dunn, ed., *Provinces: Provincial Politics in Canada*, 2nd edn (Peterborough: Broadview Press, forthcoming).

42 John McCallum, 'National Borders Matter: Canada–U.S. Regional Trade Patterns', *American Economic Review* 85 (June 1995), 615–23; William Watson, *Globalization and the Meaning of Canadian Life* (Toronto: University of Toronto Press, 1998); John F. Helliwell, *Globalization: Myths, Facts and Consequences* (Toronto: C.D. Howe Institute, Oct. 2000); George Hoberg, 'Canada and North American Integration', *Canadian Public Policy* 26, 2 [2000], S37–48; W. Mark Brown, 'Overcoming Distance, Overcoming Borders: Comparing North American Regional Trade' (Ottawa: Statistics Canada, Apr. 2002), photocopy.

43 Coalition for Secure and Trade Efficient Borders, 'Rethinking Our Borders: A Plan for Action' (Ottawa, Dec. 2001); Canada. Department of Foreign Affairs and International Trade, 'The Smart Border Declaration'; Manley, 'Notes for Address to Can-Am Border Trade Alliance'.

44 T.S. Axworthy, 'A Choice not an Echo', 6; Thomas S. Axworthy, 'Our Lack of Preparedness Is the Emergency', *The National Post*, 8 Nov. 2002, A14.

45 Compare T.S. Axworthy, 'A Choice not an Echo', and Lloyd Axworthy, 'Choices and Consequences in a Liberal Foreign Policy', papers presented to a conference on 'Searching for a New Liberalism', Toronto, 27–9 Sept. 2002; on Internet at: www.newliberalism.ca. See also Lloyd Axworthy, 'Liberals at the Border: We Stand on Guard for Whom?' Keith Davey Lecture, Victoria University (Vancouver: Liu Centre for Study of Global Issues, 11 Mar. 2002).

46 Pollara Inc., 'Canadians' Views of the Economy and the Innovation Strategy' (Ottawa: Industry Canada, Feb. 2002); Ekos, 'Canadian Attitudes Toward International Trade'; Ekos, 'North American Economic Dimensions', 9; Mendelson, Wolfe, and Parkin, 'Globalization'; Centre for Research and Information on Canada, 'Border Lines Survey'.

47 Matthew Mendelsohn, 'Canada's Social Contract: Evidence from Public Opinion', report to Canadian Policy Research Networks, Sept. 2002, photocopy; Mendelsohn, Wolfe, and Parkin, 'Globalization'.

48 T.S. Axworthy, 'A Choice not an Echo', 3.

49 Methodological changes resulted in Canada's slipping from third to tenth in 'growth competitiveness', an assessment of capacity for future economic growth, between 2001 and 2002. Canada has ranked between sixth and twelfth in current or microeconomic competitiveness since 1998. Roger L. Martin and Michael E. Porter, 'Canadian Competitiveness: Nine Years after the Crossroads' (Toronto: Rotman School of Management, Jan. 2000), photocopy; Peter K. Cornelius, 'Executive Summary',

Global Competitiveness Summary: 2002–2003 (New York: Oxford University Press, 2002), 5; Michael E. Porter, 'Building the Microeconomic Foundations of Prosperity: Findings from the Microeconomic Competitiveness Index,' in Peter Cornelius et al., *Global Competitiveness Summary: 2002–2003* (New York: Oxford University Press, 2002), 9; Jacqueline Thorpe, 'Think-Tank Glitch Mars Canada's Rank', *The National Post*, 13 Nov. 2002, A1.

50 Jack M. Mintz, 'Northern Tiger: Canada in North America' (Toronto: C.D. Howe Institute, 26 Sept. 2002).

51 Ibid.; Mintz, 'Smart Sovereignty'; T.S. Axworthy, 'A Choice, not an Echo'; Rock, 'A New Canadan Confidence'; see also Thomas J. D'Aquino and David Stewart-Patterson, *Northern Edge: How Canada Can Triumph in the Global Economy* (Toronto: Stoddart, 2001); Thomas J. Courchene , *States of Mind: Towards a Human Capital Future for Canadians* (Montreal: IRPP, 2001); Jack M. Mintz, *Most Favoured Nation: Building a Framework for Smart Economic Policy* (Toronto: C.D. Howe Institute, 2001); Conference Board of Canada, *Performance and Potential: 2001–02* (Ottawa: Sept. 2001).

52 Conference Board, *Performance and Potential: 2001–02*, 3; Conference Board, *Canada 2010*, 17, 105–9.

53 Thomas J. Courchene and Richard G. Harris, 'From Fixing to Monetary Union: Options for North American Currency Integration' (Toronto: C.D. Howe Institute, June 1999); Willard Z. Estey, 'The Quiet Hijacking of Corporate Canada', *The Globe and Mail* [Toronto], 16 Dec. 1999; Jayson Myers, 'Canada: Meeting the Challenge of North American Integration' (Ottawa: Canadian Manufacturers and Exporters, 2002); David Crane, 'Takeovers of Foreign Firms Cause for Concern', *The Toronto Star*, 18 Sept. 2002; for a contrary view, see Lawrence Schembri, 'Foreign Takeovers and the Canadian Dollar: Evidence and Implications', *Bank of Canada Review* (Spring 2002), 45–50.

54 Kevin G. Lynch, 'Building a Global, Knowledge-Based Economy for the 21st Century' (Ottawa: Industry Canada, Feb. 2000); Canada. Standing Committee on Industry, Science and Technology, 'A Canadian Innovation Agenda for the Twenty-First Century', *Fifth Report* (Ottawa, June 2001); Canadian Manufacturers and Exporters, *Canada's Excellence Gap: Benchmarking the Performance of Canadian Industry against the G7* (Ottawa, 1 Aug. 2001); Canada. Standing Committee on Finance, *Securing Our Future*, Tenth Report (Ottawa: House of Commons, Nov. 2001); Anne Golden, 'If We Snooze, We Lose', *The Globe and Mail* [Toronto], 11 Oct. 2002, A15.

55 Conference Board, *Performance and Potential: 2001–02*, 13–14.

56 Schwanen, 'After Sept. 11'.

57 Michael Hart and William Dymond, *Common Borders, Shared Destinies: Canada, the United States and Deepening Integration* (Ottawa: Centre for Trade Policy and Law, 2001); Canada. Standing Committee on Foreign Affairs and International Trade, 'Strengthening Canada's Economic Links with the Americas'; Pastor, *Toward a North American Community*.

58 Canada. Standing Committee on Foreign Affairs, 'Towards a Secure and Trade-Efficient Border' (Ottawa: House of Commons, Nov. 2001); Schwanen, 'After Sept. 11'; Beatty, 'Isolation or Integration'; David Zussman, 'The Challenges of North American Integration', *The Ottawa Citizen*, 8 Apr. 2002; David Zussman, 'A Future Vision for North America', remarks to the Food and Consumer Products Manufacturers of Canada (Ottawa: Public Policy Forum, 9 Apr. 2002); Drew Fagan, 'It's Time We Faced Facts: Canada's Focus Must Be on North America', *The Globe and Mail* [Toronto], 16 Aug. 2002, B8; Mintz, 'Northern Tiger'.

59 Dobson, 'Shaping the Future'; Gotlieb, 'Why Not a Grand Bargain?'

60 Mintz, 'Smart Sovereignty'; Beatty, 'Isolation or Integration'.

61 For different approaches to this issue, see Hart and Dymond, *Common Borders, Shared Destinies*, 41–4; Rogelio Ramirez De la O, 'Mexico, NAFTA and the Prospects for North American Integration', Commentary # 172 (Toronto: C.D. Howe Institute, Nov. 2002), 2.

62 Mintz, 'Northern Tiger', 5; a similar agenda can be found in Conference Board, *Canada 2010*, 95.

63 Rock, 'A New Canadian Confidence'; Pettigrew, 'The Canada We Want'; Eric Beauchesne and James Baxter, 'Free Trade Deal Should Be Even Freer, Manley Says', *The Edmonton Journal*, 25 Oct. 2002, A9; Anne Dawson, 'Pettigrew Confirms NAFTA Push', *The National Post*, 26 Oct. 2002, A1; Drew Fagan, 'Sweet Continental Harmony', *The Globe and Mail* [Toronto], 29 Oct. 2002, A19.

64 Ekos, 'North American Economic Dimensions'.

65 Pettigrew, 'The Canada We Want'.

3

More or Less Than Meets the Eye?
The New National Security Agenda

REG WHITAKER

The terrorist attacks on the World Trade Center and the Pentagon on September 11, 2001 (hereinafter referred to as 9/11) were widely viewed as opening a new, unsettling era in international relations. The decade-long transition from the Cold War was now over: a global war against terrorism was proclaimed by US president George W. Bush. A broad international coalition of nations was constructed to wage a prolonged struggle, not against another superpower or a rival bloc of threatening states, but against shadowy networks of violent non-state actors operating across borders. The dark side of globalization had reared its head. The old Westphalian system of international order based on nation states now faced a double challenge: not only the global governance of transnational economic activity, but the maintenance of order and basic security in a global state of nature that appeared alarmingly Hobbesian.

Although it happened outside of Canada, 9/11 forced a rapid internal realignment of national policy priorities. There are previous examples of such exogenous events. The sharp spike in oil prices forced by the actions of the OPEC cartel at the outset of the 1980s inspired the bold (if ultimately disastrous) innovation of the National Energy Program, brought in by the Liberal government of Pierre Elliott Trudeau. That impact was, however, restricted to the field of energy resource policy. To find an historical analogy to 9/11, one has to reach back to 1946 and the onset of the Cold War in Canada following the Gouzenko spy affair, and the series of national security measures enacted in its wake.[1] The Soviet threat was primarily a 'state-to-state' threat, while 9/11, a catastrophic attack on civil society, potentially posed a more wide-ranging challenge to public policy. However, despite efforts to portray 9/11 as an attack on all civilized nations, it was primarily an attack on *American* civil society. This US focus had the effect of diluting somewhat the direct impact of 9/11 on Canada, and also filtering the impact: Canada had to react not only to 9/11, but also to the American reaction to 9/11.

There was an initial tendency to assess Canada's response to 9/11 in the same framework as the US response.[2] Canada is indeed closer than any other country, both geographically and culturally, to the United States. But Canada did not feel the impact in exactly the same way the United States did. The shock waves were absorbed in Canada differently. The United States was facing a terrorist threat to the American homeland, and the conundrum of how to defeat it. 9/11 was an attack on the United States, on its military and economic symbols, and on American civilians. Canadians sympathized with Americans, shared their pain, and joined in their anger. Canadians recognized the need to bolster their security and expand intelligence on terrorism, both to assist a friend and to help themselves. Canadians also realize that they are not a *primary* target of Al-Qaida. The attack on the World Trade Center and the Pentagon sent a clear message, however perverse, about American economic and military power. An attack on the CN Tower and Ottawa Defence HQ would send an indecipherable message. This does not rule out terrorism as a threat on Canadian soil, but it does reduce its urgency.

9/11 brought with it another kind of threat to Canada: collateral damage to Canadian economic security as a result of American national security concerns applied to the Canada–US border. Canada faced the strains on sovereignty attendant upon measures required to assure Americans that the everyday flow of goods, services, capital, and people across America's northern frontier did not constitute a US national security risk. Some loss of sovereignty was inevitable, and has occurred. The government of Canada, while responding to the terrorist threat, was also forced to conduct a difficult series of negotiations with the United States, restructuring some key aspects of the Canada–US relationship. 9/11 forced Canada onto parallel tracks, one track being that of adjustment to the terrorist threat, the other that of adjustment to the collateral damage to Canada caused by the American response to 9/11. The first has been visible and only moderately controversial, the second less visible, yet at the same time highly controversial and indeed divisive within Canada.

This is the relatively complex field on which the response of the Canadian government to 9/11 should be assessed. From Canada's point of view, this war is occurring on more than one front. Moreover, we have to distinguish carefully what is genuinely new and linked to the impact of 9/11 as an exogenous event from what was already in process prior to 9/11, but required unblocking.

THE DIRECT IMPACT OF 9/11

9/11 rearranged the national policy agenda, pushing national security to a level of priority it had not had in Ottawa for decades.[3] We can summarize the impact of 9/11 on national policy priorities under the following headings:

- restructuring of the cabinet architecture for policy-making;
- reallocation of budgetary resources;
- military contributions to the war on terrorism;
- new or expanded legislative powers;
- restructuring of bureaucratic mechanisms; and
- negotiating border security arrangements.

The Cabinet Committee

The striking of the ad hoc Cabinet Committee on Public Security and Anti-Terrorism was a key step. It symbolized a degree of high-level attention to security matters that had hitherto been dangerously low. There had once been a cabinet committee on security and intelligence, chaired by the prime minister. Under pressure of a grave security crisis, that of the October 1970 FLQ kidnapping and assassination, this committee had exhibited a brief life, which extended into the 1970s as a consequence of prime ministerial insistence on countering the separatist movement in Quebec. Scandals that subsequently engulfed the RCMP security service and led to its civilianization in the 1980s sharply reduced the appetite of the cabinet for getting its hands dirty in the business of 'political policing'. By the time of the Mulroney Conservative governments from 1984 to 1993, this committee met rarely and apparently decided very little. Mulroney's Conservative successor, Kim Campbell, simply abolished the committee as part of a retrenchment of cabinet operations, and Jean Chrétien did not see fit to revive it upon assuming office. Thus, security and intelligence did not have any institutionalized cabinet-level representation, even though an interdepartmental committee of senior officials maintained bureaucratic continuity. The coordinating machinery for intelligence housed in the Privy Council Office had no direct cabinet-level point of entry, which could be considered a serious deficiency, especially in the Canadian version of the parliamentary system, where the prime minister and the cabinet are dominant and largely unchecked.

The establishment of the Security Committee would seem to have dramatically reversed this neglect of security and intelligence. It was set up in a crisis atmosphere of some considerable urgency. It comprises all the key cabinet players whose departments and agencies have roles in security (although curiously omitting then Health Minister Allan Rock, whose handling of the US-inspired anthrax scare was thus outside the committee's direct attention). For a time it functioned as a virtual inner, or war cabinet, while new policy guidelines were being devised and enacted— although this no longer appears to be the case. Most importantly of all, perhaps, it is chaired by John Manley, who within the past year has spanned the key cabinet posts of Foreign Affairs, Deputy Prime Minister, and now Finance, as well as carrying under his wing a number of ad hoc policy areas of particular political interest to the Chrétien government. Mr Manley quickly parlayed his chairmanship into a base for establishing a reputation as the strong man of the cabinet, rivalling Paul Martin while the latter remained, and then succeeding him in the finance portfolio following his sacking. It could thus be said that security and intelligence not only had cabinet representation, but very strong cabinet representation to boot. This was a clear demonstration that the government was not merely reacting to 9/11 with symbolic agenda readjustment, but was serious about materially restructuring government priorities so as to privilege security concerns.

The committee is an ad hoc rather than a permanent addition to the cabinet committee architecture. Its role has diminished in importance as 9/11 recedes further into the past, and it may be wound up altogether in the near future. It should be noted, however, that there is a longstanding deputy minister-level body, the Interdepartmental Committee on Security and Intelligence (ICSI), formally chaired by the Clerk of the Privy Council, but in practice usually by the Coordinator of Intelligence in the PCO, which discusses security and intelligence priorities and reviews proposals destined for Cabinet. ICSI has met more frequently since 9/11 and will continue to do so, even if the cabinet committee fades in importance.

Budgetary Reallocation

Cabinet's intentions were given some flesh with an immediate infusion of $280 million into anti-terrorism.[4] In Paul Martin's post-9/11 (and last) budget, $7.7 billion of new resources were allocated over the next five years to security and enforcement. Of this, $1 billion is allocated to immigration screening and enforcement, $1.6 billion to intelligence and policing, $1.6 billion to emergency preparedness and military deployment, $2.2 billion to aviation safety, and $1.2 billion to border security measures. CSIS, the RCMP, the CSE, Immigration, and Customs Canada will handle the bulk of these new resources.[5]

Some critics have suggested that this is too little, too late, that these resources will be insufficient to meet the challenge of terrorism, or even to satisfy the United States that Canada is adequately maintaining its part in the security of North America. It is difficult to evaluate these claims, which are, after all, dependent upon threat assessments that are themselves inherently controversial, especially in the absence of access to secret intelligence. I would make two related points. First, this figure does represent a significant shift in the priorities of the government of Canada, made all the more striking by the absence of any previous indication in the Liberal government's political program of any intention to upgrade national security significantly. Second, this is a government that, with or without Mr Martin, has a powerful overriding commitment to fiscal responsibility and to keeping current government accounts in the black. Competing claims for expenditure came, and continue to come, from the 'social' Liberal side of the party, particularly around the issues of health care and programs supporting children and families, or from 'green'

Liberals looking for environmental protection, such as implementation of the Kyoto accord. This sweeping reallocation to security, which had only weak political representation in the Liberal party, does indicate the powerful impact of 9/11, either directly or via the perceived indirect impact through new US actions harmful to Canadian economic security. Either way, 9/11 did have immediate and dramatic consequences with respect to how the Canadian government does business. An agency like CSIS, for example, which had been absorbing a decline in funding, received authority for an increase in spending of 30 per cent in fiscal 2001/2.[6]

Military Contributions

There is one striking deviation from the relative amplitude of new resources devoted to security. Although $1.6 billion was designated in the 2001 budget for 'emergency preparedness and military deployment', most of this amount has been designated for critical infrastructure protection, and preparedness for biochemical and nuclear threats. Funding for military equipment purchases and direct military support for the war on terrorism is actually quite limited. The one exception was the decision to double the capacity of Joint Task Force Two (JTF2), the elite Special Forces unit. However, increased funding for more conventional air, land, and sea capabilities is derisory in the context of the overall $7.7 billion. This omission is all the more striking in light of repeated assertions from many quarters, including the Commons defence committee, defence scholars, numerous think tanks and public interest groups, and finally the minister of National Defence himself, that very substantial infusions of cash into the Canadian forces are necessary to ward off serious decline and incapacity.[7] Given the broad range of tasks that the Chrétien government has set the military, from peacekeeping to collective security to domestic emergencies, its repeated failure to provide adequate resources to fulfill these tasks has been a source of much criticism. It is curious that the opportunity opened by 9/11 was not exploited to even begin to address this deficiency.

Despite chronic underfunding, Canada sent naval, ground, and special forces to Afghanistan in response to President Bush's call for a coalition to fight a war on terrorism. This decision was, and continues to be, supported by Canadian public opinion, and by a multiparty consensus in Parliament—even following the unfortunate incident in which four Canadians were killed by US-directed 'friendly fire'. This is in keeping with a long Canadian tradition of supporting actions in the name of collective security, including those in Korea, the Gulf, and Kosovo. In military terms, the Canadian contribution can hardly be termed substantial, but symbolically it did indicate Canadian support for the initial stages of the war on terrorism, and the overthrow of the Taliban regime on the grounds that it provided a land base and staging ground for Al-Qaida.

Canada's decision to recall its ground forces early from Afghanistan, save for a continuing presence of JTF2, is a sign that the deterioration caused by chronic underfunding is becoming quite visible. Military incapacity may also mask to a degree the breakdown of consensus in the coalition that has followed military victory in Afghanistan. Canada may not be able to provide military support for a war on Iraq, even one sanctioned by a Security Council resolution. Whether this will be as a result of political objections or simple penury may appear to be a moot question.

Legislative Powers

In the immediate wake of 9/11, Canada showed that it could expedite the legislative process under the pressure of events. Although it did not quite match the enthusiasm of the congressional stampede to enact the USA PATRIOT Act, the government quickly prepared a sweeping and comprehensive Anti-Terrorism Act (C-36) and guided it through public consultation and parliamentary debate and into royal assent at a brisk pace, considering the controversial nature of some of its provisions.[8] Considerable opposition was mounted by civil libertarians, trade unionists, social activists, and Canada's Muslim and Arab groups—who felt, not without reason, that their communities would be particular targets of 'ethnic profiling'.[9]

What had originally been billed as a companion piece, the Public Safety Act, has had a more checkered career. Mainly concerned with air safety, biochemical weapons control, and Defence department computer security, this legislation contained a highly controversial provision for the creation of military security zones. One small part of the bill was enacted separately under the gun of an impending US deadline on security requirements for aircraft flying in the United States.[10] The full bill was then withdrawn, redrafted in part to reflect criticisms, especially those of Liberal backbench MPs concerning undue ministerial discretion, and resubmitted as C-56. The new version made it clear that security zones would be limited to military installations, thus meeting criticism of anti-globalization protestors that this had been intended as a so-called 'Kananaskis Act'. The Kananaskis label referred to fears that this provision of the legislation would prevent or severely limit protests at G-7 and other global summit meetings such as the one held at Kananaskis, Alberta in the fall of 2002. C-56 subsequently died when the Prime Minister prorogued Parliament; when the government introduced the act in the fall 2002 session, it dropped the military security zone provisions altogether, apparently now relying on Orders in Council rather than a legislative mandate.

C-36 will stand for now as the main legislative response to 9/11. It is sweeping and comprehensive, an omnibus act on national security. On closer perusal, and despite the obsessive focus of most public debate and criticism, emergency anti-terrorist provisions occasioned by 9/11 actually constitute only a part of the act. Those sections that might be linked directly to 9/11 can be limited to the following:

- the legal definition of terrorism;
- the official listing of terrorist entities;
- specific terrorist funding offences;
- preventive detention; and
- investigative hearings.

The emergency character of the last two innovations was recognized by the government when, at the insistence of critics, it attached sunset clauses. Given the furor these measures occasioned in civil liberties and multicultural circles, it is interesting that neither appears to have actually been yet used by the government.[11] Whether they ever will be is an open question. Perhaps, despite the fears of critics, these devices were never seriously intended to be used, except perhaps in the event of another 9/11, this time directly touching on Canada. Their importance may always have been more symbolic than real, the symbolism intended as much to reassure the Americans as the domestic audience.

With regard to terrorist funding offences, having established the controversial idea of an official proscription list of terrorist entities subject to the criminal code, government laboured for months, and finally in late July of 2002 produced a list of seven entities—a shorter list than the equivalents in the United States and Europe.[12] There were controversies about the absences from the initial list, especially the political arm of Hezbollah, which Canada refused to proscribe, despite the contrary US example. In December 2002, after domestic political pressure, Hezbollah was added to the list. Thus the Canadian attitude seemed to be: arm yourself with a big stick, but wield it sparingly, if at all.

Despite its somewhat misleading name, the Anti-terrorism Act is actually a proto-National Security Act, most of the provisions of which have been in the pipeline in Ottawa for some time, many strongly favoured by elements within the security and intelligence community but stalled by the lack of attention paid to security and intelligence issues in pre-9/11 Ottawa. In the immediate aftermath of 9/11, it almost appears as if relevant agencies were circularized to submit their wish lists, many of which were then incorporated into the omnibus 'anti-terrorist' bill.

Among the elements of C-36 not related to 9/11 are these:

- the Official Secrets Act is replaced by a new Security of Information Act, which includes new offences, such as economic espionage;
- the Communications Security Establishment (CSE), the electronic eavesdropping agency, is for the first time given a statutory mandate, with its powers and limitations spelled out, and with an important additional power to retain Canadian communications related to terrorism;
- the Proceeds of Crime (Money Laundering) Act is amended to include terrorism as well as organized crime as its primary objects;
- serious limitations are imposed on the Access to Information, Privacy, and Personal Information Protection and Electronic Documents Acts with regard to the disclosure and retention of information relating to national security; and
- provisions regarding non-disclosure of sensitive national security evidence serve mainly to 'Charter-proof' existing evidence provisions following the *Stinchcombe* decision of the Supreme Court.[13]

Taken together with the Canadian Security Intelligence Service Act and the Security Offences Act of 1984 (the latter now augmented by An Act to Amend the Foreign Missions and International Organizations Act)[14] and C-11, the Immigration and Refugee Protection Act,[15] both passed just prior to 9/11, the latter itself amended by C-36, the Anti-Terrorism Act constitutes the basis for a Canadian national security act. The opportunity offered by 9/11 was alertly seized by the security and intelligence community, which has ended up with much more than it would likely have achieved had 9/11 not happened. Unfortunately, however, the atmosphere surrounding C-36's passage precluded an intelligent national debate on the merits of the specific elements of C-36 that were not directly related to 9/11, especially its lack of any comprehensive review and oversight mechanism for all the agencies involved. Thus the passage of the successor to the discredited and ineffective Official Secrets Act has not been accompanied by any external debate that might have illuminated its strengths and weaknesses—not a healthy way for such matters to be dealt with in a democracy, and not perhaps in the long-term interest of the security and intelligence community, which requires informed public interest and support.

Bureaucratic Restructuring
There are some new players in the Ottawa security and intelligence community. The Financial Transactions and Reports Analysis Centre of Canada (FINTRAC) plays an important role in tracking and identifying money laundering trails, both with regard to international organized crime and terrorism. The Office of Critical Infrastructure Protection and Emergency Preparedness (OCIPEP) has a dual mandate, to provide national leadership in protecting Canada's critical infrastructure—the key physical and cyber components of the energy and utilities, communications, services, transportation, safety, and government sectors—and to be the government's primary agency for ensuring national civil emergency preparedness. OCIPEP thus has a crucial role in what the Americans call homeland security. Both FINTRAC and OCIPEP pre-date 9/11, even if their roles have been boosted by the terrorist threat.

The most significant effects of 9/11 on the bureaucratic structuring of the security and intelligence community perhaps lie in the category of dogs that didn't bark. The first is the long-debated issue of a central foreign intelligence agency for Canada. This debate had always been an academic one, even when it was practitioners, or recently retired practitioners, who were debating, since there was never indication of any interest in such a project on the part of successive governments. Following 9/11, no less than John Manley, chair of the cabinet security committee, publicly mused about the need for such an agency as a real option. There apparently followed an internal interdepartmental debate around this idea—a debate sketchily and not altogether convincingly reported[16]—which, in the nature of such bureaucratic debates, appears to have fallen into a contest over turf. In this contest, the most effective turf defender seems to have been CSIS, which argued that it already had authority to collect foreign intelligence related to threats to the security of Canada. Director Ward Elcock raised a rather expansive version of this interpretation when he assured a senate committee that CSIS had a mandate exactly like that of the CIA. Even when more modestly defended, CSIS's case is still strong when the major foreign intelligence interest appears to be terrorism. Under s. 12 of the CSIS Act, the agency is empowered to collect intelligence, without restriction to Canadian territory, that relates to threats to the security of Canada (and under s. 2, 'security' may also encompass 'the interests of Canada'). Indeed, CSIS, which has in recent years been doing more foreign intelligence collection than in the past, appears to be the main beneficiary of any renewed interest in foreign intelligence.

The outcome of the debate is now clear: no new agency will be created, but CSIS will beef up its foreign dimension. This solution may appeal to cost-conscious and conflict-aversive Ottawa, but it does not answer to the main concern raised by proponents of a stand-alone agency: the need for broad, strategic intelligence input into Canadian foreign policy. If 9/11 re-stimulated the foreign intelligence debate, its focus on terrorism undermined the much broader intentions of those who advocate a new agency.

The other dog that has yet to bark is a central bureaucratic mechanism linking the community to the cabinet decision-makers, a British-style Joint Intelligence Committee (JIC), or an Australian-style Office of National Assessments (ONA). Although the resources of the PCO Intelligence Assessment Branch have been considerably beefed up, so that its roster of analysts is roughly double what it was before, it has not passed the institutional threshold into JIC or ONA status. Perhaps the window of opportunity offered by 9/11 and by the Manley committee has already closed on this set of options. The security and intelligence community, although augmented and strengthened, may thus remain somewhat fragmented and unfocused in its capacity to provide an integrated intelligence product to cabinet.

Border Security
Although sold as a response to 9/11 terrorism, negotiations on improved border security are actually more an indirect response, mediated through the frame of the US threat to Canadian economic security. Obviously, Canadians want and expect their government to secure their borders from terrorists. Government has at least an equal stake in ensuring that no terrorist enters the United States via Canada to wreak havoc in the American homeland. There never was a 'Canadian Connection' of any significance to 9/11, a fact now publicly acknowledged by the US government,[17] but not by many American politicians and media outlets. As late as January 2003, a US scare about five alleged terrorist suspects who had infiltrated into the US from Canada was soon revealed as a hoax. Yet Senator Hilary Rodham Clinton refused to apologize for blaming Canadian security even after acknowledging the incident never happened![18] Even the notorious pre-9/11 case of Ahmed Ressam, apprehended at Port Angeles, Washington on his way to bomb the Los Angeles Airport, however exploited by certain 'serial confessors' in this country unaccountably

eager to blame Canada for every American security lapse,[19] has now been put to partial rest by US Attorney General John Ashcroft, who publicly acknowledged that 'it was the outstanding co-operation of the Canadian authorities, who alerted us to the situation and allowed us to take steps that saved the lives of Americans.'[20]

Despite misperceptions on both sides of the border, Canada has never been a 'Club Med for terrorists'. In fact, Canadian standards for identifying the 'bad guys' are pretty much the same as the US criteria. After all, the two countries share a similar database on such matters. Canadian rules for dealing with terrorist suspects are not in fact notably more lax or more liberal than those in use in the United States. Indeed, in the specific matter of the non-disclosure of sensitive intelligence in court, Canadian rules are actually stiffer than American. If there was a gap between Canada and the United States in immigration security, it was an *enforcement* gap, attributable to relatively fewer resources available on the Canadian side. This had already begun to change post-Ressam and pre-9/11, and the gap is now being narrowed in the wake of the last Martin budget.[21] Whether the new resources are adequate is a different question than that addressed by the political and journalistic critics of Canadian performance, who have impugned the objectives and standards of Canadian policy, while systematically misrepresenting its basis.[22]

Nevertheless, an incontrovertible fact remains for Canada. The United States is entirely serious about enforcing its standards for security at all entry points. Either these standards will be enforced at the Canada–US border, or they will be enforced around the North American perimeter. The former case imposes unacceptable costs on the Canadian economy, not to speak of civil society. The latter is the only viable and acceptable response, but it might under certain circumstances come at a serious cost to Canadian sovereignty. The US ambassador to Canada, Paul Cellucci, called immediately after 9/11 for an ill-defined perimeter security arrangement that appeared to look vaguely like Europe, with a common labour market and a common entry policy. Similar calls were made by the Leader of the Opposition and by some provincial premiers, including the premier of British Columbia, who bizarrely demanded a 'Zip Lock bag around North America'.

There have been insistent pressures for radical action from influential voices within Canada, most notably the blue chip Coalition for Secure and Trade-Efficient Borders, composed mainly of the heads of the four major business associations: the Canadian Council of Chief Executives (formerly the Business Council on National Issues), the Canadian Manufacturers and Exporters, the Canadian Chamber of Commerce, and the Canadian Federation of Independent Business.[23] The crippling costs to Canada of tough US enforcement along the border are not in question, especially in the context of the 'just in time' production system that has developed in North America. There would be severe costs to the United States as well, of course, but these would be proportionally much lower, and, in any event, the post-9/11 mood in the United States is that national security must be purchased at whatever economic cost. A number of influential think tanks and policy gurus began to argue that 9/11 offered an opportunity to Canada to negotiate a yet closer form of economic and political integration with the United States, thereby solving not only the US security problem, but obviating such irritants to the US–Canada economic relationship as the ongoing softwood lumber dispute and other threatened forms of American protectionism. Wendy Dobson of the C.D. Howe Institute referred to this strategy as 'Big Ideas', and she has been echoed by Hugh Segal of the Institute for Research in Public Policy and by the former ambassador to the United States, Allan Gotlieb.[24]

These appeals have considerable resonance and are difficult to resist. Yet there are serious difficulties with 'thinking big', especially in the 9/11 crisis atmosphere. Expansive perimeter security schemes along European lines (common labour market, common entry policy) would entail serious costs to Canadian sovereignty. Harmonization of immigration policy, whatever the gloss put upon it, plainly means Canadian acceptance of US standards. Greater economic integration is very unlikely to be matched, à la Europe, with supranational political or juridical institutions, especially at a moment when the Bush administration is in an America-First, no-infringement-on-US-sovereignty mood. But this will probably not fly for *American* political reasons: Canada and the United States could not form a privileged inner core of NAFTA to the exclusion of the Mexicans, but free entry of Mexican labour into the United States would be unacceptable to Americans.

The Liberal government has sternly resisted the temptations of the proffered 'Big Ideas' of comprehensive integration. Instead of thinking big, Canada has pursued a strategy of *thinking small*, negotiating incremental changes that have the cumulative effect of reassuring legitimate American security concerns without trading away any more sovereignty than is necessary under the circumstances. In effect, Canada has deflected US attention away from the alleged overall border security problem by engaging US negotiators in a series of specific practical issues to be solved under the rubric of the so-called 'Smart Border' option.

The Smart Border negotiations between John Manley and US Homeland Security czar Tom Ridge have been successful from the Canadian perspective.[25] Key elements of this process involve the application of technology in order to fast track goods and low-risk people while focusing attention on higher risks. Pre-clearance of goods destined for the United States is a workable example of the original, pre-9/11, concept of perimeter security, which was emphatically *not* Fortress North America, but rather the notion of identifying and interdicting threats, wherever they appear, before they arrive at the border. Indeed, the Canada–US agreement on pre-clearance is a template being applied in Europe via the G-8, and now, via APEC, in Asia as well. With respect to the movement of people, a 'safe third country' agreement between Canada and the United States on asylum seekers (already on the Canadian books, but not negotiated) will reduce apprehensions in the United States about the entry of security risks into the United States via Canada, although at the cost of much controversy in Canada and bitter criticism from the refugee lobby.

More remains to be negotiated in this area, but the broad outlines of a settlement are clear. American national security concerns are being met, as are Canadian economic security concerns, but at relatively minimal cost to Canadian sovereignty. For instance, Canada has so far successfully resisted adopting the American (and British) practice of indefinite detention of non-citizens on suspicion, often without legal counsel. This practice is contrary to Canadian values, and to the judicial inter-pretation of the Charter of Rights. Canada does detain non-citizens, but for cause, and not without legal counsel. This is an example of a distinctive Canadian practice that can be retained, in the context of incremental negotiations that place reason-able limits on harmonization of policy.

Just how adroitly Canadian officials have handled this delicate set of issues is demonstrated by remarks of US ambassador Cellucci, who opened the perimeter security option in the first instance. The ambassador declared in the fall of 2002 that the relationship between Canada and the United States 'is a role model for the world', but added significantly that the two countries should be focusing on the need to build 'smart borders', and not be engaged in discussions about a 'more for-mal economic union like Europe. . . . I'm not saying that debate should not take place, I'm just saying that it should take place at a later date.'[26] Canadian officials could not have asked for more.

The Decline of the Security Priority

However powerful the impact of 9/11 on Ottawa, it was apparent within a year of the terrorist attacks that the salience of national security and the war on terrorism had dramatically declined on the policy agenda. Given that there were no terrorist attacks on Canada, and little perceived likelihood of such, it is not surprising that Canadians would quickly revert to previous preoccupations. Although early polling after 9/11 appeared to indicate that Canadians had radically realigned their priori-ties, this realignment proved to be ephemeral, and more an artifact of the traumatic nature of the events and the blanket media coverage than any indication of deeper long-term changes in values and attitudes.[27] By 2002, health care had returned to the top of Canadian concerns, where it had been during the 2000 election, along with the divisive issue of the ratification of the Kyoto Accord on climate change. Enduring residues of 9/11 are becoming increasingly difficult to discern, although one may be a heightened suspicion of immigrants from Middle Eastern countries, and another a stiffening resistance to asylum seekers.[28]

It was not just public opinion at work. The Liberal government was turned inward in 2002 by the controversy over the sacking of Paul Martin and the forced retirement of the Prime Minister, along with the ensuing leadership contest. It is unlikely that national security will be a leading plank in any of the leadership hope-fuls' platforms (by contrast to those of presidential challengers in the United States). Finally, the international context has also changed subtly, in ways that undermine Canadian enthusiasm for prosecuting the war on terrorism. The turn of the Bush administration to unilateralism in its foreign relations, and its obsessive focus on forcing 'regime change' in Iraq, by unilateral military action if necessary, has lost the United States much of the sense of solidarity engendered by 9/11 in Canadian opinion, both elite and mass.[29] Moreover, unresolved irritants in Canada–US relations such as the softwood lumber dispute have contributed to a Canadian perception that the anti-terrorism coalition is, from the US perspective, all take and no give. Future anti-terrorist cooperation with the United States may prove more controversial, thus enhancing the tendency of policy-makers to de-emphasize this priority and turn to more traditional concerns.

CONCLUSION

Taking all the elements of response to 9/11 together, the Canadian government acted with relative decisiveness in resetting national priorities and restructuring government security policy. 9/11 appears less an exogenous variable than an external event that facilitated certain processes already in train. Canada has modulated its direct response to 9/11 more than its US ally, which is neither surprising nor inappropriate considering its more peripheral status as a target for terrorism. 9/11 has been mediated for Canada through the lens of the Canadian-American relationship, which has necessitated Canada's managing a kind of two-front war, with the United States against the terrorist enemy, while at the same time struggling to limit the collateral damage to Canada threatened, more inadvertently than intentionally, by our ally. Canada has done reasonably well in managing this process.

The Canadian security, intelligence, and policing communities have benefited from 9/11 in the sense of gaining more resources, more prestige, and, perhaps—although this remains to be seen—more influence on policy. The defence community was unable to seize the opportunity to better its position, which may prove in the longer run to be the Achilles heel of Liberal security policy.

The longer-term effects of the 9/11 crisis on Canadian society are more difficult to assess. Although there have been few signs of the panicky authoritarian strains evident in US society, support for civil liberties and minority rights may have been damaged by the terrorist spectre. Certainly the practice of multicultural pluralism has taken some hits in the context of media demonization of Muslim groups, and risk management policing that looks uncomfortably like ethnic profiling. Parts of the Anti-Terrorism Act challenge basic elements of the liberal democratic process, but it is too early to assess the concrete effects of these provisions, or how lasting they will be. We can perhaps cautiously conclude that Canadian society has weathered the strains of the crisis relatively well, and that the federal government can take some credit for maintaining a reasonable balance between security and liberty.

To be sure, if a catastrophic terrorist attack were to take place in Canada—or elsewhere involving large numbers of Canadian victims—all previous bets would be off. We could then expect a much more violent American-style swing of the pendulum toward collective security at the expense of individual and group rights. That prospect alone is sufficient justification for maintenance of strong security measures to prevent such a lamentable outcome.

NOTES

1 Reg Whitaker and Gary Marcuse, *Cold War Canada: The Making of a National Insecurity State, 1945–1957* (Toronto: University of Toronto Press, 1994).

2 In the immediate aftermath of 9/11, a consensus was formed among media commentators that Prime Minister Chrétien's public response had been inadequate and that he had failed to match the performance of George W. Bush. However, polls that asked Canadians to assess Mr Chrétien's performance as a *Canadian* leader showed majority approval, and Liberal party fortunes suffered not at all. See Ekos, 'Security, Sovereignty and Continentalism: Canadian Perspectives on September 11', 27 Sept. 2001.

3 For the earlier situation, see Reg Whitaker, 'Security and Intelligence in a Cold Climate', in Gene Swimmer, ed., *How Ottawa Spends 1996–97: Life Under the Knife* (Ottawa: Carleton University Press, 1996), 409–41.

4 Of this, $79 million was allocated to airport security, $49 million to immigration security, $12 million to health safety, $54 million to the RCMP, $37 million to the Communications Security Establishment (CSE), and $10 million each to CSIS and the new anti-money laundering unit, FINTRAC.

5 Solicitor General Canada, 'Enhancing Security for Canadians', see web site: http://sgc.ca/Budget/FederalBudget2001-e.htm

6 Security Intelligence Review Committee, *An Operational Audit of the Canadian Security Intelligence Service*, Report 2001–02 (Oct. 2002), 31.

7 Report of the Standing Committee on National Defence and Veterans Affairs, *Facing Our Responsibilities: The State Of Readiness Of the Canadian Forces*, May 2002; J.L. Granatstein, *A Friendly Agreement in Advance: Canada-US Defence Relations, Past, Present and Future*, C.D. Howe Institute Commentary 166, June 2002; Conference of Defence Associations, *A Nation at Risk: The Decline of the Canadian Forces* (Ottawa, 2002); Daniel Leblanc, 'McCallum Seeking Money for Forces, Modern Equipment', *The Globe and Mail* [Toronto], 26 Oct. 2002, A7.

8 49–50 Elizabeth II 2001, Chap. 48 (assented to 18 Dec. 2001).

9 In a remarkable example of timely scholarly publishing, a conference in Toronto in November 2001 was turned within weeks into a 500-page collection of articles, mostly critical, on C-36. Ronald J. Daniels, Patrick Macklem, and Kent Roach, eds, *The Security of Freedom: Essays on Canada's Anti-Terrorism Bill* (Toronto: University of Toronto Press, 2001).

10 49–50 Elizabeth II Chap. 38, An Act to Amend the Aeronautics Act, assented to 18 Dec. 2001. Controversially, this act authorized release of personal information on passengers to US authorities.

11 As indicated by Richard Mosley, ADM, Criminal Law Policy, Department of Justice, to the House of Commons Sub-Committee on National Security, 10 June 2002.

12 Office of the Superintendent of Financial Institutions, 'Advisory re: Names of Terrorist Organizations Made Subject to the Criminal Code', 23 July 2002.

13 R v. Stinchcombe 1991 3 S.C.R. ordered the production in court of criminal intelligence relevant to the defence. Stinchcombe was a criminal case, and its relevance to national security cases was unclear. The evidence provisions in C-36 are in the spirit of 'better safe than sorry'.

14 49–50 Elizabeth II 2001–02, Chap. 12 (assented to 30 Apr. 2002)

15 49–50 Elizabeth II 2001, Chap. 27 (assented to 1 Nov. 2001).

16 David Ljunggren, 'No Need for Overseas Spy Service, Manley Says Existing Links Enough', Reuters / *The National Post,* 11 Apr. 2002.

17 US Department of State, *Patterns of Global Terrorism 2001* (May 2002), states unequiv-ocally, 'Media in the United States and elsewhere erroneously reported that some of the 19 hijackers responsible for crashing the four US commercial airliners had come to the United States via Canada: these allegations were proven false by subsequent investiga-tion. Overall anti-terrorism cooperation with Canada is excellent, and stands as a model of how the US and another nation can work together on terrorism issues' (61).

18 Sheldon Alberts, 'Clinton Refuses Ottawa's Call for Apology', *The National Post*, 10 Jan. 2003.

19 I have adapted the phrase 'serial confessors' from Audrey Macklin, 'Borderline Secu-rity', in Daniels, Macklem, and Roach, *The Security of Freedom*, 388. The phrase applies to the Canadian Alliance and certain private security experts, as well as to commentators in *The National Post*, the Southam press, and the CTV and Global net-works. See the Swiftian spoof of this mentality (and of his own paper) by Paul Wells: 'Thousands Die: Blame Canada', *The National Post*, 18 Dec. 2001.

20 Ashcroft interview with CTV News, 4 Dec. 2001.

21 I have made this case at greater length in 'Refugee Policy After September 11: Not Much New', *Refuge* 20, 4 (Aug. 2002), 29–33.

22 A particularly egregious example of this is the former executive director of Canada Immigration Service, James Bissett, *Canada's Asylum System: A Threat to American Security?* (Center for Immigration Studies, Backgrounder, May 2002).

23 Coalition for Secure and Trade-Efficient Borders, *Rethinking Our Borders: A Plan for Action* (3 Dec. 2001).

24 Wendy Dobson, *Shaping the Future of the North American Economic Space*, C.D. Howe Institute Commentary 162 (Apr. 2002); Hugh Segal, 'New North American Institutions: The Need for Creative Statecraft', Address to the 5th Annual JLT/CTPL Trade Law Conference, Ottawa, 18 Apr. 2002; Allan Gotlieb, 'Why Not a Grand Bar-gain with the U.S.?' *The National Post*, 11 Sept. 2002.

25 Department of Foreign Affairs and International Trade, *The Canada–US Smart Border Declaration*; see web site: http://www.dfait-maeci.gc.ca/anti-terrorism/declaration-e.asp. DFAIT News Release, 'Manley and Ridge Release Progress Report on the Smart Border Declaration and Action Plan', 28 June 2002.

26 Angelo Persichilli, 'Cellucci Says Canada–U.S. Relationship "A Role Model for the World"', *The Hill Times*, 7 Oct. 2001.

27 Among early polls were Ekos, 'Security, Sovereignty and Continentalism: Canadian Perspectives on Sept. 11', 27 Sept. 2001, and 'Economic and Public Security: The Evolv-ing Public Landscape', 14 Dec. 2001; the Strategic Council, *Maclean's*, 31 Dec. 2001. Fairly strong illiberal tendencies based on high anxiety and insecurity were detected: majorities favoured phone taps and national identification cards with biometric recog-nition technology. Majorities also favoured immediate integration of security policy with that of the United States. Liberal pollster Michael Marzolini wisely advised his client to 'ignore these shallow and useless polls entirely'. The media pollsters, he sug-gested, 'fail to understand that what they are measuring is not public opinion at all, but a venting of frustrations by a traumatized and fearful public.' Marzolini, In *Your Opin-ion*; see web site: http://www.polara.ca. Later polls showed him to be correct.

28 Léger Marketing, 'Immigration and Racism Following the Sept. 11 Attacks', 17 Sept. 2002.

29 Léger Marketing, 'How Canadians Feel about the US Threat to Iraq', poll conducted 20–5 Aug. 2002.

4

The House of Commons Under the Chrétien Government

JONATHAN MALLOY

In July 2002, Canadian media headlines reported that Prime Minister Jean Chrétien had written letters to each Liberal MP asking for policy suggestions for the new parliamentary session scheduled for the fall. This was interpreted by many journalists as a desperate act by the Prime Minister, who was losing caucus support in favour of former Finance Minister Paul Martin. It was seen as highly irregular that the prime minister of Canada would be interested in the opinions of his backbench MPs.

This anecdote illustrates the shifting status of the House of Commons under the Chrétien government. For most of the Chrétien years, the House was not dramatically different from its earlier incarnations. While there were instances of backbencher independence and influence, there was also harsh discipline and even expulsion for voting against party lines. However, following the 2000 election, MPs in both the government and opposition began to act in ways not seen for many years in the House, criticizing and undermining their own leaders. Dissent first emerged on the opposition benches, in the Canadian Alliance caucus, as a handful of members left the party to protest the leadership of Stockwell Day. Then, in 2002, it was the Liberals' turn, as government MPs began to openly urge the Prime Minister to retire. Even Progressive Conservative leader Joe Clark felt pressure from his caucus, although he announced his resignation before dissent reached a full roar.

But apart from leadership struggles, the Commons continued to operate much as always. Voting remained highly disciplined, with regular use of time allocation and closure. Members continued to feel the pressure of party whips, and parliamentary committees struggled to maintain unity while producing influential reports. Question Period remained a time of scripted theatre, and debates themselves remained dull and largely ignored.

This chapter examines the status of the House of Commons under the Chrétien government, particularly in its third term.[1] Is Parliament indeed just a rubber stamp? Has its role increased or declined in the Chrétien years? And how do the leadership challenges of 2001–2 fit in? Do they signify a new avenue of influence for MPs and Parliament, or only a temporary historical blip? To answer these questions, we look at the Commons in several contexts. In particular, we discuss the presence and influence of a large and increasingly experienced set of backbenchers in the House of Commons, and explore how this may have produced significant, but not transformative effects on the institution of the House of Commons.

The chapter proceeds as follows. First, we briefly explore some interpretations of Parliament and the enduring problems of amateurism and turnover. We then review the status of the Commons from 1993 to 2000, and the expectations following the third Chrétien victory of 2000. Then we look in detail at four different dimensions of parliamentary activity and influence: policy ideas, accountability, the passage of bills, and leadership struggles. We conclude with a discussion of whether recent changes and developments will produce any long-term gains for Parliament.

INTERPRETATIONS OF PARLIAMENT

The 'decline of Parliament' is a very old cliché. MPs, journalists, academics, and Canadians of all kinds have long lamented that the House of Commons appears to have lost any substantive power over national affairs, and that ordinary members on both the government and opposition benches are little more than rubber stamps, trained seals, or a host of other metaphors. Implicit in these laments is that there was a time when Parliament did have true influence, and ordinary MPs exercised real power.

Indeed, in the early years of Confederation, parliamentary discipline was far more flexible than today, and many non-ministers did wield considerable personal influence in an era of limited government and extensive patronage. But throughout the twentieth century members of Parliament complained that they no longer possessed any real power, that the Commons had been allowed to decline, and that its role in Canadian politics had been much diminished, if not lost entirely.

Has Parliament indeed declined? The answer is not as simple as many assume. Members do have less time to debate and consider bills, and have less personal access to busy ministers than in an earlier age. But MPs in the twenty-first century enjoy much greater resources than did their predecessors of a few decades ago, including better staff and office resources, greatly enhanced standing committees, and a daily Question Period. Commons proceedings are nationally accessible through television, which among other things ensures greater visibility and profiles for at least some MPs. The decline thesis is certainly not as obvious as some assume.

Similarly, assessing the role of the Commons in the Chrétien years is difficult. Do MPs have more or less influence over policy than before? How effective is the Commons at holding government to account? Do members have less or more effect on the passage of bills? And do legislators have greater or lesser influence on their leaders? The evidence is mixed, particularly because we lack accessible and widely accepted criteria by which to reach conclusions. Key aspects—such as the dynamics of private party caucus meetings—are inaccessible, while other data, such as the frequency of closure and time allocation, may not tell the whole story.

Observers such as C.E.S. Franks argue that interpretations and assessments of Parliament are inevitably shaped by differing conceptions of and assumptions about its purpose.[2] Conceptions that stress the influence and power of individual MPs clash with others that emphasize the responsibility of Parliament to seek the national interest and assure clear lines of accountability. Proceeding from these different assumptions, members and observers alike make different assessments of the House of Commons and its role. Some measure the institution by the autonomy of individual MPs and their influence with respect to legislation and policy. But others assess it by its ability to produce legislation, and assess legislators by their ability to scrutinize bills and hold government to account for its actions. Many argue that members tend too much toward the first conception, and fail to appreciate the nuances of the second.[3]

TURNOVER AND CAREERS IN THE HOUSE

Confusion and disagreement over the role of the House of Commons stems partly from the rapid turnover of its members. Since 1968, the turnover of House membership has averaged 36 per cent—that is, after each election over a third of MPs are new to the House and its ways.[4] Since 1984, turnover has been even higher: an average of 41 per cent, including a dramatic 69 per cent in the 1993 general election. These patterns have crucial effects on the role of Parliament.

High turnover means that Canadian MPs have relatively short careers compared to legislators in other countries. From 1984 to 1997, backbench MPs served an average of only 7.4 years in Parliament, and frontbench leaders served 12.6 years.[5] While seven years may seem reasonably long, it is often insufficient for members to become familiar with the institution, develop expertise in issues, and generally become comfortable with their role as parliamentarians. Thus Docherty classifies MPs with less than five years service as 'rookies', those with five to twelve years as 'seasoned', and only those with at least twelve years experience as 'veterans'.[6]

It has long been argued that turnover and short parliamentary careers prevent the House of Commons from building a firm identity in the Canadian political system, to the point that Franks argues that longer careers would be 'the greatest single change that would strengthen Parliament'.[7] Lacking a critical mass of experienced backbench MPs, the Commons faces continual identity crises as its membership comes and goes. New members must take time to understand the complex and varying demands and expectations surrounding their job, and to develop their own identities and roles as parliamentarians. This is a long process, particularly for ambitious rookies who put their hopes in promotion through party loyalty, or for members who lack experience in elected office or familiarity with the federal political scene. Only after their initial ambitions have been brought down to earth and their knowledge strengthened can they begin to develop distinct and satisfying roles as parliamentarians, by which point they are on average likely to face electoral defeat.

Turnover in the Chrétien Years

These patterns of member socialization and career path are important for understanding and assessing the status of the Commons under the Chrétien government. As mentioned, the Commons experienced a staggering 69 per cent turnover when the Chrétien government was first elected in 1993; 208 of 301 MPs were newly-elected. But the two subsequent general elections produced much lower turnover. In 1997, a more typical 31 per cent of the House was newly elected.[8] And in 2000, turnover was a mere 17 per cent—the lowest in Canadian history.[9]

These patterns mean that a large number of MPs were raw rookies in 1993, but by 2000 were seasoned and experienced legislators. In the fall of 2002, no fewer than 109 MPs (36 per cent of the House) were 1993 veterans—including 61 Liberal MPs. While some of these Liberals sat in cabinet, the majority had not moved from the backbenches since their election nine years before. A further 69 MPs (23 per cent of the House) had been elected in 1997 (or in by-elections between 1993 and 1997)—36 of whom were Liberals.

In other words, while in 1993 208 MPs were completely new to Parliament, by 2002 178 MPs had between five and nine years experience in the House—including nearly a hundred government members. This pattern, with a large number of MPs moving simultaneously from rookie to seasoned status, is different from that of previous periods. Turnover was less dramatic and more even, for example, during the Mulroney years. In the landslide Conservative victory of 1984, House turnover was 49 per cent (compared with 69 per cent in 1993); when the Conservatives were re-elected in 1988, turnover was still 41 per cent (compared with 31 per cent in 1997 and 17 per cent in 2000).

The presence of a large number of new MPs in the mid-1990s *and* an increasingly experienced group of backbenchers after 2000 poses an interesting hypothesis about the House of Commons in the Chrétien era. We can speculate that in the early years of the government, the inexperienced MPs may have been ambitious and restless, but lacked the institutional memory and knowledge to establish clear and workable roles as parliamentarians. But by 2000, this same group had sufficient understanding of and comfort with the House of Commons, and this—combined with dashed ambitions and weakening leaders—prompted them to seek more autonomous yet sustainable roles. In the following pages, we will test this hypothesis against the reality of the Chrétien era both before and after 2000.

THE COMMONS 1993–2000

Following the 1993 election, it was difficult to know what to expect from the House of Commons. Dramatic changes had of course occurred not only in its membership, but also in the configuration of parties. In particular, the Reform party was elected on a commitment to introduce parliamentary reforms—to increase the number of free votes, to place constituency views ahead of party positions, and to generally reduce what it saw as petty partisanship in the House. And indeed, the 35th Parliament (1993–7) saw a number of significant events and challenges to existing parliamentary norms, leading Docherty to conclude in 1997 that 'the initial years of the 35th Parliament were unlike any in recent memory'.[10] Both the Liberal and the Reform caucuses experienced a number of noticeable incidents of dissent, with MPs on both sides challenging the party line and being disciplined by party leaders. (The Bloc Québécois, on the other hand, expressed relatively little dissent.)

But overall, the House of Commons from 1993 to 2000 was not significantly different from its previous incarnations. While members may have spoken more freely, leaders also exacted discipline with few qualms or restraints. Standing committees continued to operate with limited autonomy, and Question Period remained a place of verbal combat, but not enlightenment or government accountability. While the Reform party displayed some tolerance of members who grounded their dissent in constituency opinion, many of its initial symbolic practices, such as a strict alphabetical seating in the Commons, with leader Preston Manning in the third row, were soon discontinued.

Hence, while there were occasional attempts to break from party lines, and other acts of autonomy, the pattern of Commons activity did not alter significantly. This is not to say things were unchanged. For example, procedural reforms in 1994 allowed bills to be sent to committee after first reading rather than after second reading, as had been the norm. This would allow committees more freedom to rewrite bills before the House approved them in principle. But this procedure was rarely used, and remained an extraordinary measure. In another development, government use of time allocation and closure increased significantly in the 36th Parliament (1997–2000), after dropping slightly in 1993–7 in comparison to the practice of the previous Mulroney government.[11] Yet the significance of this is unclear. When governments use measures to speed up legislation, is this a sign of arrogance and contempt toward Parliament? Or does it indicate a feistier opposition, and a proportionate response by the government? The data defy easy interpretation or explanation.

It seems clear that in the mid- to late 1990s, the large crop of rookie MPs were still trying to establish their roles as parliamentarians. Many had been elected with strong expectations that were either broken down by party pressure and by other institutional norms, or that simply proved unrealistic and unworkable. This process

of socialization and institutionalization took time, and included occasional erup-
tions and flares of dissent, such as when three Liberal backbenchers voted against
the government's gun control legislation in 1995 and were promptly disciplined. But
this period, whatever it was exactly, did not represent dramatic change in the role or
activities of the House of Commons.

The Commons After 2000

After the Liberal election victory of 2000 there was heightened anticipation of changes
to Parliament, and new activism among backbench MPs was predicted in the media,
for several reasons. As previously mentioned, the turnover of members in 2000 was 17
per cent—miniscule by Canadian standards. Observers noted the larger than usual
contingent of experienced government backbenchers, and predicted that these MPs
would be more willing to seek important roles than in the past. The lack of a major
post-election cabinet shuffle demonstrated yet again that they were unlikely ever to
make it to cabinet. Having completed six years in the House, they were eligible for full
pensions—thus reducing the risks and costs of defiance that might end their political
careers. And having grown thoroughly familiar with the House and national policy
issues, they were positioned to carve out new and sustainable roles for themselves.

However, once again dramatic change failed to appear—initially. The election of
a new speaker in March 2001, in which several candidates promoted themselves as
parliamentary reformers, resulted in the choice of a respected but traditional parlia-
mentarian, Peter Milliken. High expectations also surrounded the Special Committee
on the Modernization and Improvement of the Procedures of the House of Commons, which produced a June 2001 report recommending extensive but not ground-
breaking changes to a range of Commons procedures and practices.

But over time, there were a number of indications that the 37th Parliament might
indeed be more assertive than its predecessors. Government backbenchers did begin
to flex their muscles and demand changes to government legislation. Committees
began to operate somewhat more independently. And, of course, two party leaders,
including the prime minister of Canada, were forced to announce their resignations
after losing the confidence of their caucuses.

To explore further these post-2000 developments, we need to deal with key dimensions in addition to the general patterns of turnover and parliamentary careers. As
indicated, these include government legislation and its passage, government accountability, the generation of policy ideas, and the determination of party leadership. Taking
this approach, we can see that the 37th Parliament does appear to have a somewhat
heightened and more autonomous role in the political system, although it is only with
respect to the fourth of these dimensions that we see a dramatic break with the past.

PASSAGE OF LEGISLATION

The first and probably most prominent role of Parliament is lawmaking—considering and voting on legislation. However, this role quickly produces conflicting expec-

tations. In the Westminster system of responsible government, governments proceed on the assumption that their legislative proposals will pass through the House without hostile amendments. In this interpretation, the role of Parliament is to provide a period of scrutiny and consideration during which arguments for and against the policy are aired, even though the bill is likely to be passed by the government majority. Yet many legislators, particularly in their rookie years, argue that they should have the power to amend or even stop bills.

It is difficult to track reliably what effect members have on the passage of legislation. Certain bills are undoubtedly scuttled if government members express strong concerns in caucus—a place closed to researchers and the media. Similarly, as noted above, data on time allocation and closure is difficult to interpret with any certainty. However, several incidents in the 37th Parliament, and particularly in the spring of 2002, suggest that MPs' influence over legislation has increased. The experience of the anti-terrorism and cruelty to animals bills in particular seemed to hint at a new assertiveness.

Following the 11 September 2001 attacks, the government introduced two key anti-terrorism bills, C-36 and C-42. Both were roundly criticized by opposition MPs and other observers. But while C-36, which gave new powers to police and law enforcement, was passed in December 2001, C-42, which gave broad declaratory powers to cabinet, was delayed and eventually replaced, with much of the credit going to resistant government members.[12] Its replacement, C-55, was not brought to second reading before the prorogation of the parliamentary session in September 2002.

Another bill, C-15B, concerning cruelty to animals, also received unexpected resistance—from two different Liberal camps. The species at risk act was criticized by Liberal MPs from rural constituencies for its alleged impact on livestock farming practices, leading the chair of the rural caucus to advocate supporting a Canadian Alliance motion against the bill. But Liberals on the Standing Committee on the Environment introduced their own amendments to strengthen the bill and its conditions, amendments that the government reversed on the House floor.[13] While the bill eventually passed in the Commons in June 2002, fifteen months after its introduction, the difficulties it experienced gave evidence that government MPs of all stripes were no longer as willing as they had been to toe the party line and restrict their criticisms to caucus meetings.

Do these events indicate a great change in Parliament? Not necessarily, although they certainly hint that government backbenchers have become more willing to press for changes not only within but beyond the privacy of the party caucus. As we look at further dimensions, we continue to see a mixed picture.

HOLDING THE GOVERNMENT TO ACCOUNT

Scrutinizing government actions and holding the government to account is not a popular role among MPs, who tend to rank it last among their perceived responsibilities.[14] While Question Period remains the highlight of the parliamentary day, with its scripted opposition indignation and government responses, members appear less interested in reviewing department reports or investigating all but the most sensational issues. As Dobell and Ulrich conclude, 'Although [Commons] committees pay considerable attention to changing societal conditions, they have not vigorously reviewed programs or their effectiveness. In addition, committees rarely use departmental performance information that might well help make these connections. Nor do they recommend specific improvements to this potentially important source of information.'[15] Again, this is tied to the larger issue of differing expectations. Members seeking autonomous influence view accountability as oriented to the past, rather than influencing the future (even though their investigations may lead to future reforms, as noted by Dobell and Ulrich).

When one examines Question Period since 2000, things appear unchanged from previous eras. Much time was spent in 2001 on the Shawinigate affair, in which the Prime Minister was accused of influencing a crown corporation for personal benefit, just as in the previous Parliament many weeks of questioning were devoted to the HRDC affair. This sustained period of daily scrutiny produced a number of benefits. Both accusations and responses received full attention, allowing each side to make its case before the nation. But real answers and enlightenment were rare. Much of the actual information and details were not revealed first in Parliament, but rather in the press. Much dissatisfaction and confusion remained about the Prime Minister's role. And government backbenchers remained largely silent throughout the debate.

However, when one looks beyond Question Period one can find deeper and more significant activities related to accountability. This is shown most consistently in the work of the Standing Committee on Public Accounts, and its investigations into the Groupaction scandal and related matters in the spring of 2002. This case concerned the overpayment of advertising agencies for government work. Opposition members spent several Question Periods quizzing ministers on this matter, to little avail (beyond Public Works Minister Don Boudria's admission that the government could not even find a copy of one report, for which it paid $500,000). The real work and the extraction of information was undertaken by the public accounts committee, in conjunction with the auditor-general. Despite clear government attempts to moderate committee inquiries, one and occasionally more government members sided with opposition demands that more answers be given and that key public servants be examined.

Overall, though, there is little evidence to suggest that the 37th Parliament has enhanced its accountability role in meaningful ways. But this may be more a function of MPs' general indifference to the accountability function than of government recalcitrance. While some government members appear willing to hold the government to account on certain issues, there is admittedly no obvious trend of increasing activism or vehemence.

GENERATION OF POLICY IDEAS

A third dimension of the Commons, its ability to generate and discuss prospective policy ideas, also illustrates well the dilemma of conflicting expectations for Parliament. For MPs who seek autonomy and influence, the role of *discussing* policy, rather than deciding on it, is not very attractive. But policy work can also be seen as a fundamental role of Parliament, and one that it is uniquely suited to play.[16] The resources and profile of the Commons and its committees provide a prominent forum for the discussion of public issues, through hearings and formal reports. Yet many MPs do not appear to value this role, since they have little control over the impact of their reports, nor have they the ability to determine policy on their own.[17]

Observers have long noted the difficulty of simultaneously maintaining interest in policy issues at both the committee and government levels. When committees initiate studies on their own and produce all-party reports, the issue is often a low priority for the government and simply fades off the agenda. When a government does take an interest in an issue, there is usually a government position at stake; as a result, hearings are more combative and partisan, committee consensus is less likely, and members' willingness to invest time and effort in the activity is reduced.

One area where a committee's policy roles have increased under the Chrétien government is the pre-budget consultations of the Standing Committee on Finance. Since 1994, the committee has held extensive annual consultations on government fiscal policy, often travelling across Canada to hear witnesses' views on government taxation and spending (other committees may also hold similar pre-budget hearings). This is generally seen as a successful innovation by the Commons. Although committee recommendations may or may not be implemented, the exercise fulfills several functions. Not only does it give members an opportunity to discuss prospective policies in a somewhat relaxed manner, but it also gives both the Department of Finance and Canadians in general opportunities to venture new ideas and proposals in an appropriate public forum.

However, this is not a recent innovation; it dates from the very beginning of the Chrétien era. Furthermore, rather than a committee-initiated move, the pre-budget consultations are part of a larger government shift toward open budget-making, characterized by extensive consultations rather than the secretive practices of the past. Hence, this may be less a case of members' pushing the envelope than a new style of budget-making, which, while significant, does not necessarily signify the existence of a more assertive Commons either at the start of the Chrétien era or today.

Looking at the Commons' role in policy discussion in the more recent post-2000 Parliament, we continue to find a mixed picture—even in areas where the government has indicated an interest in a committee's work. An example of apparent futility is the work of the Standing Committee on Health on reproductive technologies and stem cell research. In May 2001, then Health Minister Allan Rock introduced a draft bill on assisted human reproduction and referred it to the Health committee for discussion (this mechanism was the rarely-used provision introduced in 1994 mentioned above). The committee devoted considerable effort to the investigation and in December produced a unanimous report recommending amendments to the bill. However, when a new bill was introduced in May 2002, its treatment of stem-cell research was radically different from what was recommended by the committee. This led to considerable indignation among committee members, who interpreted it as a sign of government lack of interest in (rather than simple disagreement with) the committee's work.[18] The government justified this by noting that the committee leaned strongly to one side of the stem-cell research debate, while the bill attempted to follow a middle path that was closer to the proposals of the research community. However, committee members from all parties felt slighted and ignored by the government, particularly since it had solicited the committee's views in the first place.

In conclusion, the role of the Commons in policy generation and discussion remains mixed, and there is little evidence of an accelerated role after 2000. However, as with accountability, members have also indicated less interest in this role than in others.

DETERMINING PARTY LEADERSHIP

While there may have been changes and new developments in some of these dimensions of parliamentary activity, none presents a dramatic break with the past. Not so for the fourth dimension—the determination of party leadership. The full details of the undermining of Stockwell Day and Jean Chrétien (leaving aside the more murky case of Joe Clark) do not need to be repeated here. But the contributions of the parliamentary caucuses to the leadership struggles suggest a renewed and powerful role for MPs.

Unlike some other Westminster systems, Canadian parliamentary caucuses have for many years had little influence on the selection of party leaders. Instead, leaders are both chosen and nominally removed by the party as a whole, either by delegates in convention or, more recently, by the direct votes of all members. The swift removal of a party leader by caucus vote, such as happened to Margaret Thatcher in Britain in 1990, has been impossible in Canada for many decades. And, while leaders such as Joe Clark in the early 1980s or John Diefenbaker in the 1960s faced dissent in caucus over their leadership, few members spoke publicly or broke from caucus over the issue.

This tradition made it all the more shocking when, in April 2001, Canadian Alliance house leader Chuck Strahl and former interim leader Deborah Gray resigned their positions and eventually chose to leave the caucus to protest the leadership of Stockwell Day. Over the next months, nearly a dozen Alliance MPs broke at least briefly with the caucus over dissatisfaction with Day, and several formed a 'Democratic Representative Caucus' and forged a temporary alliance with the Progressive Conservatives. Day's eventual resignation came after pressure from the party executive and other extra-parliamentary members. But it remains highly significant that so many Alliance MPs were willing to publicly defy their leader and take the risks of leaving caucus over the issue. (Following Stephen Harper's selection as leader, all but one dissenter returned to the caucus.)

In 2002, it was Prime Minister Jean Chrétien's turn to face caucus unrest over his leadership. In the spring and summer of 2002, several Liberal MPs made very clear public statements urging the Prime Minister to resign, and the *Hill Times* newspaper published a stunning list classifying Liberal MPs as either supporters of Chrétien or supporters of former Finance Minister Paul Martin, with the latter outnumbering the former, even after several corrections by MPs who claimed loyalty to the Prime Minister. No Liberal MPs resigned from caucus, although Martin had been dropped from cabinet because of his obvious ambitions to succeed Chrétien. And as with Day, Chrétien's eventual announcement setting a 2004 retirement date was not prompted solely by caucus pressures, but followed even greater unrest among party members and constituency associations. Still, the precedent of open criticism of a party leader by so many MPs, much less criticism of a popular sitting prime minister, marks a substantial departure from past parliamentary practices.

What led caucus-members to rebel against their leaders? Several factors were likely at work, apart from the qualities and limitations of the leaders themselves. The overwhelming electoral position of the Liberals may have contributed to backbencher restlessness on both sides of the House: Liberals may have felt there were few risks in breaking ranks, while Alliance MPs may have been frustrated at Day's inability to make electoral gains. In either case, they may have felt there was little to lose. (In contrast, the 1988–93 Progressive Conservative caucus remained tightly loyal to Brian Mulroney in part because of fears that dissent would only further cripple the unpopular Conservatives.) As well, Martin made vague promises of parliamentary reform that undoubtedly attracted some MPs to his side—a point explored a little further in the conclusion below.

Undoubtedly another key factor emboldening members actually to speak and defy their leaders was the fact that more and more of them were experienced parliamentarians. It is difficult to establish a firm link between their sense of freedom and their experience, but the presence of a large number of seasoned MPs on both sides of the House is strong circumstantial evidence. These MPs were thoroughly familiar with the Commons and the roles expected of them by their leaders and, on the government side, had few prospects for promotion left. This laid the conditions for eventual rebellion and public dissent on the part of members who were willing to be bolder and more assertive than they had been as rookies. Day's various missteps and the Martin-Chrétien struggle then provided an opportunity for dissenters to raise their voices, particularly in the government caucus.

One cannot be sure how much influence the caucuses had in undermining these leaders, compared to other forces within the party. Nor can we be sure what explains members' behaviour in this context. But there is no doubt that the role of MPs in recent leadership struggles has been greater than for many years in Canadian politics. Having become more assertive and willing to carve out an expanded role for themselves, Members contributed clearly—and likely decisively—to the downfall of two key party leaders in the House of Commons.

CONCLUSION: THE COMMONS POST-CHRÉTIEN

This chapter has discussed the role of the House of Commons under the Chrétien government, particularly after 2000. It has suggested that for most of the Chrétien years the Commons was not dramatically different from past incarnations. After 2000, there was some evidence of greater activism and independence among MPs, but it is only in the party leadership struggles that we see a major break from the past. Explanations for these trends remain speculative, but undoubtedly the career cycles of MPs and the progression by which 1993 rookies have become post-2000 veterans is an important factor. But what about the future? Will the slight gains in autonomy and assertiveness become part of the institution? Or have they been only temporary blips in an otherwise unchanged parliamentary tradition? We briefly consider these questions, focusing on the issue of turnover and veteran MPs.

If the Liberal electoral dominance continues, it will likely mean continuing low turnover and an ever more experienced House of Commons. If this is the result, MPs may seek out greater roles and influence, and provoke truly dramatic changes in all dimensions of Commons activity. An early indicator of this potential was the amendment of the House standing orders in November 2002 to elect standing committee chairs by secret ballot. This was a dramatic and significant event, as 56 Liberal MPs voted against the Prime Minister and cabinet to support an Alliance motion on the issue. But the Alliance motion was itself prompted by the pledges of Paul Martin, who is likely to play a pivotal role in any future changes. In the fall of 2002, Martin made clear commitments to parliamentary reform, including the tolerance of more dissenting votes and greater autonomy for committees. The combination of experienced MPs and Martin's apparent commitment to reform might well produce a truly and dramatically different House of Commons.

However, if the electoral situation becomes more unstable and turnover increases, the Commons may lose some of its apparent gains. The loss of its seasoned and veteran MPs would reduce the House's ability to act cohesively and realistically to build a role in the Canadian political system. Even the precedent of challenging leaders may wither away if the balance of MPs shifts to a new crop of ambitious rookies who do not see it in their interests to rock the boat.

In conclusion, the long-term prospects of the Commons remain unclear. The Chrétien era has seen a number of significant developments in parliamentary roles and activity, but the overall effect of these developments has been mixed. The Commons may have found an enhanced role in the Canadian political system in the dimension of selecting party leaders. But this has not been accompanied by major changes in other areas, suggesting that Parliament will continue to struggle with differing expectations and assessments of its place in Canadian politics.

NOTES

1   This chapter does not discuss the Senate of Canada, which, while an equal partner in Parliament, has a different set of dynamics and poses different issues than the elected House of Commons. While the experience of the Senate under the Chrétien government is interesting in and of itself, it cannot easily be incorporated into the research approach of this chapter, especially given space limitations.

2   C.E.S. Franks, *The Parliament of Canada* (University of Toronto Press: Toronto, 1987).

3   Jennifer Smith, 'The Canadian House of Commons at the *Millennium*', *Canadian Public Administration* 42, 4 (Dec. 1999), 398–421.

4   Calculations by the author, taken from figures on parliamentary web site: www. parl.gc.ca.

5   David Docherty, 'Political Careers in Canada', in Brenda O'Neill and Joanna Everitte, eds, *Citizen Politics: Research and Theory in Canadian Political Behaviour* (Toronto: Oxford University Press, 2001), 342.

6   David Docherty, *Mr Smith Goes to Ottawa* (Vancouver: UBC Press, 1997).

7   Franks, *The Parliament of Canada*, 78; see also Michael M. Atkinson and David Docherty, 'Moving Right Along: The Roots of Amateurism in the House of Commons', *Canadian Journal of Political Science* 25, 2 (June 1992), 295–318.

8   These and subsequent figures have been calculated by the author using data from the parliamentary web site.

9   In 1980, turnover was 19 per cent.

10 Docherty, *Mr Smith Goes to Ottawa*, xiv.

11 Yves Yvon J. Pelletier, 'Time Allocation in the House of Commons', *Canadian Parliamentary Review* 23, 4 (Winter 2000-1).

12 'Ottawa to Dump Much-Debated Anti-Terrorism Bill', *The Globe and Mail* [Toronto], 25 Apr. 2002.

13 'Backbench Revolt Puts Another Bill on Hold', *The Ottawa Citizen*, 30 Apr. 2002.

14 Docherty, *Mr Smith Goes to Ottawa*, 190.

15 Peter C. Dobell and Martin Ulrich, 'Parliament's Role in the Budgetary Process', *Policy Matters* (Montreal: Institute for Research on Public Policy, 2002), 13.

16 Ian Marsh, 'State Capacity for Policy Making: Has It Diminished? Can It Be Renewed?' (unpublished paper, Australian National University, May 2001).

17 Jonathan Malloy, 'Reconciling Expectations and Reality in House of Commons Committees: The Case of the 1989 GST Inquiry', *Canadian Public Administration* 39, 3 (Fall 1996), 314–35.

18 'MP Revolt Looms Over Stem-Cell Bill', *The Ottawa Citizen*, 18 May 2002, A3.

5

Reconciling Energy and Climate Change Policies: How Ottawa Blends

DEBORA L. VANNIJNATTEN AND
DOUGLAS MACDONALD

The Chrétien government is currently working to resolve the inherent contradiction between two of its stated policy goals: first, the extraction and sale of fossil fuel in order to contribute to economic development, and second, reductions in fossil fuel consumption in order to contribute to global efforts in relation to climate change.[1] The horns of that particular dilemma were made particularly apparent when the House of Commons ratified the Kyoto Protocol at the end of the 2002 parliamentary session.

Ratification, once the international climate regime comes into effect, will finally commit Canada to bringing annual emissions of carbon dioxide and other greenhouse gases 6 per cent below 1990 levels by no later than 2012—a considerable task, given that they are currently 19.6 per cent above the 1990 level. Alberta Premier Ralph Klein has stated that ratification would turn Alberta into a 'have not' province, and business groups spent a good part of 2002 brandishing reports with doomsday predictions of the implementation costs of Kyoto. Failure to ratify, on the other hand, would have deprived the Chrétien government of whatever small environmental reputation it still has within the country, and significantly damaged Canadian international credibility. It would also necessarily have led to a Canadian withdrawal from the international process and adoption of the much-maligned

American approach—efforts to reduce energy intensity, but without a specific CO_2 reduction target.[2]

A variety of policy options are being considered by the Chrétien government as it attempts to both meet an international Kyoto commitment and continue using energy policy as a major element of economic development. Three have emerged as the most prominent, yet they vary in the degree to which fundamental change in Canada's emissions profile is sought. The first involves moving to a lower-carbon economy; that is, replacing some oil and coal with natural gas and, more generally, shifting energy sources from fossil fuels to renewable sources such as wind or ethanol and (perhaps—the joker in the deck) nuclear. Particular elements of the oil and gas industry are already moving in that direction, which means that assisting in a transformation of the fossil fuel industry into a supplier of renewable energy is a plausible policy objective—though certainly the most challenging to the status quo. The second potential means of reconciliation is technological development to reduce the carbon intensity of manufacturing and transport. This will produce economic benefits, through both energy savings and the export of new technology goods and services, while reducing greenhouse gas emissions. This is analogous to the assistance given to the pulp and paper industry for modernization in the 1970s, which was driven by competitiveness but also led to pollution reduction. Thirdly, Canada might meet its Kyoto commitment largely by gaining credit for carbon sinks and clean energy exports—in effect, by moving to a less demanding policy objective—while at the same time spending on greenhouse gas reductions made in other countries through the purchase of international emissions credits and/or joint development mechanisms. By December 2002, it had become apparent that the federal government was also using the policy instrument of spending as a bargaining chip in its negotiations with industry, promising to cap abatement costs at $15 per tonne.

The contradiction between the Chrétien government's energy objectives and its climate objectives could be resolved by a combination of these three measures, but only if the Prime Minister and cabinet provide leadership far more clear and consistent than any seen to date. Cabinet, for its part, has appeared divided and uncertain, a problem compounded by the failure of heir apparent Paul Martin to take a clear stand on the issue. In addition, throughout 2002 national energy and climate policy were being developed against the background of raucous federal-provincial debate. The sleeping dogs of Canadian federalism—regional conflicts based in economics and identity—have again been awakened by the failure of the government to turn its mind to the difficult but not impossible task of negotiating a national climate policy in which 'no region is asked to bear an unreasonable share of the burden'.[3]

Moreover, the lack of a coherent strategy at the political level is replicated at the administrative level. Although there has been greater coordination of energy and climate policy objectives and programs over the past few years, the *development* of climate policy continues to rest with Environment Canada, whose raison d'être is environmental protection, while *implementation* rests with Natural Resources

Canada, the premier energy department. This division of responsibilities, we argue, must give way to more organizational and program coherence.

THE FEDERAL POLICY LEGACY

Climate change may well be 'the most pervasive and far-reaching environmental issue ever dealt with by the international community'.[4] The natural presence of so-called 'greenhouse gases' (GHGs)—carbon dioxide (CO_2), methane, nitrous oxide, chloro-fluorocarbons (CFCs), and ozone—trap outgoing radiation, cause the overall tempera-ture of the earth to be warmer, and make life on earth possible. Yet the transition to coal from wood as the primary fuel in the early nineteenth century, and then to oil and natural gas in the twentieth, resulted in large increases in the production of CO_2 especially, as a result of the burning of these fossil fuels. The overwhelming majority of scientists agree that the build-up of CO_2 and other GHGs is resulting in an accelera-tion in the warming of the earth's atmosphere that will have serious consequences, especially with respect to polar and inland temperate zones. The response, according to those concerned about climate change, must be movement toward a less carbon-intensive global energy system. The international commitment made at Kyoto, Japan in 1997 to reduce GHG emissions by 5 per cent below 1990 levels is seen by most experts as merely a first step along the road toward what is truly needed, something like a 50 per cent reduction. This requires tough choices on the part of both the inter-national community, faced with a truly global collective-action issue, and individual governments, understandably tempted by the concomitant possibility of free-riding.

Climate change poses a particular challenge for those countries, such as Canada, whose economies are reliant on the production and consumption of fossil fuels. In fact, kicking the fossil fuel habit in Canada is, if anything, becoming more difficult, given that the development of offshore resources in the Atlantic, and now, possibly, in the Pacific Northwest, will increase the number of provinces whose economic for-tunes are tied to oil and gas production. The balance of this section sets out the con-text for the chapter by discussing the recent history of Canadian energy and climate change policy.

Energy Policy
It is the provinces that have jurisdictional responsibility for resource management—including energy development—within their borders. Federal powers in energy pri-marily cover interprovincial and international movements of energy, energy projects that extend beyond a province's boundaries, uranium and nuclear power undertak-ings, and resource management on frontier lands. The federal government thus con-cerns itself with such activities as pipeline and powerline construction, offshore oil and gas developments, energy exports, energy efficiency standards, and energy sci-ence and technology.[5]

Natural Resources Canada (NRCan) has lead responsibility for federal energy pro-grams. Doern and Gattinger note that '[i]f Canadians have any clear image of NRCan and its predecessor EMR [Energy, Mines and Resources], it is probably of a department whose job it is to support the development of its economic constituency, namely mining and metals, energy (oil, gas, nuclear), and forestry industries.'[6] Indeed, energy policy up to and including the 1970s was almost solely producer-oriented, and was characterized by considerable support for the domestic fossil fuel industry via supportive tax and export policies, as well as pipeline development.[7]

In the 1970s, Canada, like most industrialized countries, attempted to respond to an OPEC oil embargo and then a quadrupling of world oil prices. The result was the interventionist National Energy Policy (NEP). The NEP consisted of a series of measures designed both to secure the domestic energy supply (for example, enhanced support for Canadian-owned companies; tax incentives for exploration on federal lands) and to achieve equality of pricing across the country (for example, taxing western exports to the United States and using the proceeds to subsidize eastern consumers). The NEP also included incentives for conservation and the use of renewables, in order to decrease fossil fuel consumption. Not surprisingly, these measures—along with the federal government's move to take an increased share of oil and gas revenues—soured relations between Ottawa and western Canada.[8]

From the mid-1980s to 1993, state intervention in energy markets declined and federal energy policy reflected the free market orientation of successive Conservative governments. The Mulroney government dismantled the NEP by deregulating the oil and gas industries and promoting continental energy markets. Conservation programs were collapsed down into a tiny administrative unit. In 1988, the Canada–United States Free Trade Agreement (FTA) enhanced the framework for energy trade by preventing differential pricing systems and supply restrictions, as well as by securing market access. The North American Free Trade Agreement of 1993 for the most part extended the energy provisions of the FTA.

The advent of the Chrétien Liberals in 1993 signalled both change and continuity in federal energy policy. A reorganization of the federal government resulted in the creation of a new department, Natural Resources Canada (NRCan), responsible for three major economic sectors—forestry, mining, and energy. NRCan's Energy Sector became one of four line sectors in the new department, garnering approximately one-third of its resources. Federal energy policy continued its free market orientation, but it also has had to respond to the Liberals' 'sustainable development' and 'innovation' agendas. Traditional resource development objectives must now mesh with environmental concerns, a focus on the new knowledge-based economy, and, increasingly, the climate change imperative. Thus, NRCan is in the position previously occupied by EMR—being asked to pursue the conflicting goals of stimulating production and encouraging conservation.

These contradictory influences are reflected in NRCan's current energy policy objectives: to develop a competitive and innovative energy sector, to encourage environmental stewardship, and to establish secure access to energy resources.[9] NRCan defines sustainable energy development as 'maximizing energy's contribution to economic growth and to the development of the Canadian economy while enhancing environmental quality and meeting the needs of present and future gen-erations'.[10] In an attempt to meet these objectives, NRCan has worked to develop a more diversified set of energy programs, fostering a limited renewable energy pro-gram while at the same time courting its traditional fossil-fuel clientele (especially its more 'high-tech' elements) and continuing its work on energy efficiency.[11] NRCan also has attempted to position itself—with considerable success—at the centre of federal environmental technology implementation, especially with respect to initia-tives relating to GHG emissions.

Indeed, the need to address GHG emissions has become increasingly prominent on the energy policy agenda—climate change ranks among four major 'domains' that the department believes will influence energy politics in the coming years (along with deregulation of markets, the nuclear question, and frontier develop-ment).[12] Yet the continued growth of Canadian energy production and exports—of the conventional variety—is at odds with the objective of GHG reduction. Currently, energy production from all sources contributes 7 per cent of GDP and $26 billion in exports (over 50 per cent of which are destined for the United States). Total Cana-dian oil production is forecast to increase by about 19 per cent between 1995 and 2020, and oil exports by approximately 23 per cent over the same period.[13] Gas pro-duction is rising even faster. Unlike pollution-control issues that can be addressed by relatively modest abatement spending, climate change poses a fundamental eco-nomic challenge.

Moreover, energy production and consumption is regionalized. Alberta is respon-sible for more than 60 per cent of the energy produced in Canada, and it is the largest producer of all fossil fuels (coal, oil, and gas). Canada's oil sands, located primarily in Alberta, represent one-third of the world's known petroleum resources, and production levels are expected to surpass conventional and offshore production by 2010. While Ontarians and their industries consume one-third of all energy nationwide, Alberta, because of its energy production industry, is the second-largest consumer. GHG emission forecasts, of course, tell a similar story. Alberta and Ontario are expected to experience the largest increase in GHG emissions between 1990 and 2010 (67 Mt and 31 Mt, respectively). Yet the increase in emissions in cen-tral Canada (Ontario and Quebec) over the same period will be about half that in western Canada (Alberta and Saskatchewan).[14] Thus, any attempt to bring about GHG reductions nationally risks re-opening the 1980 National Energy Program fault lines between oil-producing (primarily western, but now also some maritime) provinces and other provinces that are less reliant on fossil fuels, such as Quebec and Manitoba. This has become one of the primary challenges to federal energy—and, by extension, climate change—policy.

Climate Change Policy
Although Canada was an early leader in pushing for international action on climate change, the term 'laggard' might be more appropriate as a current descriptor.[15] In 1988, as scientific research on climate change gained momentum, Canada hosted

the much-publicized Toronto Conference on the Changing Atmosphere, at which Prime Minister Mulroney called for 'an international law of the atmosphere accord'.[16] In the ensuing international meetings between 1989 and 1991 aimed at formulating such an accord, Canada joined the Europeans in pressing for firm targets and timetables, and seemed vindicated in doing so by the scientific concerns expressed in the *First Assessment Report* of the Intergovernmental Panel on Climate Change (IPCC). In 1990, Canada made a domestic commitment to stabilize CO_2 emissions at 1990 levels by 2000.

American negotiators, under pressure from their well-funded fossil fuel lobby as well as from vocal critics of the science on which action was to be based, indicated that they might not even sign an agreement.[17] As the June 1992 Rio Earth Summit drew nearer and negotiations became more intense, Canadian officials began to focus more on the costs of achieving CO_2 reductions and on protecting Canadian business. The resulting United Nations Framework Convention on Climate Change (UNFCCC), signed by 155 countries (including the United States), was a 'rather vaguely worded' document that acknowledged increasing concentrations of GHGs but required no action—countries were asked to voluntarily implement emission reductions in order to return to their 1990 emission levels.[18] Since Canada had already unilaterally made such a commitment, this international agreement was seen as relatively benign, and was quickly ratified by the Mulroney government.

The Chrétien Liberals came to power in 1993 on a pro-environment platform containing an ambitious CO_2 reduction target designed to better the Mulroney record; the party's campaign manifesto, the 'Red Book', advocated a 20 per cent cut from 1988 levels by 2005.[19] That promise seemed quickly forgotten, however, and the Prime Minister did not initially engage himself in the climate change issue that promptly engendered fierce battles among his ministers.[20] The Natural Resources minister at the time, Ann McClellan, was successful in defending her Alberta constituency against the push by Environment Minister Sheila Copps for GHG reductions implemented via a legally binding framework. In fact, the 1995 *National Action Program on Climate Change* (NAPCC), developed through federal-provincial negotiation under the aegis of the periodic Joint Meetings of Energy and Environment Ministers, was based almost completely on the instrument of voluntarism.

At the first Conference of Parties (COP) to the UNFCCC in Berlin, in 1995, almost all signatories (including Canada) admitted that they had achieved little in the way of actual emission reductions, and the conference called on states to adopt a binding protocol by 1997. Also in 1995, the IPCC released its *Second Assessment Report*, which concluded that 'patterns of atmospheric temperature suggest a discernible human influence on global climate', and critics of the climate change science found themselves with somewhat less ammunition.[21] In the run-up to the 1997 meeting in Kyoto, Japan, European countries impressed upon Canada—via the Prime Minister himself—the importance of the country's active support for a binding protocol containing substantive reduction measures. The Americans, meanwhile, were pressing for tradable emission permits, something opposed by the Europeans.

Canada, facing these conflicting pressures in addition to considerable domestic opposition, began advocating 'flexibility' in achieving emission reductions—including credits for activities in developing countries, trading of GHG permits, and recognition of carbon sinks.[22] Europeans and environmentalists were not impressed. In the end, the Kyoto Protocol struck a compromise whereby steeper, differentiated reduction targets were set (6 per cent and 7 per cent below 1990 levels by 2008–12 for Canada and the United States, respectively) in exchange for flexibility in implementation. Here at home, first ministers met immediately after the Kyoto compromise was struck and agreed, first, that extensive consultations would be held before Canada made a final decision on whether or not it would actually honour its Kyoto commitment (by ratifying the Protocol) and, second, that no one region would be required to carry the bulk of the cost.

The COP meetings that followed in Buenos Aires in 1998, Bonn in 1999, and The Hague in 2000 focused on negotiating the details of implementation, with little success. Canada, while pushing for definitions of the joint implementation and clean development mechanisms favourable to its interests, continued to insist that managed forests and agricultural lands be eligible carbon sinks. The EU and environmentalists were strongly opposed.[23] Domestically, the fall of 2000 saw the release of the federal-provincial National Strategy and the *Canadian Climate Change Action Plan*—the fruit of extensive and detailed national consultations over the previous two years. The National Strategy was presented as an interim program, to be updated periodically while a final decision on ratification was awaited. It still relied primarily upon voluntary actions, despite the failure of the 1995 NAPCC. The federal government, in the *Action Plan*, emphasized existing technology and conservation initiatives that were to receive greater support. The 1998 budget provided $150 million for the Climate Change Action Fund, to be spent on public education and policy development, as well as on science and technology development. This was followed two years later by budget spending of $625 million, including $100 million for the Sustainable Development Technology Fund.

The Kyoto process was then dealt a near-fatal blow in March 2001, when the newly elected administration of George W. Bush announced that it would not ratify the Kyoto Protocol, because of its likely economic impacts. Instead, the Americans would adopt a made-in-the-USA approach to GHG reduction that focused on voluntary action on the part of industry and incentives for clean technology development, with no specific CO_2 reduction target. Shortly before, the Bush administration had released its National Energy Policy, which called for increasing the domestic and continental energy supply through accelerated oil and gas exploration, as well as coal use. The international process recovered, however, at the Bonn meeting of July 2001, at which agreement was reached on specific measures to implement the Kyoto agreement without US participation. At that meeting, Canada was successful in gaining acceptance of its argument that it be allowed to include sinks such as forests and agriculture lands as part of its Kyoto objective. Prime Minister Chrétien stated immediately afterward that, as a result of this concession, his government could seriously consider ratification in 2002.

An international climate regime that does not include the United States, however, poses significant difficulties for the Canadian economy, which has become so fully a part of one integrated North American market. The Bush administration's pull-out strengthened the hand of Kyoto opponents within Canada, who could now argue that they would be at a severe competitive disadvantage in their most important export markets—markets that could be expected to expand under the US NEP. The Plan focuses on energy security in terms of North American (Canadian and Mexican) supply sources, and this presents new energy export opportunities for Canada, particularly the 'blue-eyed sheiks' of Alberta. As Alberta's Energy Minister has noted, 'Let's get on with a North American solution to this where we do business. Canada does not fit within the framework of the Kyoto Protocol.'[24]

On 2 September 2002, the Prime Minister stated that the House of Commons would vote on ratification before the Christmas break. In response to demands by the anti-Kyoto forces, the federal government released on 24 October 2002 a plan for energy conservation, which was discussed, inconclusively, at a federal-provincial energy and environment ministers meeting on 28 October. Then on 21 November 2002 the government released the most definitive document to date, titled *Climate Change Plan for Canada*. On 17 December 2002, after votes in the House of Commons and the Senate, Environment Minister David Anderson presented the Canadian ratification document to the United Nations in New York.

THE BROADER POLICY CONTEXT

Federal policies with respect to climate change and energy have been influenced by a complex of domestic and international forces. Far from displaying mastery at a two-level game, however—using international pressure to strengthen its hand at home, and vice-versa—the Chrétien government has been moving its pieces on both boards without apparent coordination or coherence. Internationally, it has pursued a strategy of seeking concessions by the UNFCCC parties that would effectively reduce the contribution Canada must make to the global effort. This was done first by supporting the American effort for the use of economic instruments in the international regime and then by seeking credits for sinks and, now, clean energy exports. The Chrétien government did not follow the American lead in abandoning Kyoto, however, which seems to indicate that European pressures and a desire to preserve its internationalist reputation still mattered. With regard to the government's domestic policy, it has been difficult to discern any consistent strategy at all, which in part reflects the multi-faceted pressures that have been brought to bear on federal decision-makers by interest groups and provinces.

Domestic Forces
Coordination of national policy in the face of regional and language-based conflict has been a central challenge faced by every Canadian government since 1867. In the fields of energy and the environment, the primary mechanism used over the past

thirty-odd years has been councils of ministers, supported by federal-provincial committees made up of officials at the deputy minister and assistant deputy minister levels. Thus, the National Air Issues Steering Committee, made up of federal and provincial deputy ministers, was created in 1993 to support the efforts of the Canadian Council of Ministers of Environment to develop and implement national air pollution policy, including, at that time, climate change. Since the late 1980s, however, climate as an energy issue had been addressed by the corresponding secretariat of federal and provincial energy ministers. Beginning in 1993, energy and environment ministers began to meet together on the issue, in what has come to be known as the Joint Meeting of Ministers of Environment and Energy (JMM). They were supported at the staff level by the National Air Issues Co-ordinating Committee—Climate Change. In 1998, the JMM created another coordinating body, the National Climate Change Secretariat.

Such intergovernmental organizations have not been successful in reducing federal-provincial conflict over national climate change policy, however. The provinces have been engaged in conflict with the federal government (and each other) over Kyoto ratification since the Protocol was signed in 1997, with provincial positions determined by both economic interests and, to a lesser extent, political philosophy.[25] Opposing provinces, including Alberta, British Columbia, and (sometimes) Ontario, have argued that the federal government has not been clear with respect to how the Kyoto target is to be implemented and how the costs will be allocated among provinces. Quebec, for its part, has a clear interest in profiting from increased hydro-electricity sales as North America moves away from oil and gas, and is, along with Manitoba, Kyoto's biggest fan. Saskatchewan, another province with oil and gas interests, has neither endorsed nor opposed the Protocol explicitly.

Federal-provincial conflict reached new heights in the summer and fall of 2002 as provincial positions hardened. Alberta's Environment Minister warned that his oil-rich province would consider all options to fight Ottawa's decision to ratify Kyoto—including a court challenge to the constitutionality of ratification. It also bowed out of federal-provincial discussions on a Kyoto implementation plan and subsequently formulated its own 'made-in-Canada' CO_2 reduction plan. Ontario and British Columbia, now joined by Newfoundland, have become more outspoken in their opposition. Quebec, meanwhile, became more impatient for ratification, to the point of storming out of an intergovernmental meeting.

Business and environmental interests have also been centrally involved in the development of Canada's climate policy.[26] Environmental groups, most notably the Suzuki Foundation and the Pembina Institute, but also a number of other ENGOs united in the Climate Action Network (CanNet) coalition, largely speak with one voice. They have called for ratification as a first step, but do not see a 6 per cent reduction as anything like sufficient. They have also kept up continual pressure on federal decision-makers in an attempt to aid Environment Canada's position, pointing out flaws in voluntary programs and attempting to shame Canada at the international level. They call, instead, for significant changes to land-use planning and public transportation policy, and a switch to alternative and renewable energies. Further, these demands have been backed up by an extensive research effort.

The national business organizations initially advocated a 'go-slow' approach. However, once the Prime Minister leaned heavily toward ratification in the summer of 2001, they moved to a straight-up 'stop Kyoto' position. Driven by the need to remain competitive in the US market, they began lobbying for a continental approach, with Canada playing the role of junior partner in the Bush administration program. These organizations are largely supported by sectoral trade associations, such as the Canadian Association of Petroleum Producers (CAPP). CAPP's president summed up their position by asking, 'How do you make a domestic Canadian climate change policy operate to meet international obligations while at the same time operating in a continental energy market where none of the other countries have targets to reduce emissions?'[27]

During the spring of 2002, the Canadian Council of Chief Executives, Canadian Manufacturers and Exporters, and the Canadian Chamber of Commerce released a flurry of position papers, arguing that Canada should not ratify Kyoto. Several themes were dominant: first, business agrees that climate change is a real problem and action must be taken; second, adherence to the 1997 international commitment is not possible, because of the short time-frame, and, furthermore, the attempt to do so will impose a significant cost upon those selling into the American market; and, finally, major costs will also be imposed directly upon individual Canadians.[28] By September 2002 business had pulled out the big guns, running full-page newspaper advertisements warning of the cost to individual citizens and urging them to instead support a 'made-in-Canada' solution. These were then supplemented by a major television advertising campaign in Ontario, funded by a variety of industry sectors and the same three broad-based associations.[29] By that time, Kyoto ratification had achieved greater media prominence than any environmental issue since acid rain in the early 1980s. The attempt by business to influence national policy was the most vigorous seen since the 1988 Canada–United States free trade debate.

The oil industry is not entirely of one mind, however. Imperial Oil, following the lead of Exxon, is staying the course, but British Petroleum and Shell are moving to explore investments in renewable energy.[30] Such investments have been spurred both by competitive instincts, in that European governments currently provide generous incentives to companies that develop wind and solar power technologies that can then be sold abroad, and, likely, by the need for some 'green PR'. Meanwhile, Transalta Corp. has undertaken a project with the Canadian Wind Energy Association to encourage the Alberta government to increase its wind generating capacity, and Suncor Energy Inc. has struck a deal with Europe's EHN, a group of renewable energy companies, to develop wind energy projects in Canada. The nuclear and hydroelectric industries also have stepped up their own PR campaigns, touting the benefits of emission-free energy generation.

One of the more interesting developments on the Canadian scene has been the formation of the Clean Air Renewable Energy (CARE) coalition, in which energy companies such as Transalta, Westcoast Energy, BP Canada, and Shell Canada have teamed up with environmental groups such as the Pembina Institute, Friends of the Earth, and Pollution Probe to lobby the federal government for expanded tax credits for renewable energy sector R&D and credits for consumers who buy energy generated from renewable sources.[31] Thus, business interests have become more and more divided by quite different economic and political interests.

The American Influence
In addition to the multi-directional domestic pressures discussed above, forces emanating from outside the country influence Canadian climate and energy policy in often contradictory ways. As we have seen, Canadian representatives in international climate change negotiations have attempted to juggle the expectations of their neighbour and closest trading partner, the United States, whose approach has been cautious at best, obstructionist at worst, with those of the more proactive European countries and their allies.

There can be little doubt, however, that Canadian policy-makers pay more attention to events south of the 49th Parallel than those across the Atlantic. As Russell and Toner have noted,

> The US has several powerful coal companies and unions, and coal producing regions. It is also home to the majority of major multinational oil companies. The US is also the largest producer of carbon dioxide. Consequently, climate change politics in all of North America has got caught up in the peculiarities of American domestic politics.[32]

Yet these American domestic forces are not as unidirectional or coherent as they are often portrayed. Certainly, the US NEP and Bush's anti-Kyoto stance appear to indicate that the opponents of GHG reductions have the upper hand, especially after Republican gains in the House and Senate in the 2002 mid-term elections. This makes Canadian implementation of Kyoto decidedly more difficult. However, policy developments at both federal and state levels in the United States are quite positive in support of climate change actions, and this, too, will have implications for Canadian policy.

First, although the Bush administration's NEP contains only limited incentives for renewable energy and for conservation, the administration's 'alternative to Kyoto' will likely include more aggressive support for science and technology relating to nonconventional energy sources as well as for energy conservation. The US federal government already has a number of innovative programs for reducing GHG emissions,[33] and these may receive increased support. Such a focus will no doubt be vigorously pushed in Congress by environmental groups, which have been galvanized by the administration's overt focus on oil and gas development, and which are not (contrary to Canadian popular wisdom) powerless in a Republican-dominated Congress. In addition, a coalition of business, environmental, and political leaders has been pushing for legislative, R&D, and taxation measures to support lower carbon and carbon-free technology and applications.[34] More serious support for nonconventional energy sources also makes sense in light of the continuing debate between the administration and Congress on air quality problems resulting from coal-fired electric utilities.

Renewable energy innovations also are being spurred at the subnational level. A number of states engaged in energy deregulation are in the process of implementing such mechanisms as minimum renewable electricity standards (or quotas), renewable energy funds (charging a small fee on electricity sold to support renewable energy development), and net metering (which allows customers who themselves generate electricity to feed it back into the system and benefit financially),[35] in order to encourage alternative energy producers. And the 'California Effect' may once again be in operation, this time in relation to GHG reductions. In 2002, California passed a new law mandating reductions in GHG emissions from vehicles, which has again sparked a nation-wide debate and may result in policy and technology change beyond California's borders. Finally, the New England states have joined forces with eastern Canadian provinces in establishing a cross-border regime for CO_2 reductions. Thus, domestic policy developments in the United States may in fact help to push Canada toward renewable energy sources and new energy-efficiency technologies regardless of the international climate regime.

FEDERAL DECISION-MAKING AND THE CLIMATE CHANGE FILE

The responsibility for federal climate change policy rests with Environment Canada and NRCan. Environment Canada was initially assigned lead responsibility for the climate change file when it first emerged as an issue in the late 1980s. As climate change policy came to be seen more and more as an energy issue, NRCan's role became more significant. Tensions between the two departments with regard to the climate file were evident throughout the 1990s, and attracted critical comment from the federal Commissioner for the Environment and Sustainable Development. Although there has been greater coordination in recent years, with federal decision-makers beginning to look more closely at the options for Kyoto implementation, tensions and challenges remain—and these are rooted primarily in the division of responsibilities between the two departments. In 1998, when the Secretariat was created to coordinate federal responsibilities, Environment Canada became responsible for taking the lead in international negotiations, while NRCan's primary responsibility lay in domestic policy. Since then, however, as judged by media visibility, the Environment Minister has assumed primary responsibility for the domestic file as well. Nevertheless, and compounding the confusion, NRCan possesses the actual programs and analytical expertise for reconciling energy development and GHG reduction.

Within Environment Canada, responsibility for both climate change science and policy development originally rested with Atmospheric and Environment Services (now Meteorological Service). The science responsibility has remained there ever since. The policy function, on the other hand, soon moved, and by the early 1990s had been transferred to the Environmental Protection Service (EPS). After Canadian ratification of the UNFCCC in December 1992 the department was faced with the task of both working with the provinces to develop a national program to implement that commitment and working with other parties to the Convention in the continuing task of developing the international regime. By the mid-1990s, both responsibilities had been moved from EPS to the Policy and Communications branch, where they were housed in two separate units. The two were then reintegrated within a new section of that branch, the Climate Change Bureau, after the Kyoto meeting of parties in December 1997. The Bureau remains the primary internal unit of Environment Canada responsible for the issue with respect to international negotiations, the federal-provincial process, and coordination with other federal departments.

Under the federal *Action Plan 2000 on Climate Change*, NRCan is responsible for the majority of initiatives,[36] and most of these are lodged with the department's Energy Sector, which has placed ever more emphasis on the challenge for its programs and policies posed by climate change.[37] Departmental officials estimate that work related to climate change accounts for about 70 per cent of the Energy Sector's budget and the activities of more than half of its staff.[38] A brief look at the Energy Policy Branch shows how the climate change issue has insinuated itself into the Sector's ongoing activities. The Branch houses Policy Analysis and Coordination (concerned with coordinating and managing sector-wide issues such as climate change), Domestic Environment and International Environment (both of which cite climate change as their main focus), Energy Forecasting (whose main responsibility is 'the development of Canada's long-term energy and energy-related emissions projections'), and Economic and Fiscal Analysis (concerned with analyses related to energy economy and climate change, with specific responsibility for emissions trading and other GHG mitigation strategies).[39]

Activities related to the climate change program are sprinkled among the Sector's other four branches, with the Office of Energy Efficiency and the Office of Energy Research and Development garnering the lion's share of resources. Renewable and alternative energy programs were given higher profile in a new Division and were consciously sheltered from budget cuts under (surprisingly) Ann McLellan's watch, although these programs remain relatively small. The recent arrival of a new deputy minister, George Anderson, has also served to energize NRCan climate change activities. Fresh from the Privy Council Office, and with earlier experience in EMR as head of the Energy Policy Branch, Anderson has encouraged the department to take a more hands-on approach to climate change.

Throughout the 1990s, the government relied upon the Prime Minister's Office and the Privy Council Office to manage interdepartmental climate change discussions. Over the past two years, however, a complex network of trans-governmental mechanisms has been established to bring about greater synchronization. This network stretches from the program and sectoral levels, through deputy ministers and ministers, and finally to full cabinet. The interdepartmental activity is coordinated by the previously mentioned Climate Change Secretariat, which brings together bureaucrats working on the climate issue in various departments, and which also coordinates the national climate change consultation process.

The Climate Change Management Council (CCMC), with an interdepartmental membership convened under the auspices of the Climate Change Secretariat, is the federal forum that manages the climate change file and directs program-related work. Weekly meetings of the CCMC, which can last three to four hours, are attended by assistant deputy ministers from NRCan, Environment Canada, Finance, and the PCO, as well as NRCan officials working on various implementation programs. Every six weeks or so, the Secretariat brings CCMC members together with officials from other departments with an interest in climate issues, such as Transport or Agriculture.

The CCMC serves as the 'window' into the Climate Change Reference Group of Ministers, which actually takes two forms: a 'broader' group of twelve ministers whose departments have a stake in the climate change issue[40] and a 'core' group of four ministers—Finance, PCO, Environment, and Natural Resources—who play the lead role. The Climate Change Reference Group of Ministers is not a decision-making body, but rather a forum for cabinet-level discussion. Formal responsibility for climate change policy rests with the Cabinet Committee on the Economic Union and the full cabinet. A recent addition to this process is the Reference Group of Deputies, which also has both broader and core incarnations, mirroring those of its ministerial counterparts. Decision-making under this system percolates upward, though not necessarily in a perfectly linear fashion. The PCO acts as the facilitator between the interdepartmental process and the Prime Minister's Office.

Certainly, this network of mechanisms has brought greater coordination across departments between the formulation of policy and its implementation, as well as between the climate change and energy files. Memoranda to cabinet emerge out of the CCMC, interdepartmental meetings are held at various levels, and the outcome is a multi-departmental product. However, this process does not alter the reality of divided responsibility for climate change decision-making and implementation. Neither does it effectively resolve NRCan's conflicting objectives—the simultaneous pursuit of GHG reductions and oil and gas development. In fact, the inability of the federal government to fully reconcile the energy and climate change files was made clear in the Prime Minister's decision to create an Energy Reference Group of Ministers after the release of the Bush administration's NEP—to discuss Canada's role in supplying US energy needs. Energy and climate change, it would seem, remain on parallel, rather than merged, tracks.

CONCLUSION

Our examination of the failure of the federal government to develop one coherent energy and climate policy package has led us to the following conclusions: Canada can survive the current spate of regional wrangling, just as it has survived many others before this one; and something must be done to resolve the anomaly of policy decisions' being made by one department while the instruments for implementation are developed by another. In both these realms, political leadership is critical.

The Alberta-Quebec public argument over who will pay what portion of the cost of implementing Kyoto is indicative of the basic dynamic of Canadian federalism: in all policy fields, each provincial government defends the economic interests of its province. Alberta Premier Ralph Klein mused briefly on the possibility of Alberta's separating to avoid the horrors of Kyoto ratification, but then abandoned that position the next day. For whatever reason, though the economic union is increasingly fragmented by north-south continental trade, the political union is ever less threatened by the spectre of separatism. Given appropriate federal leadership, a bargain on regional allocation of the Kyoto costs can be struck and then continually renegotiated in the years ahead. As both the American and Canadian jurisdictions turn their attention to reducing the carbon intensity of their economies, independently of the international regime, regional strains will lessen.

The necessary federal leadership, however, is dependent upon changes in the current arrangement for energy and climate policy formulation and implementation. As noted, energy departments at both levels of government have an inherently schizoid need to both consume and conserve the Canadian supply of fossil fuel buried underground—which poses a problem for a coherent climate and energy policy. Yet the Energy Sector of NRCan has undergone a considerable shift in its mandate, its programs, and its policies toward addressing the climate change imperative, and there is evidence to suggest that these new priorities have begun to permeate the mining and forestry sectors as well. The question is whether this shift, which has put in place a new set of incentives, can be made to operate department-wide.

Certainly, moving energy conservation into a new, separate department might make the conservation-development conflict more transparent, allow it to be played out using the normal processes for working out interdepartmental conflict, and give it an organizational profile corresponding to the visibility and urgency of the issue. On the other hand, the experience of environmental policy has shown that vesting a new, and probably junior department with responsibility for implementing a horizontal policy issue requiring action by many of its more powerful sister departments is not likely to be effective. An alternative to departmental change might be the creation of a new cabinet committee, which combines the currently separate political discussions of energy and climate policy, and reinforces coordinating mechanisms at the administrative level. Whatever the solution, the federal government can only extract itself from the energy vs climate change dilemma through organizational and policy coherence.

There can be no doubt that the role played by the prime minister will continue to be significant, even as the holder of that office changes some time during the winter of 2003–4. Jean Chretien's involvement with the issue has oscillated between benign neglect and strong-handed intervention. Several analysts have noted that Chretien seems particularly susceptible to pressure from other heads of state, especially at G8 meetings. Presumably, his late conversion to the 'legacy' of social issues also explains his recent actions. Whatever the reasons, the effect of this zig-zag course has been that the moves to renewable energy and to technological development for energy efficiency have not been given the policy prominence and the leadership they require. To date, Paul Martin has also done his best to ignore this issue. If Martin does become prime minister, though, he will have to implement the ratification decision made by his predecessor. Unless he first develops his own means of reconciling energy and climate policy, he will have to face this problem when it becomes unavoidable, at which point the necessary federal leadership required for an effective blending of the two policy goals may be impossible to achieve.

NOTES

1 With reference to the Chrétien government's climate goals, see Liberal Party of Canada, *Creating Opportunity: The Liberal Plan for Canada* (Ottawa, 1993), 70; Government of Canada, *Canada's National Report on Climate Change* (Ottawa: Environment Canada, 1994); Government of Canada, *National Action Program on Climate Change* (Ottawa: Environment Canada, 1995); Government of Canada, *Government of Canada Action Plan 2000 on Climate Change* (Ottawa: Supply and Services Canada, 2000). With reference to the Chrétien government energy goals, see Natural Resources Canada, *Energy in Canada 2000* (Ottawa: Energy Publications, 2000).

2 In fact, the February 2002 Bush administration climate plan is expected to result in a 30 per cent *increase* in American emissions over the Kyoto time period. Government of Canada, Discussion Paper (Ottawa, 2002), 9.

3 Principle adopted by the first ministers at their meeting of 11–12 December 1997; quoted in Commissioner of Environment and Sustainable Development, *Report of the Commissioner of the Environment and Sustainable Development to the House of Commons: Global Challenges* (Ottawa: Public Works, 1998), 3–10.

4 D.J. Russell and G. Toner, 'Science and Policy When the Heat Is Rising', Global Change Strategies Inc. Accessed at web site: www.gcsi.ca/risingheat.html 22 July 2002.

5 Natural Resources Canada, *Energy in Canada 2000*, chap. 1.

6 G. Bruce Doern and M. Gattinger, 'New Economy/Old Economy? Transforming Natural Resources Canada', in L. Pal, ed., *How Ottawa Spends 2001–2002: Power in Transition* (Don Mills: Oxford University Press, 2001), 225.

7 G. Bruce Doern and G. Toner, *The Politics of Energy: The Development and Implementation of the NEP* (Toronto: Methuen, 1985), 67. See also Natural Resources Canada, *Energy in Canada 2000*, chap. 1.

8 See Doern and Toner, *The Politics of Energy.*

9 Natural Resources Canada, *Energy in Canada 2000*, chap. 1.

10 Ibid., Introduction.

11 See Doern and Gattinger, 'New Economy/Old Economy?' 223–46, and D.L. VanNijnatten, 'Getting Greener in the Third Mandate? Renewable Energy, Innovation and the Liberals' Sustainable Development Agenda', in G. Bruce Doern, ed., *How Ottawa Spends 2002–2003: The Security Aftermath and National Priorities* (Don Mills: Oxford University Press, 2002), 216–33.

12 Natural Resources Canada, *Energy in Canada 2000*, chap. 1.

13 Ibid., chap. 3.

14 Government of Canada, *Canada's Emissions Outlook: An Update* (Ottawa: National Climate Change Process, Analysis and Modelling Group, Dec. 1999), 51.

15 H. Smith, 'Canadian Federalism and International Environmental Policy Making: The Case of Climate Change', Working Paper, Institute for Intergovernmental Rela-

tions, Queen's University. See web site: www.qsilver.queensu.ca/iigr/pub...s/working
_paper_series/Hsmith.html 07/22/2002, 1.

16 P.R. Samson, 'Canadian Circumstances: The Evolution of Canada's Climate Change
    Policy', *Energy & Environment* 12, 2/3 (2001), 201.

17 See P. Newell, *Climate for Change: Non-State Actors and the Global Politics of the
    Greenhouse* (Cambridge: Cambridge University Press, 2000), chap. 3.

18 Smith, 'Canadian Federalism and International Environmental Policy Making', 3.

19 Liberal Party of Canada, *Creating Opportunity: The Liberal Plan for Canada* (Ottawa,
    1993), 70.

20 Russell and Toner, 'Science and Policy', 6.

21 Ibid., 4.

22 Samson, 'Canadian Circumstances', 205.

23 Ibid., 206–7.

24 Canadian Press, 'Alberta Works on Proposal to Reduce Greenhouse Gases Through
    NAFTA, Not Kyoto', 15 Apr. 2002. See Web site: www.gcsi.ca/risingheat.html

25 Doug Macdonald et al., *Ratification of the Kyoto Protocol: A Citizen's Guide to the
    Canadian Climate Change Policy Process* (Toronto: Sustainable Toronto, 2002), avail-
    able at web site www. sustainabletoronto.ca, 62.

26 Samson, 'Canadian Circumstances', 210.

27 Canadian Press, 'Alberta Works on Proposal'. See web site: www.canoe.ca/National
    Ticker?CANOE-wire.Kyoto-NAFTA.html 7 July 02.

28 Macdonald et al., *Ratification of the Kyoto Protocol.*

29 Hugh Winsor, 'Questions Lurk Beneath the Surface of Ads on Kyoto', *The Globe and
    Mail* [Toronto], 8 Nov. 2002.

30 Ian Rowlands, 'Beauty and the Beast? BP's and Exxon's Positions on Climate
    Change', *Environment and Planning C: Government and Policy* 18 (2000),
    339–54.

31 Matthew MacKinnon, 'Tax Breaks Proposed for Green Consumers', *The Globe and
    Mail* [Toronto], 27 Dec. 2000. See web site: www.globeandmail.com

32 Russell and Toner, 'Science and Policy When the Heat Is Rising', 9.

33 M. Bramley, *A Comparison of Current Government Action on Climate Change in the
    U.S. and Canada*, Pembina Institute for Appropriate Development, May 2002.

34 Russell and Toner, 'Science and Policy When the Heat Is Rising,' 9.

35 S. Clemmer, B. Paulos, and A. Nogee, *Clean Power Surge: Ranking the States* (Cam-
    bridge, Mass.: Union of Concerned Scientists, April 2000), 5. Three states—Con-
    necticut, New Jersey, and Massachusetts—have adopted all four of these policies,
    while New York, Maine, Illinois, and Pennsylvania have adopted three of the four.

36 Government of Canada, *Natural Resources Canada: 2002–3 Estimates* (2002), 23.

37 A comparison of the Energy Sector Business Plans for 1996–9 and 1998–2001 shows
    this shift: whereas the 1996–9 Plan mentions climate change in passing as one of the
    'international factors' to be considered, the 1998–2001 Plan notes that climate
    change is 'our biggest challenge over the planning period'. Natural Resources
    Canada, *Energy Sector Business Plan 1996–99* (Ottawa, 1996); Natural Resources
    Canada, *Energy Sector Business Plan 1998–2001.*

38 Ibid., 4.

39 See web site: www.nrcan.gc.ca/es/epb/eng/enghome.htm

40 These include Environment, NRCan, Agriculture, Industry, Finance, Health, DIAND,
    Transport, Fisheries, Foreign Affairs and International Trade, PCO, and Intergovern-
    mental Affairs.

6

The Federal Role in Health Care Reform: Legacy or Limbo?

GERARD W. BOYCHUK

Roy Romanow, head of the Commission on the Future of Health Care in Canada, has publicly stated that if Prime Minister Chrétien wishes to leave a lasting legacy, there is no more important area in which he could seek to do so than in health care reform.[1] In keeping with the broader search for a legacy agenda, Ottawa had been laying the groundwork for a major initiative in health care throughout 2002. After some midsummer prevarication, the Throne Speech in the fall of 2002 reiterated that the Chrétien government was indeed planning a major initiative to put the Chrétien stamp on a new federal-provincial health care deal following the release of the Romanow Commission report and the report of the Standing Senate Committee on Social Affairs, Science and Technology (the Kirby Committee) on its Study on the State of the Health Care System in Canada. Such an initiative seems the natural culmination of a series of federal moves over the past three years suggestive of 'a major shift in federal strategy and federal spending in the health care field'.[2]

However, the successful achievement of a major federal health care reform initiative faces two major obstacles. Both are rooted in broader, more perennial issues, yet at the current juncture both are sharply conditioned by the politics of the federal Liberal leadership. First, health care is an area of primarily provincial jurisdiction. Any strategy designed to significantly reassert federal government leadership in the health care field—and provide a worthy and lasting legacy—will require a significant financial commitment. The provinces are well positioned to wrestle large financial concessions from the federal government—federal transfer restraint has significantly contributed to the problems in the health care field, while Chrétien's ability to deal forcefully with the provinces has been seriously undermined by the internal challenge to his leadership. Secondly, at the same time, the wrangling over the Liberal leadership has significant implications for the politics of federal budgeting that will act as a brake on the federal commitment of new funding. The questions, then, are these: will the Chrétien government manage to salvage the major health care initiative for which it has been striving since early 2000, or has the window of opportunity for bold federal action in health care already passed? Will the federal government be forced to settle for a more modest package, which increases funding but falls short of fundamental reform?

This chapter first provides an overview of the main substantive issues confronting the federal government in the field of health care. It then considers the politics of the federal role in health care reform and how this has been affected by the politics of both the Chrétien legacy agenda and the federal Liberal leadership. Finally, the chapter provides a brief overview of the reports of the Kirby Committee and the Romanow Commission and considers whether the two sets of recommendations taken together seem likely to provide a promising blueprint for federal health care reform in Prime Minister Chrétien's final period of tenure. As the fate of both sets of recommendations rests very heavily on an increased federal financial commitment, the grounds for optimism seem slim.

THE FEDERAL ROLE IN HEALTH CARE: THE ISSUES

The federal government plays a role in five aspects of health care: the financing of health services provided by the provinces, research and evaluation, the provision of health infrastructure, the promotion of health in the population, and the direct provision of health services to specific population groups. The most visible of these and the most significant in terms of federal expenditures is the transfer of funds for health care to the provinces under the Canada Health and Social Transfer (CHST), governed by the five principles enshrined in the Canada Health Act (CHA). Four broad themes encompass the various issues related to reform of this aspect of the federal role:[3] What changes can be made in health care delivery that could have an impact on the amount of federal funding required? What form should federal funding for health care take? How should the federal government raise revenue for the purpose of health care or constrain provinces in how they may raise revenues? Finally, who should be covered under public health care insurance and what services should be covered? These are the central issues currently facing the federal government in determining what its role will be in the reform of the health care system in Canada. These are also the questions to which any major federal initiative or proposed blueprint for reform will have to provide answers.

The aspects of health care delivery that most Canadians likely perceive as being most important, such as how physicians are reimbursed, how primary care is organ-

Table 6.1

Central Issues in Federal Health Care Financing

Theme	Specific Issues
Changes in Health Care Delivery	• Improving Efficiency and Effectiveness • Primary Care Reform • Regionalization of Health Services • Contracting Private For-Profit Facilities • Health Promotion and Population Health
Form of Federal Funding for Health Care	• Matching Conditional Cost-Sharing • Maintaining Current Block-Funding (CHST and CHA) • Improving CHST • Converting CHST to Tax Point Transfers • Converting CHST Cash Transfers to Medical Savings Accounts • Enrichments to federal health funding through tax expenditures for health care costs to individual Canadians

Raising Government Revenue for Health Care	• allowing/encouraging provinces to do so through
	  ○ user charges
	  ○ income tax on health care
	  ○ health care premiums

Public Health Care Coverage	Expanding Coverage
	• Pharmaceuticals
	  ○ national Pharmacare program
	  ○ tax initiative to protect against drug expenses
	• Homecare
	  ○ national Homecare program
	  ○ tax credit and tax deductions for homecare
	  ○ tax measures for informal caregivers
	• More restricted definition of medically-necessary services

Adapted from The Standing Senate Committee on Social Affairs, Science and Technology, *The Health of Canadians: The Federal Role; Volume Four: Issues and Options* (Sept. 2001), xxiii.

ized and delivered, whether services are offered in public facilities or contracted out to private facilities, fall largely outside the ambit of direct federal control. Yet, paradoxically, the federal government has a significant interest in these issues, because they have important implications for the overall costs of public health care provision, and, as a result, repercussions for the federal contribution to health care financing. Provinces demand that federal contributions to health care keep pace with increasing costs, and yet it is the provincial governments that control the most significant levers of cost control, not the federal government. Thus, the issue for the federal government in relation to health care delivery is not so much finding the most efficient and effective way to deliver health care services, but rather leveraging its ability to encourage provinces to do so.

The main role of the federal government in regard to alternative mechanisms of revenue generation for health care has largely been one of prohibiting certain of them, such as extra-billing and user fees. The federal government has faced significant pressures from provincial governments on this score. The latter must absorb increasing health care costs while federal restrictions significantly limit the means available to them by which to do so. As a result, provinces are forced to devote increasing proportions of their overall budgets to health care.[4] It is not surprising that they, in turn, demand that federal contributions match increases in costs. As a result of this dynamic, the federal government has faced the ongoing question: should it increase its own financial commitment to health care, or relax CHA restrictions against various methods of revenue-generation, such as user fees or extra-billing?

The form of federal funding for health care is clearly under direct federal control, and the two main issues are stability and visibility. From the provincial point of view, the federal government has been a notoriously unreliable partner in terms of its financial contributions to health care. As a result, the federal government has publicly faced pressure from provincial governments and from outside observers such as both the Kirby Committee and the Romanow Commission to stabilize federal contributions to health care. For its part, the federal government's concern in regard to funding is to maximize predictability and control, leverage over provincial health care delivery, and federal visibility. The Kirby Committee has noted that one of the major weaknesses of the CHST is a lack of federal visibility: 'Federal visibility is weak under the CHST because it is no longer possible to identify, even notionally, the actual level of the federal contribution to health care.'[5] With respect to leverage, federal cash transfers have a mixed record as means for enforcing federal principles such as those enshrined in the CHA—which is a serious problem, considering that this is their main rationale. Federal penalties have been very effective in discouraging user fees and extra-billing. On the other hand, the federal government 'has never penalized provinces for non-compliance with the five principles [of the CHA]', despite the fact that 'there are outstanding cases of non-compliance, involving the patient-oriented principles of portability, comprehensiveness, and accessibility'.[6] Another option for the federal government would be to consider alternative methods of contributing financially to health care, such as medical savings accounts.[7] Alternatively, the federal government may also choose to shift some of its spending away from direct transfers to provinces to transfers to individuals through the tax system, with primary candidates here including pharmaceutical and home care expenses.

With respect to the scope of coverage, the restrictions enshrined in the CHA are limited to medically necessary hospital and physician services. However, medical necessity is determined by the provinces, and it is the provinces that thus, under the current system, have the ability to delist services. One option for the federal government would be to allow provinces to define medical necessity more narrowly than is currently the case, such that a narrower range of health services would be exempt from restrictions against user fees, extra-billing, or private provision.

Another option would be for the federal government to outline more specifically those services that are to be considered medically necessary and allow the provinces greater flexibility in the provision of services outside this range of core health services. A related possibility is for the federal government to expand public funding of health services beyond just hospital and physician services. The two obvious potential candidates for expanded coverage under some form of federal program are pharmaceuticals and home care. Possibilities here range from a new federal cost-sharing program for pharmaceutical coverage, through an expansion of the CHST and its principles to include pharmaceutical coverage, to a federal tax initiative to alleviate pharmaceutical costs.[8] A similar range of possibilities exists for home care.[9]

THE POLITICS OF THE FEDERAL
ROLE IN HEALTH CARE REFORM

In late 2001 and early 2002, the federal government was laying the groundwork for a major initiative in the health care field, one major element of which was an attempt to improve the tenor of the relationship between Ottawa and the provinces. By the fall of 2002, the federal government formally signalled its intent to pursue a major health care initiative with the provinces following the release of the Kirby Committee and Romanow Commission reports. However, the possibilities for and the politics of health care reform had been transformed over this period by simultaneous developments outside the health care field—namely, the politics of the federal Liberal leadership.

Laying the Groundwork

Federal-provincial debates over health care in early 2002 promised to be rancorous. In the late fall of 2001, Ontario and Alberta had engaged the federal government in a vociferous, sometimes personal, debate over user fees. Alberta declared that it would implement user fees.[10] The Ontario government argued that federal underspending on health care would force it to implement user fees and informed the federal government that it would consider imposing them when a four-week deadline had passed.[11] Of course, the federal government rose to the bait, with Federal Intergovernmental Affairs Minister Stephan Dion virtually daring the Alberta government to violate the strictures of the CHA and forfeit federal funding.[12] With the release in early January 2002 of Alberta's Mazankowski Report outlining a blueprint for provincial health care reform, another direct confrontation with the federal government seemed, to most observers, inevitable.[13]

However, the expected confrontation between Alberta and the federal government did not materialize. Rather, the federal response was to praise aspects of the report and to encourage a debate on some of its more controversial elements, such as an increased role for the private sector, while urging provinces to wait for the report of the Romanow Commission in November before moving ahead.[14] The federal response, while perhaps simply a tactical manoeuvre, seemed indicative of a new spirit of accommodation, which many observers in the national media obviously found surprising—perhaps even disappointing.

In keeping with these federal moves, less than a week after the release of the Mazankowski report Allan Rock was replaced by Anne McLellan as the federal minister of health. It was reported that McLellan launched her tenure as health minister 'by defending the record of her home province of Alberta, declaring public health care should not be "frozen in time" and stating that she is "open" to changes in the Canada Health Act.'[15] Senator Marjorie LeBreton, deputy chairperson of the Kirby Committee, was quoted as stating that, while she doubted that Allan Rock was open to significant change, '[t]he whole debate on health care can now go down new avenues.'[16] Alberta's health minister viewed the appointment as 'a strong signal from the federal government that we're going to enter into a phase of constructive discussion and dialogue on health care.'[17] In the first week of her tenure as federal minister, McLellan issued a number of statements 'suggesting that the federal government is now more open to medicare changes already underway in provinces such as Alberta and Ontario'; she declared that she had 'no problem with the introduction of private hospitals, so long as provinces continue to respect the principles of the Canada Health Act'.[18] The same day, Alberta Premier Ralph Klein stated in his annual state-of-the-province television broadcast that the province planned to delist non-necessary services and begin to charge user fees for those services.[19] The following day, the Ontario Health Minister Tony Clement announced that Ontario was 'planning to increase the role private-sector companies play in providing publicly financed health-care, including using them to build and pay for hospitals and operate clinics'.[20] Ottawa's reaction appeared muted—as a result of which the new minister drew criticism, including some from Liberal MPs.[21]

The federal strategy was to maintain this more accommodating stance even as provinces argued that they would move ahead with health reform on their own without waiting for the Romanow Commission to report. In September, the federal minister clearly signalled to the provinces that the federal government would take a hands-off approach unless reforms were clearly in violation of the CHA.[22] A week later, Alberta announced that it had given permission for a private, for-profit medical centre for groups falling outside of public health insurance coverage such as those covered by workers' compensation.[23] The federal minister referred the matter to Health Canada officials for study, although her public reaction was that 'this is a matter of health care delivery in the province of Alberta'.[24] It was reported that the federal minister 'scolded' Alberta for expanding the clinic—not for the substance of the decision, but rather for not waiting for the Romanow Commission report to be released.[25] It was in this new context of federal flexibility that the Speech from the Throne in fall 2002 committed the federal government to 'convene a First Ministers meeting early in 2003 to put in place a comprehensive plan for reform, including enhanced accountability to Canadians and the necessary federal long-term investments, which will be included in the next budget'.[26]

The Politics of the Liberal Leadership

Of course, the development of the federal health care strategy cannot be divorced from the politics of Chrétien's legacy agenda and the Liberal leadership. The federal policy agenda over the course of the spring was dominated by the search for policy issues that could be incorporated by Prime Minister Chrétien into a legacy agenda. However, the legacy agenda was thrown sharply off track and, subsequently, into high gear when Finance Minister Paul Martin's long-standing leadership campaign burst spectacularly into the open in early summer—a process that culminated in Martin's removal from cabinet. After vigorous leadership jockeying, Chrétien announced in August that he would be stepping down in February 2004, giving himself enough time to fulfill what he argued was his electoral mandate of the 2000 election—including at least one more budget.[27] The Throne Speech of fall 2001 indicated that health care would be a central element in that final Chrétien budget.

As the time to negotiate a health care reform deal with the provinces arrives, Chrétien is in a defensive position in regard to both his own party and the relationship between the federal and provincial governments. Provincial premiers enter negotiations secure in the knowledge that if federal initiatives are forestalled for much more than a year, the clock is likely to be restarted under a new federal leader. The other side of the coin is that the next Liberal leader may enjoy considerably more solid ground from which to wrestle a health care deal. At the same time, a number of provincial elections are also slated to take place over the next year, and provincial premiers may be anxious about facing their electorate if a health care deal has not been struck. The premiers may therefore be anxious to strike a deal with a weakened federal leader desperate to put his personal stamp on a policy portfolio—possibly any policy portfolio. The politics of the federal Liberal leadership have put the ball squarely in the provincial court. Chrétien would likely be unable to muster the political strength required to wrangle a health care deal that was less than favourable to the provinces. This is likely to translate into provincial demands for more federal health care funding and minimal federal intrusion into the health care field.

At the same time, the internal politics of the Liberal leadership have set the politics of health care reform on a collision course with the politics of budgeting. In late August 2002, McLellan was reported as stating in a major address to the Canadian Medical Association that the federal government would implement major health reforms within months of the release of the Romanow report, and that these would include putting more money into health care.[28] The same day, Finance Minister John Manley was reported as having 'cast doubt . . . on an immediate cash boost for health care' and having 'sent a strong warning that the shrinking surplus could derail short-term plans to shake up health care'.[29] According to *The Globe and Mail*, 'Mr Manley said that if Mr Romanow calls for an injection of new federal money, that probably won't be possible because of the shrinking federal surplus.'[30]

The replacement of Martin with Manley as minister of finance has had important implications for the politics of budgeting. Much of Martin's current political capital is based on his image as having almost single-handedly tamed the federal deficit. The appointment of John Manley, at the time still an unofficial challenger for the Liberal leadership, to the post of finance minister guaranteed a continued strong focus on fiscal restraint. Manley stated publicly that he would resign before bringing down a deficit budget.[31] Manley himself clearly cast the issue in terms of leadership politics: 'If we end up with a budget deficit, where does that leave me? I get a bus ticket to the minor leagues.'[32] For similar reasons, he also publicly demonstrated his extreme opposition to increases in taxes—especially the politically unpopular Goods and Services Tax (GST)—even in support of new health care initiatives.

Yet, at the same time, key players on all sides of the health care issue have called for more federal funding. Manley's public comments in August drew immediate and vociferous criticism from Romanow, who was reported as stating that '[t]he federal government will be committing "political suicide" if it fails to heed public calls to put more money into the health care system'.[33] For its part, the CMA demanded that 'any government spending in the fall should reflect public concern over the state of the country's health system'.[34] Provincial ministers have warned Ottawa that it should not expect to exercise any influence upon the reformation of the health care system if it does not increase health care funding significantly.[35] Provincial demands in the fall of 2002, before the release of the Kirby and Romanow reports, were for the federal government to increase transfers to the provinces by $5 billion per year. Most recently, in October 2002 the Kirby Committee report called for $6.5 billion per year in increased federal health spending, of which $5 billion would be raised from new sources, and in November the Romanow report called for $15 million over 3 years—escalating from $3.5 billion in 2003 to $6.5 billion in 2005— increasing after that according to a negotiated escalator.

Thus, the first major challenge to a significant federal role in health care reform is for the federal government to come up with new funding in the context of a federal leadership race in which existing expenditures are jealously guarded, and the spectres of budgetary deficits and increased taxes are both anathema to leadership contenders. Secondly, provincial demands for enriched transfers have traditionally created serious difficulties for the federal government in committing new funding to health care: '[A]ny indication by Ottawa of having resources available for health care is guaranteed to generate trenchant provincial demands for increases to the cash component of the . . . CHST . . ., transfers that provide little direct political benefit to Ottawa'.[36] The federal government has been reluctant to direct new spending to new program initiatives, rather than simply enriching the CHST. The last major federal attempt to do so was Allan Rock's plan in early 2000 to 'save medicare', which included a major new initiative for a federal-provincial cost-sharing program for home care. The plan drew a vociferous response from the provinces, which demanded that the federal government first restore CHST transfers. The plan was dead within months.[37] In light of this abysmal failure, the federal government will certainly have to develop a more sophisticated strategy as it proceeds with new spending programs. It is not clear, however, that either the Kirby or the Romanow report offers substantial suggestions in this regard.

THE KIRBY COMMITTEE AND
ROMANOW COMMISSION REPORTS

The reports of the Kirby Committee in October 2002 and the Romanow Commission in November 2002 had long been heralded by the federal government as marking the point at which health care reform would be undertaken in earnest.[38] Despite what appeared earlier to be quite widely divergent positions,[39] the final reports were considerably more similar than many observers originally anticipated.[40] Both faced the same essential conundrum: how to maximize federal leverage and visibility in a field that is primarily the jurisdiction of the provinces. Both resolved this conundrum by suggesting that the main—in fact the only—bargaining chip the federal government should bring to the federal-provincial negotiating table is cash. From a provincial perspective, the recommendations can be argued to offer little else. As a result, the political feasibility of both sets of recommendations rests heavily on the internal politics that determine the scope of the federal financial commitment.

Both reports endorse relatively minor adjustments to the status quo of federal-provincial arrangements, and recommend that growing federal-provincial tension be eased, primarily by means of the commitment of significantly increased federal funding. The overall annual cost of the Kirby recommendations would be $6.5 billion—$4 billion in increased direct federal spending and $2.5 billion in increased transfers to the provinces (of which $1 billion would ostensibly be 'transitional'). The overall cost of the Romanow recommendations would also be $6.5 billion annually, phased in by increases of $3.5 billion in 2003, $5 billion in 2004, and $6.5 billion in 2005.

Kirby and Romanow: The Recommendations
Broadly, the basic formula of both sets of recommendations is to maintain federal transfers to the provinces for provincially-provided health services (under some variant of the CHST), which would continue to be governed by principles enshrined in federal legislation (an unaltered CHA in the case of Kirby and an expanded CHA in the case of Romanow). Both recommend that these arrangements be grounded within a broader national philosophic framework or commitment in the area of health care—a national health care guarantee in the case of Kirby and a 'Canadian Health Care Covenant' in the case of Romanow. Finally, both recommend that this philosophic and fiscal framework be complemented by a set of new, more limited federal-provincial programs targeted to specific issue areas—with a two-year period of transition in the case of Romanow. In both cases these would include, for example, catastrophic drug coverage and specific forms of home care.[41] Thus, the reports can be argued to reflect a relatively similar view of the appropriate federal and provincial roles in health care: '[b]oth recommend highly centralized solutions with

federal cash attached by strings designed to "buy change".[42] Both, in fact, use this very language.

In order to 'buy change', both reports recommend shoring up federal transfers. The Kirby report recommends shifting the basis for existing federal CHST funding so that it is generated by an earmarked tax comprised of a stipulated proportion of the 7 per cent Goods and Services Tax (GST); the report suggests half of that tax, which would represent an increase in transfers of $1.5 billion per year.[43] In addition, the report raises the possibility of using the contingency fund of $1 billion that is one of its recommendations to enrich transfers to the provinces on a 'transitional' basis— although the politics by which the transfer funding would later be retracted are far from clear. The earmarking of a portion of the GST would be a significant improvement on the current situation, in that it would insulate federal transfers to the provinces for health care from the caprice of federal budgetary politics while still allowing the federal government to maintain leverage in enforcing national principles such as those enshrined in the CHA. In exchange for the increased transfers and the stability of an earmarked transfer fund, the provinces would continue to be subject to current restrictions under the CHA, and to new federal restrictions designed to enforce a new national health care guarantee.

For its part, the Romanow Commission proposed that the health portion of the CHST be enriched, converted to a dedicated cash-only transfer, and modified to include the requirement that an escalator be negotiated and then established for five-year periods. This escalator provision would 'ensure [that] future funding is stable [and] predictable' and that funding would increase 'at a realistic rate, commensurate with our economic growth and capacity to pay'.[44] The report proposes that this escalator be set to match projected increases in provincial health expenditures or, alternatively, at a fixed rate relative to gross domestic product (GDP) growth based on historical patterns in the ratio of growth rates in health care spending to GDP growth.[45]

In regard to the conditionality of these transfers, neither report suggests any major change to the national principles of medicare, as enshrined in the CHA. While the Kirby report recommends that the Act be left completely unchanged, the Romanow report suggests adding a new principle (provincial accountability), as well as expanding the CHA to include diagnostic services and priority home care services.[46] Both reports, however, suggest constructing a broader national philosophic framework for health care. In the Kirby report, this would take the form of federal enforcement of a national health care guarantee (guaranteeing timely access to health care) through federal-provincial agreement, or, if not, through federal legislation with financial penalties similar to those of the CHA. The Romanow Commission recommends the establishment of a 'Canadian Health Covenant', which would symbolically outline the rights and responsibilities of citizens in health care provision, as well as those of both levels of governments.

With respect to health care provision at ground level, both reports recommend that the federal government use funding to leverage specific federally-identified models of health care delivery in areas primarily falling under provincial responsi-

bility, including, for example, hospital remuneration, organization of health authorities, and primary health care delivery. Thus, some of the most significant innovations in health care provision recommended in both reports are aimed, primarily,
not at the federal government but at provincial governments. In order to achieve
these innovations, both reports recommend new programs for federal-provincial
matching conditional cost-sharing, including programs for catastrophic drug coverage, some aspects of home care, and primary care reform, although Romanow recommends that these be time-limited.

The two reports differ more considerably on how to raise new funds for health
care spending. The Kirby report *insists* that $5 billion annually come from new
funding sources.[47] The report implies—if taken at face value—that if the government is unwilling or unable to raise additional funds, the demise of the one-tier universal public health care system is preferable to the diversion of funds from other
policy areas. However, the insistence on finding new sources of funding appears primarily geared toward deflecting provincial complaints that new federal spending in
health care is coming from funds that ought otherwise to be transferred to the
provinces. It is not surprising that the report also insists that '[n]ew federal funding
for health care should not be given to the provinces and territories under the mechanism of the Canada Health and Social Transfer'.[48] If the federal government raises
new funds that are earmarked for health care, it will neatly avoid the problem of
provincial claims on those funds.

However, this suggestion overlooks a potentially serious political problem: the
new federal taxes or premiums, as structured, may not necessarily be seen by Canadians as a contribution to the most visible elements of health care (physicians and
other health care professionals; hospitals), but as premiums for narrower federal
programs, such as catastrophic drug coverage and home care, which may not have
the same universal appeal as do health care services defined more broadly. Ultimately, the report does not outline a fundamental rationale explaining why new
dedicated funding for health care—raised from the fabled 'one Canadian taxpayer'—
should go exclusively to federally controlled health programs rather than to the
provinces, who have primary responsibility for the provision of health care. In this
light, the report appears more clearly concerned with issues of federal-provincial
jockeying than with issues directly related to health care.

Both reports highlight the fundamental conundrum of federal involvement in
health care provision and both reach the same conclusion in resolving this conundrum—significant injections of new federal money. Given enough new money, federal eagerness to provide leadership in the field and provincial resistance to federal
intrusions can likely be reconciled temporarily. In the absence of such a financial
commitment, the prospects for reform are infinitely dimmer. Thus, both reports
have bet almost exclusively on the ability and willingness of the federal government
to make a serious commitment to large increases in the federal financial contribution to health care. The first and most important question that must be answered in
order to determine the ultimate fate of either set of recommendations appears to be

how big a financial commitment the federal government is willing to make. Given the historical record of federal-provincial relations in this field and the fact that both reports recommend only marginal changes to the existing set of federal-provincial arrangements, the residual question will then be how well and for how long divergent federal and provincial interests can be reconciled, given such a commitment.

Kirby and Romanow: The Reactions

The reactions to the reports have been, for the most part, predictable, with one notable exception—that of the federal health minister. The immediate and predictable reaction of the minister of finance was that the cost of the recommendations was higher than the federal government could possibly commit. However, Manley did allow that 'multi-billion-dollar increases will be necessary—over an appropriate period of time'.[49]

For their part, the provinces reacted to the Romanow report recommendations in ways that seemed almost scripted. The response of Ontario has been that the recommendations are too little, too late. Premier Eves also criticized the Romanow report's emphasis on public delivery of health services.[50] Alberta Premier Ralph Klein reacted by threatening not to accept additional federal dollars if there were to be strings attached: 'We don't need someone to tell use how we should spend our health-care dollars.'[51] Other provinces, including Manitoba, Saskatchewan, Prince Edward Island, and, to a more limited degree, New Brunswick and Nova Scotia, were more supportive. The most vociferous response came from Quebec Premier Bernard Landry, who argued that the Romanow Commission recommendations represented a 'frontal attack against Quebec's identity'.[52] Provinces complained that spending for new programs should come after increased funding for more pressing needs, that cost-shared programs would divert cash from other crucial areas, and that, in some case, the priorities identified by the Romanow report did not adequately represent the specific challenges faced by individual provinces. Provincial reactions provide little evidence that the release of the Romanow report itself did anything to shift the provinces away from a business-as-usual approach to federal-provincial wrangling.

On the other hand, the federal government's response to these provincial reactions did not conform to traditional patterns. This seems to reflect the fact that to some significant degree both the Kirby and Romanow reports run contrary to the tenor of federal-provincial relationships as the federal government was attempting to develop them over the course of 2002. The federal minister's reaction to the Romanow report, and her interactions with her provincial colleagues, were clearly in keeping with a more accommodating approach than is implicit in both reports and than is probably required to implement either set of recommendations. At the initial meeting of federal and provincial ministers of health, 'it was clear the feds were signaling sympathy for provincial concerns'.[53] McLellan's response to provincial concerns was that she 'is intent on allowing the provinces flexibility'.[54] When pressed by reporters, 'Ms McLellan would not say she supports Mr Romanow's recommendation to tie health dollars to particular programs or areas.'[55] This relatively accommodating federal stance has been argued by some observers, perhaps pre-emptively, to signal the fact that the federal government is more concerned about achieving a health care deal than the about the deal's actual substance: '[T]he truly contentious Romanow recommendations—a national public health institute to mon-itor provincial performance, a dedicated federal health-care transfer, strict targeting of funding, national pharmacare and home care programs—are off the table, proof that Ottawa truly wants a deal.'[56]

Nevertheless, the reports taken together will likely provide the context in which health care reform is considered in the immediate future. First, both put the provinces on the defensive in regard to the demands of certain of them for the latitude to implement user fees or to more aggressively pursue market-oriented options for health care provision. These issues seem likely to be off the table, at least in the short term. Secondly, the reports may actually have increased the federal latitude for manoeuvre. Because both suggest solutions that significantly strengthen the federal government's role in health care, a federal stance more accommodating to the con-cerns of the provinces may appear to the provinces (and perhaps to the Canadian public) relatively reasonable in comparison. At the very least, federal initiatives that fall short of the Kirby and Romanow recommendations seem less likely to be suc-cessfully sold by provincial premiers to the public as jurisdictional intrusions war-ranting provincial resistance than they would have been in the absence of the reports.

At the same time, the political dynamics generated by the reports made it basi-cally impossible for the Chrétien government not to act—not to make some increased commitment, even if a limited one, to health care funding. Secondly, the insistence in both reports that the federal government use increased funding to 'buy change' generated expectations that it will do something beyond simply enriching existing unconditional transfers. Thus it is not surprising that, in initial discussions with the provinces, McLellan did not agree to unconditional reinvestment, even if she would not clearly outline how far the federal government would go in attaching conditions to federal funding. She chose instead to reiterate continually that the fed-eral government 'unequivocally accept[s] the important principle of flexibility'.[57] The reports left Chrétien with little latitude to escape dealing with the issue in some fash-ion, and, partly as a result, forced him with ever greater urgency to stake his legacy agenda on federal health care reform. At the same time, both reports simultaneously increased the challenges faced in securing a deal, and raised the costs of failure.

CONCLUSIONS: LEGACY OR LIMBO?

The challenges to major health care reform in Canada are always great; however, by late 2001 the federal government appeared relatively well situated to meet those challenges. Over the course of 2002, however, the political context for this reposi-tioning shifted dramatically, primarily as a result of the politics of the Liberal lead-ership. The Kirby Committee and Romanow Commission reports have had an important impact on the politics surrounding health care reform; however, neither shifted the underlying political context and neither provided a blueprint for significantly reordering the dominant constellation of political forces in this policy area. Certainly, the federal government will attempt to deliver something in the way of health care reform in 2003. The question is whether the federal initiative will represent a significant and fundamental reform of health care or simply reinforce the status quo. It will take considerable skill for the Prime Minister to successfully deliver meaningful health care reform, leave a lasting legacy, and keep Ottawa's role in health care reform from again being consigned to limbo.

NOTES

I would like to thank Kevin Wipf for his research assistance on this project and the other contributors to this volume for their comments. I would especially like to thank Bruce Doern for his flexibility and patience in allowing this chapter to be submitted late in order to incorporate a discussion of the Romanow Commission report.

1 Colin Freeze, 'Legacy May Hinge on Medicare Reform', *The Globe and Mail* [Toronto], 22 Aug. 2002, A5.
2 Gerard W. Boychuk, 'Federal Spending in Health: Why Here? Why Now?', in G. Bruce Doern, ed., *How Ottawa Spends 2002–3003: The Security Aftermath and National Priorities* (Don Mills: Oxford University Press, 2002), 132.
3 The following discussion draws from Standing Senate Committee on Social Affairs, Science and Technology, *The Health of Canadians: The Federal Role*, vol. 4, Issues and Options (Ottawa, Sept. 2001), 55–61.
4 Gerard W. Boychuk, 'The Illusion of Financial Unsustainability of Canadian Health Care', *Policy Option-Options politiques* (Nov. 2002), 20–4.
5 Standing Senate Committee, vol. 4 (2001), 56.
6 Ibid., 17.
7 Under such a system, 'some part or even the totality of the current CHST transfer would be transformed into separate individual health care accounts. Each account would be set up by depositing an amount equivalent to the average amount the federal government now spends per capita on health care, and everyone would control their own account.' Ibid., 59. See 59–60 for a discussion of the various options for alternative MSA designs.
8 Ibid., 77–80.
9 Ibid., 80–5.
10 Jill Mahoney and Brian Laghi, 'Klein Plans to Implement Health-Care User Fees', *The Globe and Mail* [Toronto], 11 Nov. 2001, on-line edition.
11 Edward Greenspon, 'Health Care Wars Return with a Vengeance', *The Globe and Mail* [Toronto], 8 Nov. 2001, on-line edition.
12 Canadian Press, 'Alberta Braces for Showdown with Ottawa over Canada Health Act', *The Globe and Mail* [Toronto], 8 Nov. 2001, on-line edition.
13 Alberta. Premier's Advisory Council on Health, *A Framework for Reform: Report of the Premier's Advisory Council on Health*, Dec. 2001.

14 Brian Laghi, 'Rock Asks for Patience on Medicare Overhaul', *The Globe and Mail* [Toronto], 9 Jan. 2001, A1. See also Tom Arnold, 'Alberta Wants Health Revolution . . . and Ottawa Reacts Warmly', *The National Post*, 9 Jan. 2002, on-line edition; Luiza Chwialkowska, 'Rock Impressed by Alberta Report, Romanow Is Not', *The National Post*, 9 Jan. 2002, on-line edition.

15 Luiza Chwialkowska, 'McClellan Brings Hope for Health Reform', *The National Post*, 16 Jan. 2002, on-line edition.

16 Ibid.

17 Ibid.

18 Shawn McCarthy, 'McClellan Supports Private Hospitals', *The Globe and Mail* [Toronto], 21 Jan. 2002, on-line edition.

19 Allison Dumfield, 'Klein Calls for Changes in Health Care', *The Globe and Mail* [Toronto], 21 Jan. 2002, on-line edition; Jill Mahoney, 'Albertans Urged to Open Wallets', *The Globe and Mail* [Toronto], 22 Jan. 2002, A7.

20 Richard Mackie, 'Private-Sector Role in Health to Increase, Ontario Says', *The Globe and Mail* [Toronto], 22 Jan. 2002, A7.

21 Robert Remington, Joan Bryden, and Ian Bailey, 'Klein Authorizes Health Revolution: Will Accept All 44 Mazankowski Proposals; Liberal MPs Push McClellan to Resist Alberta', *The National Post*, 23 Jan. 2002, on-line edition; Steven Chase, 'Provinces Have Taken Control of Health Care, Group Warns', *The Globe and Mail* [Toronto], 25 Jan. 2002, A4.

22 Mark Kennedy, 'McLellan to Allow Private Clinics: Health Minister Clarifies Position, Tells Provinces She Won't Interfere', *The National Post*, 6 Sept. 2002, on-line edition.

23 Brian Laghi and Dawn Walton, 'Alberta Opens Private, Overnight Health Facility', *The Globe and Mail* [Toronto], 13 Sept. 2002, on-line edition.

24 Brian Laghi, 'McClellan Scolds Alberta for Expanding Clinic', *The Globe and Mail* [Toronto], 17 Sept. 2002, A4.

25 Ibid.

26 Canada, *Speech from the Throne to Open the 2nd Session of the 37th Parliament of Canada* (Ottawa: House of Commons, Sept. 2002).

27 Shawn McCarthy, 'Manley Sees Only One More Chrétien Budget', *The Globe and Mail* [Toronto], 20 Sept. 2002, A1.

28 Tom Arnold, 'Minister Vows "Swift" Action on Health Care', *The National Post*, 21 Aug. 2002, on-line edition.

29 André Picard and Heather Scoffield, 'Manley's Warning Touches Off Health-Care Dispute', *The Globe and Mail* [Toronto], 21 Aug. 2002.

30 Ibid.

31 Shawn McCarthy, 'Manley Sees Only One More Chrétien Budget', *The Globe and Mail* [Toronto], 20 Sept. 2002, A1.

32 Ibid.

33 Tom Arnold, 'Political Suicide to Ignore Report, Romanow Says', *The National Post*, 21 Aug. 2002, on-line edition.

34 Vernon Clement Jones, 'Doctors Disappointed by Manley's Views', *The Globe and Mail* [Toronto], 21 Aug. 2002, on-line edition.

35 Brian Laghi, 'Ottawa Told to Boost Health Funding', *The Globe and Mail* [Toronto], 26 Aug. 2002, on-line edition.

36 Boychuk, 'Federal Spending in Health', 122.

37 Ibid., 126.

38 Standing Senate Committee on Social Affairs, Science and Technology, *Highlights, Volume Six: Recommendations for Reform, Final Report on the State of the Health System in Canada*, Oct. 2002, 24; Roy J. Romanow, *Building on Values: The Future of Health Care in Canada, Final Report*, Commission on the Future of Health Care in Canada, Nov. 2002.

39 See Boychuk, 'Federal Spending in Health.'

40 Jeffrey Simpson, 'Proud Parents of Health-Report Twins', *The Globe and Mail* [Toronto], 3 Dec. 2002, A25.

41 The Kirby report also recommends increased federal investment in a number of areas more clearly within the federal ambit, including health care technology, human resource development, health promotion, and disease prevention. The Romanow approach is to recommend matching conditional cost-sharing to achieve these various objectives under the rubric of various transitional funds: Rural and Remote Access Fund, Diagnostic Services Fund, and Primary Health Care Transfer. See Romanow, 71–2.

42 Simpson, 'Proud Parents of Health-Report Twins'.

43 The report also argues that the provinces would collectively save an additional $1.5 billion per year from health care they would no longer have to provide after the report's recommendations were implemented.

44 Romanow, xxv.

45 The escalator for health care transfers suggested by the report is 1.25 times the growth in GDP, which 'is based on the long-term trend (1960–2000) between growth in total health expenditures relative to the growth of the Canadian economy.' Romanow, 70.

46 Romanow, xxiv.

47 The two alternatives outlined in the report are a 1.5 per cent National Health Care Sales tax and a Variable National Health Care Insurance Premium. The latter would be income contingent and range from $0.50 per day for low-income Canadians to $4.00 per day for those in the highest tax brackets. Of the two, the latter option is favoured by the committee. However, as the report notes, the important point here is not *how* federal funding *will* be raised, but *that* new federal funding *must* be raised (highlights, 28).

48 Ibid., 24.

49 'Romanow Wants Too Much, Too Soon: Manley', *The National Post*, 28 Nov. 2002, on-line edition.

50 Richard Mackie, 'Health Care Proposals Insufficient, Eves Says', *The Globe and Mail* [Toronto], 29 Nov. 2002, on-line edition.

51 Rod Mickleburgh, 'A Provincial Chorus of Complaints', *The Globe and Mail* [Toronto], 29 Nov. 2002, on-line edition.

52 Rhéal Séguin, 'Romanow Call for Greater Control May Lead to Spring Vote in Quebec', *The Globe and Mail* [Toronto], 30 Nov. 2002, on-line edition.

53 John Ibbotson, 'Why Roy Will Sing the Blues,' *The Globe and Mail* [Toronto], 7 Dec. 2002, on-line edition.

54 Brian Laghi, 'Extra-Cash Conditions for Health Care Split Ministers', *The Globe and Mail* [Toronto], 7 Dec. 2002, on-line edition.

55 Tom Arnold, 'Provinces, Ottawa Still Disagree on Health Care: McLellan Unwilling to Provide Funding Without Strings', *The National Post*, 10 Dec. 2002, on-line edition.

56 Ibbotson, 'Why Roy Will Sing the Blues'.

57 Arnold, 'Provinces, Ottawa Still Disagree'.

7

The Chrétien Governments and Higher Education: A Quiet Revolution in Canadian Public Policy

ALLAN TUPPER

Since 1997, the government of Canada has invested heavily in the research capacity of Canadian universities.[1] Federal expenditures on university research are now significant budgetary commitments. Armed with an ambitious agenda and with strong support from universities, Ottawa has defined university research and university research infrastructure as national priorities.

Federal policy has certainly responded to universities' arguments about the importance of higher education for Canada's future well-being. In turn, Ottawa's initiatives have shaped university priorities. Federal policy for university research has also altered federal-provincial relations with respect to post-secondary education and generated new links between senior university administrators, prominent university researchers, and federal officials. To an unprecedented degree, Canadian universities are engaged as instruments of national economic policy.

This chapter examines four recent federal programs—the Canada Foundation for Innovation (CFI), the Canada Research Chairs (CRC), the Canada Millennium Scholarship Foundation, and Canadian Institutes of Health Research (CIHR). These programs are centrepieces of Ottawa's new relationship with universities.[2] They establish Ottawa as the driving force in Canadian higher education, notwithstanding the provinces' substantial financial and policy roles and formal constitutional authority. Apart from the Millennium Foundation, Ottawa's strategy promotes research as a university priority.

The chapter also links Ottawa's agenda for university research with the Innovation Agenda of 2002. The Innovation Agenda both reflects and extends Ottawa's ambitious agenda in higher education, as well as promoting other national objectives. The next major step in Ottawa's relationship with universities is likely to be a continuing federal program for the indirect costs of research. Finally, the chapter examines the implications of Ottawa's aggressive policies for university research. Issues examined include federal-provincial relations, the impact of federal policy on university priorities, and the accountability of university research.

Public policy with respect to higher education has been badly neglected by Canadian scholars, as has public expenditure in that policy area. There is a pressing need for careful assessment of the federal policy innovations of the last decade. Has performance met expectations?

OTTAWA AND THE UNIVERSITIES

This section details Ottawa's major policies since 1997 with respect to post-secondary education, with special attention to three recently established programs related to university research and one concerned with access to undergraduate education. It first examines the Canada Foundation for Innovation and then turns to the Canada Research Chairs, a 2000 budget program that complements CFI but adds a major new dimension to federal policy. CFI stresses research infrastructure, while CRC emphasizes the recruitment and retention of research professors. These two policy thrusts—superior research infrastructure and the sustenance of researchers themselves—parallel long-standing priorities in the United States, where national governments have fostered strong research and a national elite of researchers. A third project, Canadian Institutes of Health Research (CIHR), established in 2000, constitutes a new federal approach to health science research. CIHR embodies Ottawa's major policy interests in university research, notably encouragement of interdisciplinary research, closer links between researchers and business, and the development of elite Canadian researchers.

The Canada Millennium Scholarship Foundation, established in 1998, represents a different strand of federal policy. Its focus is students, not researchers. Its priority is access to post-secondary education, not advanced research. Moreover, Millennium Scholarships, while substantial in scope, simply add a major new federal program to a policy area in which both levels of government are already active. CFI, CRC, and CIHR, on the other hand, raise more complex federal-provincial issues. These agencies influence government priorities not only in relation to universities, but in other areas as well, such as human resources and industrial development.

The Canada Foundation for Innovation

The Canada Foundation for Innovation was established by federal legislation in 1997. It received an initial endowment of $800 million and a mandate to strengthen the research capacity of Canadian universities, hospitals, and non-profit agencies. Research is defined broadly as a process that involves the discovery of new things, the reinterpretation of existing insights, and new ways of applying knowledge in 'science, health, engineering and the environment'. Research infrastructure is also defined broadly to include software and hardware, as well as conventional physical plant and equipment. In a significant recent change, CFI now supports the operating costs of infrastructure projects that it funds. It also engages in joint ventures with researchers abroad.

The Foundation has defined its specific purposes as the development of advanced research infrastructure as an element of economic competitiveness, as a way to attract and retain research talent in Canada, and as a vehicle to promote interaction between researchers and research institutions. One of its major programs, the Innovation Fund, encourages projects that strengthen institutional research capacity in priority areas. The New Opportunities Fund provides infrastructure support to new faculty members engaged to work in priority areas.

CFI operates on the premise that public funds should be levered to embrace partners and other funding sources. It insists that, if institutions want projects to be realized, they must find partners and/or use their own resources. To this end, CFI's contribution to projects averages only 40 per cent of eligible costs. Eligible partners include foundations; departments and agencies of the government of Canada, excluding the research granting councils; provincial and municipal governments; corporations; and individuals.[3] Interestingly, provincial governments are accorded no particular priority as partners. They are one of many sources of funds. CFI estimates that it will generate nearly $9 billion of new capital investment by 2010.

CFI pursues these objectives as an independent corporation established by legislation in 1997. It enjoys considerable freedom from political direction. CFI is not subject to audit by the Auditor General. Nor can the federal government issue directives to it. The Foundation has a bicameral governance structure comprising 15 members of the Foundation and a 15-person Board. The minister of Industry appoints six foundation members, the Board chair, and six Board members. The ministerial appointments then select the remaining Foundation and Board members. Half the Foundation members and half the Board must be representative of the research community. Other members and directors must be from business and non-profit agencies. Regional balance is required.

The Canada Research Chairs

The Canada Research Chairs program stresses researchers. Established in 1999, it provides $900 million to Canadian universities for the recruitment and retention of outstanding researchers.[4] The program assumes that talented university researchers are scarce commodities. It acknowledges that universities are facing a wave of retirements in the near future. Its more fundamental premise is that public policy must support universities in the international 'war for talent'.[5] Otherwise Canadian universities and national economic competitiveness will suffer.

The CRC program is a major new federal investment in universities. Between 2000 and 2005, it will fund up to 2000 research chairs. The chairs are of two types— Tier I and Tier II. Tier I chairs are for recruitment and retention of accomplished scholars. Each chair receives $200,000 per year for up to seven years and is renewable. Tier II chairs offer promising younger scholars $100,000 for up to five years. Only universities can nominate chair holders. University nominations must reflect institutional research priorities.

The allocation of CRC chairs within and between universities has been controversial. Chairs are primarily allocated according to university performance over a three-year period in the annual competitions of the major federal research funding agencies. But this formula is biased toward larger research universities. To compensate, the CRC program allocates 6 per cent of the chairs to 'smaller universities', defined as those receiving less than one per cent of total research funding over the period.

The CRC program has also confronted the fact that universities differ in their respective emphases on medical, scientific, social scientific, and humanistic research. Federal funding for medical, scientific, and engineering research is substantially greater than for that in social sciences and humanities. Accordingly, CRC allocated 45 per cent of the chairs to natural sciences and engineering, 35 per cent to health, and the remaining 20 per cent to social sciences and the humanities. While social sciences and the humanities receive only 20 per cent of total federal funding, humanists and social scientists comprise more than 20 per cent of Canadian university teachers. CRC thus aggravated the long-standing concern of Canadian social scientists and humanists that their contributions were undervalued compared to scientific and medical endeavour. The program is governed by a 'steering committee' composed of executive officers of the federal granting councils, the president of the Canada Foundation for Innovation, and the deputy minister of Industry.

The Canadian Institutes of Health Research

The Canadian Institutes of Health Research were established in 2000 as a replacement for the Medical Research Council of Canada. In rationale and structure, CIHR represents the new federal approach to universities and to advanced research.

CIHR is an umbrella organization for a set of 'virtual' health research institutes in Canada. Each institute is a network of researchers that undertakes interdisciplinary research in broad areas of human health. The institutes embody a 'four-pillar' approach to health research. They incorporate the expertise of biomedical scientists, clinicians, experts on health care delivery, and specialists in the socio-economic determinants of health.

In common with other recent federal research policy initiatives, CIHR aims to recruit scientists to Canada, to retain talent in Canada, and to nurture a generation of researchers. As then Minister of Health Allan Rock put it, 'Our goal is to make Canada the country of choice for researchers from around the world. And we want to make our own students and researchers feel that there is nowhere else they would rather go because there is nowhere else that they can achieve so much.'[6] CIHR argues that effective health research requires a new paradigm. Implicit in its programs and rationale is the view that health research cannot be the preserve of medical scientists. Practitioners and even social scientists and humanists should also participate. CIHR urges universities and other research institutes not only to break down disciplinary boundaries, but also to think collaboratively as partners. Moreover, CIHR argues that universities must do a better job in assessing their strengths and pooling their research resources. Accordingly, CIHR sees health researchers as a collective national resource, not as employees of a variety of institutions. Finally, CIHR believes that health research must be linked with economic priorities. Health care discoveries must be commercialized. In a broader sense, its view is that health care is an element of economic and social policy.

In governance, CIHR is both traditional and innovative. The umbrella organization operates as did its predecessor, the Medical Research Council of Canada. It has a President and a governing council of 19 members, which are order-in-council appointments. It is in their structure that the governance of the institutes is innovative. Each has an Institute Advisory Board, selected from a variety of occupations, disciplinary perspectives, and sectors. As CIHR puts it, 'These members represent all walks of life and help to bridge the gap between the scientific and voluntary communities. They are health stakeholders, members from the voluntary sector, medical doctors, philanthropists and laypeople.'[7] Such boards expand the range of interests that have a stake in CIHR and federal research policy. Whether this broader base will breed critics or supporters is unclear. The advisory councils also admit a radical idea in the governance of advanced research—that non-experts should participate. Expert control over research has been an unchallenged tenet of national decision-making in Canada and other countries for decades.

Proponents of this triad of federal research policy initiatives—CFI, CRC, and CIHR—justify their support by pointing out that the world's economies are locked in competition for highly qualified workers, that social and economic policies must be better linked, and that government must adopt new roles. Furthermore, in a period of economic change, robust economies need highly developed capacities for indigenous innovation.

Federal policies for advanced university research also rest on more precise premises, such as the following:

- Universities must think more about their research priorities and pursue initiatives that build on their strengths. Universities must also think carefully about how they relate to each other and how they can better cooperate. Universities have been too insular, and as a result research capacity has been harmed.

- Wherever possible, university research should be interdisciplinary. Modern societies are increasingly interdependent, and university research, encumbered by rigid disciplinary boundaries, sometimes responds too slowly. Effective research and public policy requires the coordinated work of many disciplines. The 'traditional' model of individual scholars pursuing research in isolation, while still widespread, is giving way to the model of interdisciplinary researchers working in teams.

- Canadian industrial capacity and future economic prosperity demand that university research be more frequently and more quickly commercialized. Commercialization requires that distinctions between basic and applied research be broken down, that governments, business, and university researchers work more closely together, and that new research policy frameworks be developed. Universities should put in place necessary policies and institute 'culture change', in order to ensure that the commercialization of research is granted the priority it merits.

- University research must be inspired by a desire to be the best in the world. Only research at the highest levels of quality and supported by the best infrastructure will attract the necessary talent to Canada and retain it.

- Wherever possible, funding for university research and research infrastructure must 'lever' funds from other sources. Governments are the major force in advanced research funding. Other sectors, notably business, must contribute as well.

The Canada Millennium Scholarship Foundation

Ottawa's strong interest in post-secondary education is not limited to advanced research. The Canada Millennium Scholarship Foundation, established in 1998, provided a $2.5 billion endowment for bursaries for Canadian undergraduate students in financial need. The Foundation, unlike the new federal initiatives in research, emphasizes access to higher education. In 2000, the Millennium Foundation's major program provided bursaries of an average value of $3,043 to almost 90,000 Canadian students.[8] Such bursaries comprise 95 per cent of the Foundation's expenditures. In addition, the Foundation's Excellence Award Program provides a small number of scholarships to students who present evidence of academic achievement combined with a record of leadership and community service.

The Millennium Foundation is a major new federal entrant into the field of financial assistance for post-secondary education. It has far-reaching effects on federal-provincial relations in this area. By injecting large numbers of bursaries into the system, Ottawa caused the provincial governments to realign their priorities and to launch new initiatives. Ottawa, proceeding with determination, established agreements with provincial governments that led to the application of 'displaced' provincial moneys to new or revised provincial initiatives in student financial assistance.

To be sure, the provinces determined their own priorities for reinvestment. But equally clearly, the Millennium Foundation was the catalyst for provincial changes. Moreover, it has gone against the recent trend by which student financial assistance in Canada has shifted, in bold strokes, toward loans and away from grants and bursaries. In addition, by defining student financial assistance as a national priority, the Foundation identifies the interests of the national student body with those of the federal government. Ottawa has also established itself as a presence in the minds of Canadian parents, through tax measures that provide savings vehicles for future educational needs. In this way, at a time when education at provincial post-secondary institutions is becoming more and more expensive, the federal government has skillfully indicated that it will help Canadian families pay for it.

THE INNOVATION AGENDA

In 2002, the federal government launched its long-awaited Innovation Strategy. The strategy rests on two white papers; one, *Achieving Excellence*, was sponsored by Industry Canada,[9] and the other, *Knowledge Matters*, by Human Resources Development Canada (HRDC).[10] The white papers are wide-ranging in their content and their policy implications. They are the basis of a national consultation on options for economic and human capital policies. The consultations culminated in a National Summit on Innovation and Learning in Toronto in November 2002.

The two strands of the Innovation Strategy may be described as 'hard' and 'soft'. Industry Canada's is the hard contribution; it stresses research and development, infrastructure, and industrial policies that generate new goods, services, and processes. Its major human resource interest is policy to attract skilled personnel to Canada and retain them. The softer HRDC contribution examines labour force issues and education in broad terms. Its concerns include on-the-job training, immigrants in the work force, and Canadians who cannot participate fully in the labour market. Ideally, the soft and hard streams will interact in a way that links the 'elite', research side of innovation with societal concerns about employment in a period of economic change.

The Innovation Strategy has evoked speculation about Ottawa's underlying political strategy. Whether the consultations will yield major policy changes is unclear in light of the Liberals' leadership struggle in 2002. The Innovation Strategy, however, is testimony to the political influence of universities and their importance in federal thinking. Both papers frequently acknowledge that universities are keys to the achievement of ambitious national goals. These goals include Canada's achievement by 2010 of a ranking among the top five countries in the world with respect to research and development performance, the establishment of distinctive centres of innovation in each province, and the ranking of Canada among world leaders in the share of private sector sales attributable to innovations. The papers recommend an annual increase of graduate student intake of 5 per cent per year for a decade. There are frequent references to the need to ensure broad access to post-secondary education.

The policy influence of universities is reflected in Ottawa's willingness to under-take yet another major new program to strengthen them. This time a perennial con-cern of universities, the 'indirect costs of research', is being addressed. Federal research grants pay only for certain costs of advanced university research; as a result, the research consumes resources that are not funded. For example, university research involves wear and tear on libraries and demands new library resources; it requires that laboratories be maintained and staffed in particular ways; it requires a policy framework that demands compliance with federal and provincial regulations; it generates difficult intellectual property issues that must be addressed; it requires costly computing and telecommunications support networks; and, finally, the effort to 'commercialize' must be paid for. These and other indirect costs, generally thought to amount to at least 40 per cent of direct costs, are substantial. Other coun-tries, notably the United States, provide payments for such costs.

The federal budget of December 2001 responded to a request by Canadian uni-versities for federal support for the indirect costs of research by providing a $200 million one-time payment. The 2002 Throne Speech also made reference to indirect costs, but the government's precise intentions with regard to them will not be known until the budget is read in early 2003.

One aspect of Ottawa's support for the indirect costs of university research is noteworthy. Universities have shifted their arguments about indirect costs. For many years, their case was that a research grants system that funded only a small part of total costs caused universities to underfund undergraduate programs. This argument is less often heard today, although it is certainly still current. Universities' main argument now is that a continuing program of reimbursement for indirect costs will strengthen research infrastructure, so that better research will be done, and more research will be commercialized. In other words, Ottawa's goals in university research are now reflected in the arguments presented by universities. A confluence of university and federal priorities is evident.

THE IMPLICATIONS OF FEDERAL LEADERSHIP

How have major federal investments in university research shaped Canadian uni-versities? Put simply, advanced research has been elevated as a university priority. The federal programs described in this chapter all demand that universities think systematically about their research needs, their research priorities, and their links with other universities. Ottawa's investments have also led universities to strengthen their capacity to capitalize on federal largesse. Offices of vice presidents for research, industry liaison offices, and public affairs offices have grown and gained influence as universities have positioned themselves to receive federal moneys. Federal policy has also strengthened the growing inclination of universities to stress interdiscipli-nary studies and scholarship. Indeed, federal policy in the 1990s consistently endorsed the interdisciplinary approach as the best way to organize research. Finally, federal policy has emphasized that advanced university research must lead to demonstrable economic benefits and commercially viable goods, services, and therapies. Universities have taken up this challenge vigorously. To an ever greater extent, universities are becoming direct participants in the economy by way of spin-off companies and technology transfer activities, whereas heretofore they were content to undertake basic research and educate a skilled workforce. Some Canadian universities now define research commercialization as a university priority on a par with teaching, research, and public service. On the other hand, increased emphasis on research commercialization raises concerns about corporate influence on university priorities, the weakening of the commitment to basic 'curiosity driven' research, and a subtle, but worrisome, diminution of university objectivity.

Federal policy defines accomplished researchers as national assets. The contribution that professors make through their teaching and other university activities is only incidentally important in Ottawa. Similarly, graduate student support is increasingly justified as part of a national strategy to nurture and retain talented researchers. Federal policy is silent on how research meshes with other university priorities. The premise is that universities will adjust their priorities and that undergraduate programs will be addressed by provincial action. Such adjustments will be difficult and controversial.

Federal policy has not been unanimously endorsed. As noted, smaller universities with lesser capacity and less need to do advanced research have felt diminished in stature. Their claim is that their distinctive needs and contributions are ignored and/or belittled by federal initiatives that favour research universities. To a degree the Canada Research Chairs program responded to their concerns, as did the 2001 budgetary allocation for the indirect costs of research. The Association of Universities and Colleges of Canada (AUCC) now urges Ottawa to consider the diversity of universities in its policy-making. The long-standing debate about whether federal assistance should be concentrated in a small number of universities remains. Another long-term issue is whether smaller universities and universities without, for example, substantial health science programs will remain faithful to their distinctive instructional and scholarly activities or mimic large research universities. A former president of Cornell University, observing the tendency of small American universities to hitch themselves to the research bandwagon, called the process 'Harvardization'.[11] Canada has never formally addressed the overall roles and responsibilities of its universities. With universities continuing to change and undertake new roles, a debate on this topic is overdue. Which universities should undertake advanced research? Could more students be effectively accommodated if undergraduate teaching were to assume a greater role in some institutions? How do research and teaching interact? Should research prowess be as important as it is at present in determining the stature of a university?

Another grievance against federal policy is that it elevates the medical and natural sciences to undeserved prominence in university affairs and in the public mind. Such arguments are voiced by social scientists and humanists, who argue that the national interest demands greater attention to Canada's economic, political, and social challenges. These claims recently led Martha Piper, president of the University of British Columbia, to propose a new approach to federal support for humanities and social science research in Canada.[12] Her view is that social scientists and humanists have distinctive contributions to make to major debates about Canada's economic future, and that their disciplines should be called the 'human sciences'. 'Civil society', the domain of serious social science and humanities scholarship, should be elevated in importance as a determinant of Canada's economic well-being.

Over the past decade, the government of Canada has successfully defined itself as the motor of post-secondary education policy. CFI, CRC, and CIHR constitute a strong infrastructure that has substantially increased the research capacity of Canadian universities. Such federal policy initiatives, while creating some tensions, have been strongly advocated by universities themselves. Universities now define the federal government as their preeminent source of funding and of effective university policy.

Ottawa's dominance in post-secondary education has been institutionalized to a considerable degree. Large numbers of professors, university administrators, and students participate in the substantial number of federal advisory councils and evaluation committees that sustain the research enterprise. Industry Canada is the undeniable champion of universities' interests in federal policy-making. The department of Finance also sees universities as significant forces in Canada's economic future. The AUCC is a major national interest group whose activities meld disparate university concerns into coherent policy positions. Its activities are supplemented by such organizations as the 'G 10' group of presidents of major research universities. Such organizations engage in conventional lobbying activities. They also define and reinforce universities as part of a larger national political and public policy community. Another body that measures the importance of universities in Ottawa is the federal Liberal caucus committee on post-secondary education, whose membership burgeoned in the late 1990s.

While, as we have seen, the government of Canada aggressively appealed to Canada's universities in the 1990s and assumed a substantial role in setting their priorities, the relationship between the provincial governments and universities in the same period has been distant, business-like, and sometimes fractious. To be sure, several provinces, notably Alberta and Quebec, have defined provincial universities as instruments of economic and industrial policy. Alberta's Heritage Foundation for Medical Research successfully built a substantial community of health scientists in that province. Provincial governments have also endorsed federal support for the indirect costs of research, and often match Canada Foundation for Innovation funding.

On the other hand, throughout the 1990s provincial governments restrained funding for universities, imposed regimes of performance accountability, and shifted their funding from unrestricted operating grants to more directed contributions. Moreover, they put in place controversial policies for tuition fees. Some provinces, notably Quebec, British Columbia, and Manitoba, strictly regulated tuition as a matter of public policy. Other provinces put in place formulae that allowed for tuition increases but imposed ceilings and other restrictions. The Liberal government of British Columbia elected in 2001 changed course, and now allows provincial universities unrestricted authority to set tuition and fees. Provincial governments have also tried to establish new relationships with universities, technical institutes, and community colleges. These policies have seldom satisfied students, governments, or universities.

As a result, provincial governments have borne the brunt of complaints about limited student access, deteriorating faculty salaries, weak systems of student financial assistance, and inadequate infrastructure. Federal policy is much more in tune with university ambitions. It situates universities as key forces in the economy and important determinants of national well-being. As a result of the establishment of the Millennium Foundation, Ottawa is seen as a progressive force on the issue of student access, and it has received accolades for its financial contributions.

Federal-provincial relations with respect to higher education require serious thought. In recent years, Ottawa's Quiet Revolution in university research has established the federal government as the decisive force. Ottawa's focus on advanced research highlights an activity that, while vitally important, is only one of several major university obligations. Moreover, the long-standing division of labour by which Ottawa funds research and the provinces fund teaching and general operating expenses is obviously breaking down. For example, under certain circumstances CFI funds operating costs, and CRC, while conceived as an element of research strategy, shapes universities' teaching priorities and capacities. A plausible case can be made for more intergovernmental co-operation, in recognition of Ottawa's aggressive role, the resultant weight attached to research, and the greater interdependence of federal and provincial policies. The provinces may well show rekindled interest in universities and try to regain their diminished influence over funding.

In the coming years, Canadian universities face high expectations, a harbinger of which is the concern of successive Auditors General about the accountability of the Canada Foundation for Innovation, and to a lesser degree that of the other federal research agencies. The worry is that CFI enjoys excessive independence from political control and public accountability. In 2001, the Auditor General argued that the model of traditional federal research granting agencies is superior to that of endowed foundations like CFI. The federal government also wants universities to account for the expenditure of funding for indirect costs.

Auditors General have focused attention on the accountability of federal endowments. In his 2001 Killam lecture, John Evans, former president of the University of Toronto, raised broader concerns about universities' obligations. He pointed out that Ottawa expects results from its substantial investments in university research. Universities will have to prove that federal policy objectives are indeed advanced by their research. Evans speaks of a Public Research Contract, by which Ottawa provides stable, long-term funding for university research, and in return universities commercialize research, educate future researchers, and serve national policy objectives. In his words, 'If universities fail to adapt to this new challenge, as embodied by the Public Research Contract, government support will undoubtedly stall or be directed elsewhere.'[13]

The issue of universities' accountability for research results is a complex one. First, the implicit social contract under which universities operate already confers substantial independence on them. Canadian governments and probably most citizens accept the idea that universities must be free to research and teach about topics that are controversial. Such autonomy is deeply prized within universities. The Public Research Contract is not something universities can submit to lightly. Nor will governments always want to enforce its terms. Secondly, universities are heavily shaped by both federal and provincial policies. Will provincial governments allow universities to submit to an explicit federal accountability regime? Should there be an intergovernmental accord? Thirdly, university research is a complex and unpredictable process: in natural sciences and medicine, major discoveries are sometimes unintended offshoots of research on altogether unrelated matters; and the research process cannot be placed on a timetable. Nor can governments' quest for more commercialized research results be easily achieved. And disagreements will occur about whether a research project was successful or not. In these respects, university research policy differs little from other government policies whose results are hard to define. University accountability, however, is perhaps uniquely complex, because of the confluence of traditions of university autonomy, issues that arise from the federal-provincial relationship, and the nature of research itself.

CONCLUSIONS

This chapter observes a significant change in Canadian public policy. Steadily and without much fanfare, the federal government has undertaken far-reaching programs affecting research at Canadian universities. The Canada Foundation for Innovation, the Canada Research Chairs, and Canadian Institutes for Health Research have substantially strengthened the research capacity of Canada's universities. These programs stress interdisciplinary research, closer links between universities and businesses, and the development of outstanding Canadian researchers. In addition, the Millennium Scholarship Foundation, the major goal of which is to provide enhanced student access to higher education, has been instituted. Ottawa's policies reflect the greater importance attached to advanced education and research throughout the democratic world. They make Ottawa the driving force in Canadian universities.

The future of policy-making for higher education is unclear. Ottawa's Innovation Strategy of 2002 sees universities as essential to Canada's economic future. The federal government has indicated that it is committed to further financial support for the indirect costs of university research and to greater support of graduate students. At the same time, the provincial governments are concerned about the costs of postsecondary education. While Ottawa's policies are strongly supported by universities, provincial-university relationships are at best cordial, and sometimes fractious.

As time goes on, Canadian universities are likely to become an even more important element in public policy-making. Their accountability may become an issue as government funding increases and as governments and universities work more closely together. The ethical and policy challenges of biotechnology may well change and strain the relationships between Canadian governments, voters, and universities. For all these reasons, Ottawa's relationship with universities is likely to be frequently revisited in future editions of *How Ottawa Spends*.

NOTES

1 For an excellent analysis of recent federal policy see David M. Cameron, 'The Challenge of Change: Canadian Universities in the Twenty-first Century', *Canadian Public Administration* 45 (Summer 2002), 145–74. See also Jeffrey Simpson, 'There's at Least One Chretien Legacy: Universities', *The Globe and Mail* [Toronto], 9 Nov. 2002, A21.

2 Ottawa has undertaken other important initiatives, but these are not analysed here. They include increases to the budgets of the federal research granting councils and the renewal and extension of the Networks of Centres of Excellence program.

3 Canada. Canada Foundation for Innovation, *CFI Policy and Program Guide* (Ottawa, 2002), 8.

4 For a useful overview of the Canada Research Chairs Program see Canada. Canada Research Chairs, *Program Guide* (Ottawa, 2002).

5 John R. Evans, 'Higher Education in the Higher Education Economy: Towards a Public Research Contract', 2001 Killam Annual Lecture, 15.

6 Canada. House of Commons, *Debates*, 23 Nov. 1999, 1597.

7 Canada. Canadian Institutes of Health Research, *Who We Are* (Ottawa, 2001).

8 Canada. Millennium Scholarships Foundation, *Annual Report 2000: The Foundation at Work* (Montreal, 2000).

9 Canada. Industry Canada, *Achieving Excellence: Investing in People, Knowledge and Opportunity* (Ottawa, 2002).

10 Canada. Human Resources Development Canada, *Knowledge Matters: Skills and Learning for Canadians* (Ottawa, 2002).

11 Frank H.T. Rhodes, *The Creation of the Future: The Role of the American University* (Ithaca, New York: Cornell University Press, 2001), 20–1.

12 Martha C. Piper, 'Building a Civil Society: A New Role for the Human Sciences', Killam Annual Lecture, Ottawa, Oct. 2002.

13 Evans, 'Higher Education in the Higher Education Economy', 11–12.

8

The Pursuit of an Elusive Ideal: Spending Review and Reallocation Under the Chrétien Government

JOANNE KELLY

The expenditure management system in Ottawa has undergone significant modifications and shifts since the election of the Chrétien government in 1993. Exercises such as Program Review in 1994–5 and the move to 'prudent budgeting' sought to reduce spending by a sufficient increment that the deficit would be curtailed. More recent adaptations have focused on the politics of dividend spending: seeking to manage the trade-offs between tax reduction, new policy spending, and debt reduction. Yet, relatively little attention has been given to questions of how to manage the 'A-base' of the spending budget, including questions of expenditure review and reallocation. This is despite the intentions of the formal Expenditure Management System (EMS) articulated by the Chrétien government in February 1995, which stated that

> [m]inisters will identify significant new spending initiatives . . . and fund these initiatives at Budget time through concurrent reductions to, or the elimination of, lower priority programs. . . . [F]unding of unexpected increases . . . will be through reallocations.[1]

As a consequence, the expenditure management process in Ottawa remains subject to the criticism that it is highly traditional in its focus on incremental spending (or cutting) decisions and in its disjuncture between questions of funding and those of performance. Despite successive surpluses since 1997, this has led some to argue that spending in Ottawa is out of control.

This chapter examines the Chrétien government's efforts to incorporate review and reallocation into the EMS. These efforts include the Program Review exercise (1994–5), the introduction of a new Expenditure Management System (1995–current), business plans (1995–8), and two recent initiatives, Program Integrity (1999–2001) and Departmental Assessments (2001–current). The section that follows provides some initial context and explanation.

The evidence of this chapter suggests that review and reallocation are neither as elusive nor as ideal as the rhetoric would suggest. Permanent reform has been difficult, but the Chrétien government has used review and reallocation continually throughout its term in office to support its budgetary objectives. As budgetary objectives changed, new reform initiatives were introduced. Secondly, and I think more importantly, incorporating reallocation and review into the EMS is politically and technically difficult. One of the forgotten functions of a budgetary system is to resolve conflicts, whether between cabinet ministers, different interest groups, or alternative policy choices. Yet reallocation based on program review requires elected governments to continually reopen policy questions that were thought resolved. And that produces conflict. Governments will only tolerate the political turmoil associated with review and reallocation if they believe that the pain is unavoidable, or that it will be counterbalanced by rewards in other areas. Under these circumstances it is difficult to envisage any technical solution that would provide the 'best way' to encourage review and achieve reallocation, despite the rhetoric of some.

THE LIBERALS' PURSUIT OF
EXPENDITURE MANAGEMENT REFORM

Since 1994, the Liberals have introduced five different initiatives to make expenditure review and reallocation both possible and desirable. The first and most public is colloquially known as the Program Review exercise: reviews were conducted during late 1994 and early 1995; the cuts that resulted were announced in the 1995 budget and implemented over the next three years, ending in 1998. The government's intention to incorporate these practices permanently into the EMS was announced in February 1995 with the introduction of a system-wide reform intended to change the basis of budget decision-making in Canada. By 1998, however, the deficit crisis had subsided and, as a result, the argument for ongoing review and reallocation appeared less persuasive. Some ministers focused on spending the 'fiscal dividend'; others worked to overcome the 'legacy of program review'. Many of the mechanisms developed under the EMS to sustain expenditure review were either redirected toward other purposes or they were quietly dropped. In their stead the government introduced new review mechanisms: Program Integrity (1998 and 1999) and Departmental Assessments (DAs) (2000 to current). In contrast to previous reforms, these systems shifted from government-wide reforms to those focused on specific management issues. Nor were they necessarily intended to deliver expenditure restraint.

From Program Review to the 'New Expenditure Management System'

Program review shocked Ottawa. Ministers and officials did not believe that the Treasury Board (TB) would deliver on its president's mandate to 'review all aspects of departmental spending'. They did, however, believe that Finance Minister Paul Martin would be able to achieve the 3 per cent deficit target set out in the first Liberal Red Book. Such complacency was dashed by a worsening economy, criticism from the IMF, and the threat of a downgrade by the Moody's rating agency.[2] In the face of crisis, cabinet was forced to consider a more comprehensive program review, one that delivered cuts sufficient to achieve the deficit target. As a consequence, the interests of the TB and the department of Finance coalesced into 'Program Review', which led to a re-examination of government programs that was intended to achieve specific expenditure reduction targets; this re-examination played out over the six months between June and November 1994. Martin announced the resultant changes to program and government machinery in the 1995 budget, and these were to be implemented over the four years to 1999.

Yet Program Review did little to alter the established norms of expenditure management in Ottawa. Experience has shown that most new governments use their early years in office to cut some programs established by their predecessors and then use the resultant cash to fund new programs and policies. Certainly program review was a concentrated and painful exercise for many. It affected most government departments; up to 45,000 jobs were lost, programs were cut, and some significant re-engineering occurred.[3] Yet Program Review was, for all that, a one-off exercise. The expenditure plans set out in the 1995 budget were projections rather than limits, and imposed little discipline on future years. Upon completion of program review, many claimed to have 'got government right', and that the machinery for ongoing review or reallocation was superfluous. The cabinet structure supporting the exercise was disbanded and packed away even before Martin announced the results of Program Review on budget day in February 1995.

In February 1995, the government announced reforms designed to permanently incorporate the practices of review and reallocation into the EMS. Tabled by the President of the Treasury Board, *The Expenditure Management System of the Government of Canada* was presented as 'the most significant overhaul of the government's expenditure management system since . . . the early 1980s'.[4] This document presented details of a system that 'requires the ongoing review of programs and spending to reduce expenditure and identify opportunities for reallocation . . . enhances accountability . . . [and] introduces long-term strategic planning and the adjustment of programs and services'. When drawn together, the seven principles underpinning EMS were intended to establish an environment conducive to ongoing expenditure review and reallocation at three different levels.[5]

First, EMS sought to create a political demand for reallocation by limiting ministers' access to new funds and therefore forcing them to operate within 'existing resource levels'. The notion of an 'integrated' budget planning system meant that total spending levels for each department would be decided during an annual budget cycle and then held as immutable limits throughout the year.[6] This was reinforced by the elimination of the policy reserves, which had previously provided ministers with a source of funding for within-year policy decisions. As a consequence, new policy initiatives or cost increases that occurred throughout the year would have to be funded by the responsible ministry by reallocating funds from lower priorities. If new policy initiatives involved more than one department or ministry, then either the sponsoring department or the TBS had to present cabinet with the details of a 'reallocation package' to fund the policy proposal. In this way, the EMS reiterated sentiments expressed by the ill-fated Clark government, that the budget system should 'establish known expenditure limits . . . and place responsibility for saving on those who spend'.[7]

Secondly, EMS was designed to supply the information required to make reallocation decisions by requiring the 'ongoing review of programs' and continual monitoring and reporting on 'program performance'. Primary responsibility for deciding how, when, and on what basis to conduct these reviews was delegated to individual departments and ministers, who were also responsible for identifying reallocation options. Responsibility for conducting a second round of government-wide program reviews and the task of establishing a sustainable cycle of performance review were both assigned to the TBS. It was assumed that on the basis of this information the TBS could develop suggestions for reallocating funds across departments. Two assumptions underpin this aspect of the EMS: first, that options on how to reallocate within a department would be identified on the basis of review findings, and secondly, that the review of programs would inevitably provide evidence to support funding cuts and reallocation. As we shall see later in this chapter, both of these assumptions proved difficult to sustain.

Thirdly, by introducing departmental Business Plans (DBPs) and by increasing managerial flexibility, the EMS sought to ensure that reallocation decisions taken as part of the budget process were translated into actual program changes. No matter how difficult the process of identifying cuts, the practicalities of implementing those decisions are more difficult and more complex. Reallocation decisions mean that some operations must be wound down while others are accelerated, staff must by re-deployed, retrained, or retrenched, and detailed authorizations—ministerial, legal, or administrative—are often required. Often departments are frustrated in their attempts to reallocate internally by interminable demands to justify any changes; mechanisms intended to ensure probity inevitably hamper reallocation. By increasing the degree of managerial autonomy available to ministers and officials, EMS promised freedom to pursue internal reallocations unfettered by central controls and to allow 'innovative approaches to service delivery'. The newly introduced DBPs were designed to ensure that departments implemented the decisions taken in

Program Review and to lubricate the future cycles of reallocation and realignment envisaged by the EMS. In short, DBPs were intended to provide an agreed policy and management framework within which the department could reallocate resources as it saw fit; they were also intended to enable TB to track changes and to ensure that the budget decisions were implemented, not deferred.

In sum, the three strands of the EMS were intended to establish both the incentives and the means for reallocation. In a world of limited resources, parliamentarians, individual ministers, and departmental officials seeking to implement new policies and programs would demand information on how to fund these initiatives through reallocation. Both the performance reports and the more specific reviews of ongoing programs would supply the information required by these actors to identify reallocation options. And, once decisions were taken at the level of 'policy' in the budget, responsibility for ensuring that the decisions were implemented fell to departments working with the TB and TBS through the DBPs.

Yet moving the EMS from a plan to an operational reality was always going to be difficult. Control over the budgetary system in Ottawa is diffused among three central agencies, all of which work toward distinct objectives. Very simply, we can say that the main focus for Finance is fiscal discipline and tax levels, the Privy Council Office (PCO) focuses on questions of policy direction and priorities, and the TBS focuses on ensuring that departmental programs are well managed once they become part of the A-base. The period of fiscal crisis that underpinned the Program Review exercise and the development of the EMS provided a common goal for all three agencies into which these different perspectives could be integrated. But as the fiscal environment began to change, so the tensions between the three agencies became more apparent and the design of EMS began to shift.

Without the binding effect of a fiscal crisis, commitment to the annual, integrated budget planning cycle underpinning EMS began to collapse, and was abandoned altogether once surpluses were achieved. First, the notion that funding would only be available during the budget planning session began to give way. Although central policy reserves were eliminated, they were replaced by less obvious reserves, such as TBS's operating reserve, but more fundamentally by Finance's use of both explicit and implicit 'prudence factors', which created an informal reserve by using overly conservative figures in the fiscal framework. Initially the government used the excess revenues to show smaller and smaller budget deficits. By 1998, however, Finance was releasing an increasing proportion of these 'prudence' reserves to fund new policies near the end of the fiscal year when it was confident that the fiscal targets would be met. Making these funds available undermined the notion of integrated budget planning and provided departments and ministers with additional windows through which to access policy money without recourse to reallocation.

Secondly, as additional funding began to flow into the system and ministers began demanding the opportunity to debate new policy initiatives, the willingness of PCO to support the principles of EMS waned. In 1998, the Clerk of the Privy Council did away with the requirement for fully funded Memoranda to Cabinet. This meant, essentially, that ministers and departments could develop policy initiatives without considering how the initiatives were to be funded. As a consequence, the trade-off between new programs and reallocation that underpinned EMS no longer held. Ministers were able to propose new programs without identifying a 'source of funds'; as a direct consequence, they no longer had to 'demand' information on how to reallocate from one program area to another and a primary driver of ongoing program review disappeared.

From Business Plans to Business Planning

Within this changing environment, TBS developed the concept of departmental Business Plans. Much has been written to explain the development and eventual decline of business planning as an instrument of TBS-departmental engagement, most of which will not be repeated here.[8] The important point for this chapter is that Business Plans (BPs) were introduced as one component in an integrated expenditure management system, became the basis for redefining TBS–departmental relationships, and finally evolved into a tool for internal departmental planning quite separate from government-wide expenditure management or budget implementation. This had the effect of removing the second EMS 'strand' (supply of information), which was intended to incorporate review and reallocation into the EMS.

DBPs were intended to support the practices of review and reallocation underpinning EMS at two different levels. The primary intention was to ensure that departments implemented reallocation decisions taken in the 1995 budget. TBS required each department to submit a DBP that was consistent with Budget targets and strategies, and with the new spending and reduction initiative. As well as identifying decisions taken in the budget, the BP of each department was to include implementation strategies; the program and resource authorities (or flexibilities) needed to deliver on these strategies, targets, and performance measures; performance information; and the challenges expected over the next two years. This information formed the basis for discussions between TB and departments, initially at the level of officials and then in presentations by the Secretariat to ministers of the TB.[9] Once the BPs were reviewed and agreement was reached, departmental managers could, at least in theory, implement the necessary changes free of TBS 'interference'. For its part, the TB would have the performance information required to identify 'new reallocation options and areas where it needs more performance information'.[10]

But TBS also saw the introduction of DBPs as an opportunity to redefine relationships between departments and the TB, to streamline the work of TBS, and to shift the focus of TB discussions from transactions to strategy. The business planning process could be used to identify the TB authorizations required by each department for the upcoming year and more easily manage the flow of TB work.[11] It was also expected that departments would eventually link this cycle of annual DBPs to their internal management and planning cycle and to parliamentary reporting documents, and would thus streamline a number of processes.[12] In short, DBPs were seen as the basis for advancing the concept of Treasury Board as a management board rather than a mechanism for ensuring implementation of specific budget decisions. Gradually the managerial objectives of BPs began to predominate.

Within this context, the gradual transition from DBPs in 1995 to business planning in 1997 and 'renewed business planning' in 1999 is more than rhetoric. As early as 1996, TBS was already speaking of 'business planning' as a process of 'dialogue and exchange' between TBS and departments, and the notion of BPs as a submission made by departments to the TB as part of the EMS was dropped. By 1999, TBS had dropped the annual cycle of DBPs in favour of a targeted and selective approach as part of the 'renewed' approach to business planning. Thereafter deputy ministers were invited to submit a business plan when they were implementing significant changes, or once every three years.

At the same time, TBS increasingly felt the need to justify its own involvement in the process. An evaluation of BPs in late 1996 focused on 'how well the Treasury Board and the Secretariat have used Business Plans, [and] what value they have added'. Line departments wanted to know how the TB used the information they had provided. In response to these criticisms, the focus within TBS shifted from ensuring a streamlined process to ensuring that the outcomes of business planning were meaningful to both TB ministers and to departments. As a result, TBS developed a number of 'tangible products', including the development of TBS Perspective Documents—an 'ever-green document that reflects the state of TBS collective knowledge of departments and agencies and the programs they deliver'—and the Report on the Integrity of Government Operations.[13] Others can debate whether these changes achieved the 'management board' objective. The point here is that the evolution of DBPs removed what was seen by the designers of EMS as a critical tool for facilitating the review of ongoing programs and resource reallocation, and for identifying both the review agenda and reallocation options.

REVIEW AND REALLOCATION IN A TIME OF PLENTY

It is perhaps surprising to learn that between 1999 and 2002, within the context of budget surpluses, the Chrétien government established two new mechanisms to facilitate the review of ongoing programs and reallocation: Program Integrity operated throughout 1999 and 2000; DAs commenced in 2001. Although generally seen as distinct initiatives, the latter is really an adaptation of the former. Both assumed the continuity of the broader EMS; both encouraged departments to review ongoing programs and to reallocate from their existing resource base. In contrast to EMS, these were discrete initiatives intended to address specific problems of expenditure management, rather than attempts at system-wide reform. These review initiatives differed from the earlier exercise of Program Review in that they were focused more on questions of public sector management than on delivering expenditure cuts—not surprising given that they were introduced during a period of budget surpluses.

Program Integrity instigated a series of reviews designed to resolve critical risks to the sustainability of government programs. During the previous round of business planning, TBS had developed the *Report on the Integrity of Government Operations*, which assessed the capacity of departments to continue delivering their existing programs and policies within existing funding levels.[14] In this report TBS identified a number of 'critical risks' that threatened to undermine the 'integrity' of government programs. For example, the capital and asset holdings of a number of departments were found to be in such a state of disrepair that they presented health and safety risks. Funding shortfalls in other program areas were deemed to constitute a legal risk; in other departments increased workload meant that, given existing funding, the standard of program delivery was falling dangerously close to a minimally acceptable level.

The Program Integrity exercise operated in three stages. First, TBS worked to identify an agenda for review that focused on problems that could not be ignored or 'put off'. Two different types of review were carried out: reviews that focused on specific departments and those that focused on a series of horizontal issues. The latter focused on program management problems common to a number of departments, with TBS analysts acting as review co-ordinators and advisors. Next, TBS and departmental analysts worked together to review the problems and find possible solutions. If TBS assessed that departments had the capacity to fund the solution through reallocation, it would be recommended. If reallocation was not possible, then TBS recommended whatever additional funding was required. After the TB ministers discussed these findings, the president made recommendations for additional funding to the minister of Finance and the prime minister as part of the budget process. In this way Program Integrity broadened the focus of budgetary debates to include additional funding for existing programs, as well as for new policy initiatives.

The fact that the Program Integrity reviews were carried out in an environment of surplus budgets affected the initial design. Many thought it would be well-nigh impossible during a time of surplus budgeting to persuade ministers and departments to engage voluntarily in a review exercise that would have led to reallocation. Consequently, the first round of Program Integrity sought to ensure that review departments received at least some additional money to resolve their problems. The longer-term objective was to make access to new policy funds conditional on resolving program integrity problems, and therefore to force departments to reallocate from within their own funds.

The second round of Program Integrity reviews were completed in an environment in which the department of Finance was warning that Canada faced an impending recession and needed to ensure fiscal discipline. Finance criticized the Program Integrity exercise as generating additional pressures on the public purse, arguing that without the exercise, departments would have been forced to solve their internal management problems through reallocation. This argument has intuitive appeal: Program Integrity certainly encouraged departments to focus on issues they had hitherto ignored, and it provided significant funding to address at least some of their problems. Whether continued neglect by the central agencies would have produced more reallocation or an even larger crisis is, however, debatable, as is the question whether early intervention prevented even greater increases in costs both to the taxpayer and to program sustainability.

The launch of DAs in 2001 attempted to dampen the emerging fiscal pressures while allowing legitimate reallocations to occur. In contrast to Program Integrity and the 1995 Program Review exercise, the DA process was not driven by pre-stated fiscal, managerial, or policy objectives. Referencing the principles of EMS, the process assigned responsibility for internal reallocation to individual ministers and departments. It restated that, under conditions of limited resources, ministers and departmental managers would pursue reallocation as way of funding new policy initiatives and resolving any problem associated with ongoing programs. As a result, departments wishing to pursue internal reallocation would initiate a DA in the hope that cabinet would provide the political backing or cabinet authorizations necessary to achieve the desired changes. The primary role of central agencies was to validate the claims of departments and then facilitate the requested reallocation actions.

It is too early to comment on the success or otherwise of the DA process, but two issues are worth noting. First, even the most successful DA will not lead to reallocation across departments. This is not a criticism of the process, merely an explicit feature of its design. Second, in concept at least, the DA process provides the means for reallocation without any explicit requirement for program review. It is assumed of course that departments continually review their ongoing programs and have robust performance information that provides the knowledge required for reallocation. The intervention of central agencies is overly cautious at best. When we compare this system to the aspirations of the EMS, we see a very different ethos of expenditure management, one in which the interests of the centre and those of departments have become clearly separated rather than reinforcing each other. We can only wait to see whether this is sustainable. However, statements made by both the Prime Minister and by the Minister of Finance in the run-up to the 2003 Budget have focused on 'reallocation for transformation'.[15] This suggests that the Chrétien government is still not satisfied with the balance and that we will see yet further efforts to encourage reallocation and review in the near future.

We can conclude from the above analysis that the Chrétien government has throughout its time in office established mechanisms to encourage the ongoing review of government programs *and* the reallocation of resources. Many of these mechanisms seemed quite sensible at their inception, and, in theory at least, were supported by some quite powerful actors within the bureaucracy and by ministers. Yet the initiatives themselves were often short-lived: some were dropped, and often they were replaced by other initiatives with apparently similar objectives. The following section seeks to explain these events, and to draw out some lessons for the future.

REVIEW AND REALLOCATION: WHY DID THE
LIBERALS TRY TO RE-OPEN THE BOX?

That expenditure review and reallocation impose new problems is well known to both ministers and academics.[16] Writing about the US federal budgeting processes, Naomi Caiden summarized the 'politics of subtraction' as follows:

> Whereas the politics of addition act to assuage conflicts, those of subtraction not only are the source of increased conflict but also undercut the accepted means by which this was previously resolved.[17]

Why then did the Liberals attempt to incorporate review and reallocation into the EMS? Our account of the various programs suggests that three distinct, yet related objectives underpinned the various efforts by the Liberals to promote review and reallocation. These were fiscal and expenditure discipline; reprioritization and program renewal; and the improvement of public sector management. It is significant that these budgetary objectives reflect the primary emphases of the three central agencies. When these three objectives have come together there is evidence of a unified impetus to institutionalize mechanisms of review and reallocation.

This commonality of purpose among central agencies explains the apparent unanimity concerning the need for review and reallocation in 1994–6 and why such a concerted effort was expended during this period. There was general agreement at this time among ministers and across the three central agencies that the fiscal crisis was real and ongoing.[18] Ministers accepted that they would need to reduce existing spending in order to implement new policies. Under these circumstances there was political mileage to be made from reallocation—it showed that the government was restoring fiscal sovereignty. There were also benefits in review: the government could claim that it had undertaken a zero-based review to ensure a better alignment of government resources and priorities and to get government right. Program Review was the immediate response; EMS was to permanently entrench these activities.

Once the fiscal crisis abated, however, commitment to the principles outlined in EMS declined among ministers and within the central agencies. First, continuing to reallocate made little sense politically—it was much more sensible to declare a victory on the deficit, and use the 'fiscal dividend' to fund new policies. Thus, the cabinet shifted the focus of its discussions to questions of policy development, and PCO sought to increase the number of policy initiatives flowing through cabinet by allowing unfunded policy proposals. Coincidentally, this shift removed the expenditure discipline underpinning the EMS. Although Finance argued for ongoing reallocation, it began to 'spend' the additional fiscal flexibility first by releasing tracts of new funding at the end of the fiscal year and then by means of massive tax cuts. Even if presidents of the TB had supported reallocation in principle, it made little sense for them to promote this option when the other two 'guardian' ministers were focused on spending. Secondly, while TBS continued to promote the ongoing review of existing programs, this review focused on questions of program integrity and good management rather than on reprioritization as envisaged in the EMS. Given that new money was flowing through the system, it is not surprising that TBS attempted to use the review findings to encourage ministers to fund the ongoing program base. By doing so, it broke the nexus between review and reallocation that was implied by the EMS.

The department of Finance's warnings of impending fiscal doom, repeated frequently since 1999, can be seen as an attempt by the department to recreate an environment of restraint and to support its longstanding advocacy of review and reallocation. But, like the boy who cried wolf, those who falsely predict a fiscal crisis will be believed for only so long. Eventually the actual figures must be revealed. Over the longer period 'surprise' surpluses only encouraged ministers and officials to avoid the tough decisions required to reallocate, in the expectation that sufficient fiscal flexibility would emerge, whatever Finance forecasts suggested. This situation has dampened any commitment to the principles of reallocation on the part of departments. It has also led to the stop-start program of reform that we have witnessed.

The experience of Program Integrity highlights two additional lessons for expenditure management: review and reallocation are not inextricably linked, and budgetary objectives can sometimes clash. If we assess the Program Integrity exercise by asking whether it facilitated the review of ongoing programs, then we can say that the exercise was successful at a number of levels. The exercise identified solutions to problems within departments and built up the knowledge of A-base issues inside TBS. It provided a legitimate focus for dialogue between the TBS and departments (confirming the drift away from budget planning). It also involved ministers in the review process, and provided an additional source of information for the process of budget planning. If, however, we look for explicit reallocation decisions as the criteria for success, then the exercise appears to have failed. The objective of TBS analysis had been to 'push back' departments wherever reallocation seemed to be a viable option. However, no explicit reallocation recommendations or decisions were made, and reallocation options were left to departments. As a consequence, the visible outcome of this process was recommendations for additional funding. This created the perception that reviewing ongoing programs was undesirable, because it caused additional budgetary pressures, and set up a clash between the two budgetary objectives of fiscal discipline and the improvement of public management.

This situation goes to the heart of conflicts over the primary objective of review and reallocation. Should we, in the pursuit of fiscal restraint, review ongoing programs to identify possible options for reallocation? Or should programs be reviewed in the pursuit of better public sector management, with reallocation standing as just one possible outcome? Program Review was certainly in the former camp; Program Integrity was in the latter. Similarly, should programs be reviewed without the discipline of an explicit expenditure limit? If so, it is likely that additional funding will be recommended at least occasionally. As a result, the fiscal and managerial objectives of expenditure management will be in conflict. Given the relative strength of the Finance department in the budget process, it is not surprising that it is able to block funding to initiatives perceived as threatening its primary objective, fiscal restraint. Hence the demise of Program Integrity reviews.

A related point is that the least successful efforts to incorporate review and reallocation into the EMS have been those introduced to improve public sector management and good governance. These objectives underpinned the original EMS, Program Integrity, and the DAs. Under this model, reviews are conducted for a variety of purposes, including assessments of efficiency and effectiveness, of program design, and of performance evaluation. Reallocation is one expected outcome of review, but others are also possible, including additional funding, restructuring or outsourcing, and 'strategic' investments. Both priorities and total spending may remain constant, but there would be changes in the way programs are delivered or in the mix of activities (programs), and these changes would be based on the results of evaluations and assessments of specific program areas or management practices.

The evidence presented above provides a number of explanations for the lack of success in using review and reallocation to support a 'good management' objective. First, if review and reallocation are to facilitate better public management they must be permanently incorporated into the EMS. Yet TBS—the primary instigator of these reforms in Canada at the moment—has limited authority over the government budget system. The demise of Program Integrity provides an example of what is likely to occur when the objectives of TBS clash with those of Finance. Secondly, as we have already seen, the establishment of an EMS built around review and reallocation contradicts traditional budgetary norms, which are designed to resolve conflict, not exacerbate it. When reallocation and review are used as tools to address issues affecting existing programs, the focus of negotiations is moved from the increment to the A-base. As a consequence, issues previously seen by interest groups, program providers, and elected officials as 'settled' are re-opened, and system-wide reform is introduced in an area that is, by its very nature, rife with conflict.

Under the current balance of power then, TBS should limit any review or reallocation initiatives to the specific areas over which it has authority, and these should not be dependent on the annual budget system for implementation. There are several reasons for this. First, the budget system is an area over which PCO and Finance have primary authority. Whatever course of action TBS and the TB decide, their recommendations will always be vulnerable to the vagaries of PCO and Finance if they require approval through the budgetary process. Secondly, the budgetary environment has become increasingly turbulent over the past few years; it is therefore all but impossible to develop a regular cycle of review around this process. Thirdly, the core politics of budget negotiations are primarily focused on the allocation of new money. Any review undertaken in this environment will attempt first and foremost to provide a justification for more funds. Fourthly, the interests of TBS extend to questions of program design, performance, and management. Reviews focused on such questions may have little to do with the total funding levels per se. Hence, they are unlikely to gain sufficient attention.

Perversely, the incorporation of reallocation into TBS reforms may make implementation even more difficult. At the political level, reallocation will be difficult to sell. Ministers may accept the need for a balanced budget, but they are more likely to achieve it by deferring new policy initiatives or 'non-essential' capital upgrades than by cutting current programs or personnel. Similarly, announcing reallocations in the budget may win the acclaim of economists and credit-rating agencies, but gaining the approval of program recipients will be more difficult. This suggests that TBS should either downplay the role that reallocation plays in any review, as it did with Program Integrity, or reduce the visibility of any program cuts. Further, if reallocations are to occur at the level of individual departments, then the involvement of TBS will be challenged by deputy ministers, who jealously guard any flexibility to reallocate resources within their domains. Conversely, reallocation is likely to win support from the burghers of Finance, eager to address criticisms from the economic press and the capital markets, who want to see that reallocation is occurring.

These observations lead to a final and related lesson about the direction of reform under the Chrétien government. A quick perusal of newspaper articles on the issue shows that the most vocal and public advocates of program review and reallocation are from the banking sector, business groups, economic think-tanks, and the federal department of Finance. Most frequently cited are the Canadian Chamber of Commerce, the Bank of Canada, the C.D. Howe Institute, the Conference Board of Canada, and, of course, the ministers of Finance (both Martin and the incumbent, John Manley). They have been joined recently by two former finance officials, David Dodge (now Governor of the Bank of Canada) and Don Drummond (now chief economist with the Toronto Dominion Bank).[19] These critics are themselves typically pursuing an agenda of lower taxes and paying off debt. For example, Nancy Hughes Anthony of the Chamber of Commerce is quoted as asking the government to 'refocus spending with a review of existing programs' so that the government can 'commit itself to cutting taxes, debt and spending'.[20] Similarly, Bill Robson of the C.D. Howe Institute hoped Manley would be 'inclined . . . to look to lower taxes as a key element in his program'.[21] Not surprisingly, the Liberals see these agendas as debatable. If the primary justification for reviewing existing programs is to deliver a policy agenda in which the Liberals do not believe, then it is hardly surprising they are easily distracted from the 'ideal'.

Finally, many within the government are not convinced of the necessity for fundamental reforms, because they can point to evidence that reallocation is currently occurring. Indeed, some of the chapters in this volume show where changes have occurred within policy areas and departments, where priorities have shifted and programs are being redesigned. In addition, reprioritization does not necessarily mean cutting ongoing programs; it can also be achieved through differentiated rates of expenditure growth. However, these forms of reallocation are rarely acknowledged—or even noticed—by critics, who focus on issues of fiscal management and whose primary focus is consequently the annual budget. The budget does not capture the full extent of change within the federal public service, because it emphasizes annual changes in the aggregate expenditure figures and incremental changes in specific areas of program spending. Reallocations within departments that have little impact on the bottom line will not be captured by such figures. It can be argued that the public should be informed of these programmatic changes, but, as argued above, the electoral unpopularity of reallocation makes this unlikely, and, quite perversely, may stop any reallocation that currently occurs.

CONCLUSIONS: WHERE TO NOW?

The experience of the Chrétien government provides us with some important lessons about the usefulness of review and reallocation in public expenditure management. First, the Chrétien government has used review and reallocation to pursue three distinct budgetary objectives: fiscal restraint, reprioritization, and the encouragement of better program management. Each new initiative adapted the practices of review and reallocation to address one or more of these objectives, but no single model was able to achieve all three equally well. As the budgetary environment shifted—deficits turned to surpluses or the government moved to implement new policy initiatives—new budget tools were developed. This reminds us that review and reallocation are useful tools in expenditure management, but they are not ends in themselves. Furthermore, the assumption that review and reallocation are inextricably linked is not supported by recent experience. Reviewing government programs can provide useful information for budget decision-makers, but it will not necessarily provide evidence that incontrovertibly supports reallocation. Nor will it replace the need for the government to make political choices. Finally, review and reallocation will often undermine one of the fundamental—if often forgotten—objectives of government budgeting: conflict resolution.

This evidence suggests that efforts to promote reallocation during the final stages of the Chrétien government have every chance of success. While the fiscal situation appears to be relatively healthy, pressures are being created by an ambitious policy agenda. Under these circumstances, the government is likely to accept the costs of reallocation, especially if it can be shown to improve program efficiency or policy renewal. Whether this forms the basis for the more permanent incorporation of reallocation is debatable. On the one hand, Canada's longer-term fiscal position is relatively comfortable—budget surpluses are likely to continue, and to gradually increase.[22] This will reduce the extent to which new policies must be funded from reallocation. On the other hand, Canada is facing a period of political turmoil over the next two years at least: first the Liberal leadership race and then the election. Both can be expected to provide instances of increased activity in the development of agendas for program change and policy development, and reprioritization is likely to be seen as an essential component of these agendas. Such a prolonged period of instability may provide a window of opportunity for those promoting review and reallocation as means to improved public sector management. However, the lessons of previous attempts in this direction warn that this will be difficult if these processes are played out in the political realm of public budgeting, or if they threaten to undermine fiscal discipline.

NOTES

I would like to acknowledge with thanks the helpful comments on earlier drafts of this chapter by Mike Joyce, Bruce Doern, and Peter Aucoin, and by the other authors in this edition.

1 Government of Canada. Department of Supply and Services, *The Expenditure Management System of the Government of Canada* (Ottawa, 1995).
2 The objectives were set out in Finance Canada, *Budget Plan 1994*, and in the Liberals' electoral platform, colloquially known as the 'Red Book': Liberal Party of Canada, *Creating Opportunity: The Liberal Plan for Canada* (Ottawa: Liberal Party of Canada, 1993); for the pressures, see Paul Martin, 'Minister of Finance Disappointed with Moody's Downgrade' (News Release, Department of Finance, 2 June 1994); Robert Chodos, Rae Murphy, and Eric Hamovitch, *Paul Martin: A Political Biography* (Toronto: James Lorimer & Co., 1998).
3 For examples see Gene Swimmer, ed., *How Ottawa Spends 1995–96: Life Under the Knife* (Ottawa: Carleton University Press, 1996); Peter Aucoin and Donald Savoie, eds, *Managing Strategic Change: Learning from Program Review* (Ottawa: Canadian Centre for Management Development, 1998).
4 Government of Canada. Department of Supply and Services, *The Expenditure Management System*, 1.
5 Seven basic principles underpinned the system: 1. integrating the budget planning system; 2. emphasizing the ongoing review of programs and management within available resources through reallocations; 3. eliminating central policy reserves; 4. introducing departmental Business Plans to focus on strategic changes to programs and business; 5. providing more flexibility to ministers and departments to help them manage within approved resources; 6. improving information on program performance to aid decision-making and facilitate accountability; 7. recognizing the role of the House's standing committees in reviewing the government's spending priorities for future years and introducing departmental Outlooks. This chapter does not discuss the parliamentary component of EMS.
6 In this context 'integrated' refers to a temporal integration, a single integrated 'window of opportunity' in the budget cycle when decisions on funding and policy would be taken.
7 Finance Canada, *The New Expenditure Management System* (Ottawa: Department of Supply and Services, 1979).
8 But see three studies by Evert Lindquist: 'Citizens, Experts and Budgets: Evaluating Ottawa's Emerging Budget Process', in Susan Phillips, ed., *How Ottawa Spends 1994–95: Making Change* (Ottawa: Carleton University Press, 1994), 91–128; 'On the Cutting Edge: Program Review, Government Restructuring and the Treasury Board of Canada', in Gene Swimmer, ed., *How Ottawa Spends 1996–97: Life Under the Knife* (Ottawa: Carleton University Press, 1996), 205–52; 'Expenditure Manage-

ment in the Millennium: Vision and Strategy for Integrated Business Planning', discussion paper prepared for TBS, 1998.

9 Only a limited number of presentations were made by the submitting ministers—a result primarily of limited agenda time available given the TB's continuing heavy 'transaction' load, but also a result of reluctance on the part of some ministers, who had no clear understanding or experience of the implications.

10 Government of Canada. Department of Supply and Services, *The Expenditure Management System*, 8.

11 It is worth noting that the TB did not 'approve' DBPs—whether or not it should was the subject of much debate inside TBS at the time. But the lack of any framework to make approval or, more significantly, lack of approval meaningful was the primary reason they were just 'reviewed', and only specific requests for authorities were considered for approval.

12 This information was initially provided in the Department Outlooks on Program Priorities and Expenditures. These were adapted via two phases of the Improved Reporting to Parliament Project (IRPP) (1995–8, and 1999 to current), in which Part III of the Main Estimates were split into Reports on Plans and Priorities (RPPs) and Departmental Performance Reports (DPRs).

13 Various TBS internal documents.

14 Treasury Board Secretariat, *Report on the Integrity of Government Operations* (Treasury Board Secretariat, 1999).

15 See Canada, *The Canada We Want: Speech from the Throne to Open the Second Session of the Thirty-Seventh Parliament of Canada*, 30 Sept. 2002, and Finance Canada, *Economic and Fiscal Update* (Ottawa: Department of Finance, 30 Oct. 2002).

16 For examples in Canada, the United States, and the United Kingdom see, respectively, Peter Aucoin, ed., *The Politics and Management of Restraint in Government* (Toronto: Institute of Research and Public Policy, 1981); Allen Schick, 'Micro-Budgetary Adaptations to Fiscal Stress in Industrialised Democracies', *Public Administration Review* 48 (1988); Maurice Wright, ed., *Public Spending Decisions: Growth and Restraint in the 1970s* (London: Allen and Unwin, 1980).

17 Naomi Caiden, 'The Politics of Subtraction', in Allen Schick, ed., *Managing Economic Policy in Congress* (Washington: American Enterprise for Public Policy Research, 1983), 100.

18 For an interesting account of this period see E. Greenspon and A. Wilson-Smith, *Double Vision: The Inside Story of the Liberals in Power* (Toronto: Doubleday Canada, 1996).

19 For example, see comments by David Dodge, in Eric Beauchesne, 'Dodge to PM: Hold Off on Spending', *The Ottawa Citizen*, 4 Sept. 2002.

20 Quoted in Eric Beauchesne, 'No Spending Spree Business Tells PM', *The Ottawa Citizen*, 23 Sept. 2002, A4.

21 Quoted in Alan Toulin, 'Manley Likely to Confirm $Billion Debt Cut: Pressure For Budget', *The National Post*, 17 June 2002, A4.

22 See Alan Toulin, 'Manley Predicts $70 billion in Surpluses: Five Year Compilation', *The National Post*, 31 Oct. 2002, A1.

9

Taking Stock: Governance Practices and Portfolio Performance of the Canada Pension Plan Investment Board

MICHAEL J. PRINCE

The purpose of this chapter is to describe and understand the Canada Pension Plan (CPP) Investment Board in terms of its origins, its corporate governance, and its investment policy and performance. Created in 1998, the Board is a federal Crown corporation with a mandate to invest in capital markets those CPP savings that are not required to make current benefit payments. The analysis is guided by a number of questions. Why, after the CPP had been in existence for over 30 years, was the Investment Board established? What were the circumstances and the context of its establishment? How is the Board structured and what is its mandate? Through what mechanisms are accountability, integrity, autonomy, and transparency addressed? What are the investment policies and portfolio management practices of the Board? What so far have been the results of the Board's investment decisions and the performance of its assets? What might the Board's performance mean for intergovernmental relations, public awareness and confidence, and, thus, future pension reform?

A look at the management structure and operation of the Investment Board is pertinent to current debates over corporate governance and ethical conduct. As a Canadian Senate committee noted not long ago, 'Good governance is especially critical for pension funds because, unlike mutual funds [companies that sell shares to the public and invest the money they receive] people can not move easily into and out of pension funds and there is relatively less publicly available information about their activities or performance.'[1] When considering the governance arrangements of the CPP as a program, analysts usually focus on the shared federal-provincial juris-diction over contributory pensions and supplementary benefits; the amending for-mula for approving major changes to the Plan; the opting-out provision that allows Quebec to establish its own plan, and the consequent link between the Canada and Quebec pension plans; and the administration of the CPP by Human Resources Development Canada.

The manner in which the Investment Board is governed was of special political and public interest when the Board was established, and this issue has become even more prominent in the wake of recent scandals over corporate conduct in the United States. Perhaps not surprisingly, then, the CPP Investment Board has legislated gov-ernance requirements and ethical practices that, in many respects, are exemplary for pension plans as well as for Crown corporations and other public bodies.

With the acceleration of CPP contribution rate increases over the 1998 to 2003 period, and the formation of the Investment Board, the CPP is becoming a primary vehicle in the country for investment in stocks and equities and thus for the supply of capital resources to the private sector. Within a decade, it is estimated that the Board will be administering and investing upwards of $150 billion in pension assets. This investment role and this resource flow highlight the economic and market aspects of the CPP. Typically, the CPP has been seen as a social program, and the pol-icy and intergovernmental aspects have been manifest. Although there has always been an economic and market side to the Plan, through the contributions and the labour force attachment rules for eligibility, the CPP has understandably been regarded as part of the retirement income system and the wider social union. Now, with an investment agency and related processes, the CPP is more clearly and cen-trally linked with the market economy—more specifically, with equity capitalism. This casts the CPP in a new light, raising new issues and prompting new questions, along with new implications with respect to public confidence and the political con-text of the Plan.

Presented in four parts, the chapter first examines the political context of the pension reform debate of the 1990s that informed the birth of the Investment Board. The second part looks at the Board as a public sector pension fund and financial institution. Pension governance is considered in relation to the Board's mandate and mission; the appointment criteria and process of Board members, and their powers and duties; the emerging organizational culture of the Board; and its accountability and autonomy provisions. The third part investigates the investment policy and performance of the Board, including the investment objectives and strategies, rates of return to date, and projected cash flow and assets. The final part offers a brief conclusion and some forecasts. The Board's long-term achievements in stock mar-kets and venture capital may well facilitate the expansion of CPP benefits. The suc-cess of this form of equity capitalism could therefore help bolster public confidence and overcome those obstacles that executive federalism raises—or so it has traditionally been supposed—to the realization of progressive reform in public programs.

TAKING UP A NEW INVESTMENT POLICY

Unveiled in general terms in the February 1995 federal budget, the Liberals' perspective on pension reform was motivated by a determination to control rising program costs. 'Concerning the CPP', Finance Minister Paul Martin declared, 'the most recent actuarial report was released last week and it leaves no doubt that we will have to take steps to ensure that [the] plan continues to be sustainable.'[2] The Liberal pension reform agenda became more strongly apparent in the Finance Minister's May 1996 federal budget speech. That speech criticized previous governments for not taking proper action with respect to financing the CPP; for that reason expressed concern about a potential crisis; and promised to consult with other governments before taking action to slow the growth rate of CPP expenditures.

Martin intoned sombrely that 'Canadians feel our very way of life is at risk. They look at Medicare—and feel it is threatened. They look at the pension system—and wonder if it will be there in the years to come.' He added, 'Confidence in the pension system must be restored. The party that put pensions in place for this country must now act to preserve them. The challenge is clear—it is one of sustainability. First, the CPP must be put on a sound financial footing—and done so in a way that is sustainable, affordable and fair.'[3] The Finance Minister again made reference to the latest report of the Chief Actuary to make the argument that changes were needed to restore the CPP to health. In a 1996 report, the Chief Actuary indicated that without modifications the CPP fund would be depleted by 2015, and that by 2030 the combined contribution rates would have to increase to 14.2 per cent to cover the growing benefit costs. With the 1996 actuarial report projecting an exhaustion of reserves by 2015, the need to negotiate a federal-provincial deal to maintain the funding integrity of the Plan was not really a matter of debate. If a deal was to be reached, the challenge for Ottawa was to find a high degree of consensus among governments of all political stripes. Hence the strong rhetoric of urgency and crisis of confidence among Canadians.

In 1996, as part of the statutory review of the CPP that the federal and provincial/territorial governments must do every five years, governments agreed to a joint process of public consultation across the country. The options presented in what was called a joint information paper, *Securing the Canada Pension Plan*, included a major shift in the funding principles of the Plan, involving private investment, partial funding, and accelerated contribution increases, to create a 'steady state' contribution rate. Following public consultations, federal and provincial/territorial finance ministers participated in a series of intergovernmental meetings to negotiate a consensus on changes. In the 1997 federal budget, Martin trumpeted the intergovernmental consensus that had been reached, and outlined some of the principles that had guided the reforms. Among these was the belief that the CPP must be affordable and sustainable for future generations. This requires fuller funding.

When presenting Bill C-2, the Canada Pension Plan Investment Board Act, to the House of Commons Standing Committee on Finance in October 1997, Martin described the results of the public consultations in the following words: '[T]he clearest message we heard is that Canadians want, Canadians need, and Canadians count on the Canada Pension Plan. They told us they want the CPP fixed now and fixed right—not left to drift, not privatized, and not scrapped as some have suggested. And they told us to fix it in a way that does not pass on an unbearable cost to younger generations.'[4] For the purposes of our analysis, the most important changes to the CPP were as follows:

- Moving from pay-as-you-go financing to partial funding. Contribution rates rose from 5.85 per cent of contributory earnings in 1997 to 9.9 per cent in 2003 (rather than the previously scheduled rise to 7.35 per cent by 2003), and then remain steady, rather than rising, as projected, to 14 per cent or more by 2030.
- Investing the CPP reserve fund in a portfolio of market securities, to get higher returns, something that the QPP has been doing since the start of that plan.
- Establishing an Investment Board at arm's length from governments to manage the reserve fund. The fund will grow in value from the equivalent of two years of contributions currently, to about five years of contributions.
- Changing the policy on provincial governments' borrowings from the CPP, so that provinces no longer have full access to CPP funds at preferential interest rates, but rather have access to a portion of the reserve at market rates of interest.[5]

Bill C-2 passed third reading in the House of Commons on 4 December 1997 by a vote of 167 to 73, one of the few times that opposition parties have been so significantly opposed to legislation concerning the CPP. The very same day, Bill C-2 was given first reading in the Senate. After some debate, which concentrated on the governance of the new Investment Board and the scale and possible economic effects of the contribution rate increases, Bill C-2 was passed by the Senate on 17 December. Royal Assent followed on 18 December 1997; provincial cabinets passed supporting orders in council. Upon approval, the changes to the contribution rates were retroactive to January 1997, and the benefit changes and their administration went into effect 1 January 1998. The related developments establishing the CPP Investment Board and the new investment policy were proclaimed 1 April 1998.[6]

TAKING FORM: CREATING THE INVESTMENT BOARD GOVERNANCE REGIME

The Association of Canadian Pension Management defines pension governance as 'the processes and structures used to direct and manage the affairs of the pension plan, in accordance with the best interests of the pension plan participants.'[7] On the importance of governance, the President and Chief Executive Officer (CEO) of the CPP Investment Board, John A. MacNaughton, stresses that

> good governance is central not just to better checks and balances and improved performance, but also to greater public confidence in corporations, whether in the public or private sector. As a new Crown corporation, we at the CPP Investment Board are in an ideal position to implement and test new standards of governance. We have no internal history to wrestle with—we have no negative baggage to discard. Furthermore, we are governed by forward-looking legislation that sets the blueprint for the highest standards of accountability and ethical behaviour.[8]

Indeed, in 2002, the CPP Investment Board won the Conference Board of Canada/ Spencer Stuart National Award in Governance for the public sector and was also honoured with a 'global best practice' in public pension funds by the World Bank.[9] It is instructive then to examine the structures, the culture, and the procedures of the Investment Board, in order to appreciate what good governance means in this context.

Mandate and Mission

The core statutory functions of the Board are (a) to manage any funds transferred to it under the CPP 'in the best interests of the contributors and beneficiaries' under the Plan, and (b) 'to invest its assets with a view to achieving a maximum rate of return, without undue risk of loss, having regard to the factors that may affect the funding of the Canada Pension Plan and the ability of the Canada Pension Plan to meet its financial obligations'. The Investment Board is also expressly prohibited from carrying out any business or activity or exercise any power that is inconsistent with these objects.[10] The Board has adopted the following Vision, Mission, and Long-Term Objectives:

Vision

Earn the confidence of Canadians that we are working for them to help the Canada Pension Plan keep its pension promise.

Investment Mission

- Manage the assets entrusted to the CPP Investment Board in the best interests of Canada Pension Plan contributors and beneficiaries.
- Invest in ways that over the long-term will maximize investment returns without undue risk of loss while having regard to the financial obligation and other assets of the Canada Pension Plan.

Investment Objectives

Achieve long-term investments that:
- Contribute to the financial strength of the Canada Pension Plan, and

- Earn returns that fairly compensate for the risks taken and costs incurred (that is, risk-adjusted net value added).[11]

Guided by this mandate to achieve a maximum rate of return without too much risk of loss, the Board's fundamental task is to invest funds not currently needed by the CPP. The Board's grand goal is to contribute to the Plan's long-term financial sustainability and fairness. In terms of intergenerational social policy, the role of the Board is nothing less than to create retirement income in later decades for today's younger workers, especially Canadians with low-income earning histories who do not have a workplace pension plan, contribute little if anything to a Registered Retirement Savings Plan, and cannot afford to save for their future on their own. In this context, MacNaughton sees the Investment Board as 'in the business to help them retire with dignity'.[12]

Board of Directors: Selection Criteria, Nomination Process, and Composition

A key element in good pension governance is having a board of directors that is knowledgeable in pensions and investment matters, and independent of the managers of the plan. In the case of the CPP, the board of directors must also be independent of governments, so that they are not subject to political influence or interference. The Investment Board comprises 12 directors. According to the legislation, each director is appointed by the federal cabinet on the recommendation of the minister of finance, to hold office for up to a three-year term. A director may be reappointed for one or two additional terms of office, for a maximum of nine years. The Board Chair can serve up to four terms, or twelve years. In any one year, no more than half of the directors' terms of office are to expire, so as to avoid a large turnover at once.

The enabling legislation provides for the establishment by the finance minister of a committee to advise on the appointment of directors. This nomination committee consists of a representative selected by the minister and a representative of each the nine participating provinces designated by each province's finance minister. Before making any recommendation to the federal cabinet with respect to the appointment of directors, and before making an appointment to fill any vacancy, the federal finance minister is statutorily obliged to consult with the provincial ministers. The legislation specifies two factors for consideration in recommending and making appointments to the board of directors. These factors are 'the desirability of having directors who are representative of the various regions of Canada and having on the board of directors a sufficient number of directors with proven financial ability or relevant work experience such that the Board will be able to effectively achieve its objects' (s. 10 [4]). In addition to these legal requirements, other generic attributes for all Board members and desirable qualifications of financial and investment experts were weighed, along with other considerations, including gender representation.[13] The nominating committee—which is chaired by a private sector executive and includes public officials and business leaders—has now gone through two rounds of appointments and reappointments. The Chair of the Investment Board of

Directors, Dr. Gail Cook-Bennett, was appointed by the federal cabinet, following consultation with the provinces and the full board of directors.

Through the first round of appointments to the Board in October 1998 and the second round of reappointments and some new appointments in March 2001, the directors collectively reflect a broad regional representation of the country (so far eight provinces and all five regions have been represented) and embody an impressive depth of work experience in accounting, actuarial science, banking, economics, finance, law, pension plan investment, and related fields.[14]

Powers of the Board and the Division of Power Between Board and Management
In general terms, the role of the Board of Directors is to supervise the management of the affairs of the Investment Board. More specifically, the main statutory powers and responsibilities of the Board of Directors are

- to establish written investment policies, standards, and procedures in accordance with the prudence that an ordinary person would exercise in dealing with the property of others (s. 8 [2] and 35);
- to establish procedures for the identification of potential conflicts of interest and procedures to resolve those conflicts;
- to establish a code of conduct for officers and employees of the Board;
- to designate a committee of the board of directors to monitor application of the conflict of interest procedures and the code of conduct;
- to make by-laws consistent with the Act to govern the conduct and management of the Board's business (s. 27);
- to establish an audit committee and an investment committee as well as establish other committees as it deems necessary (s. 30);
- to appoint the auditor for the Board; and
- to obtain all information and explanations from present or former staff or agents of the Board that the Board's auditor considers necessary to enable the auditor to prepare any report required by the legislation (s. 44).

With respect to the division of roles and responsibilities between the Board and management, the Act stipulates that the Board may not delegate its powers to adopt, amend, or repeal by-laws; to establish investment policies and standards; to fill a vacancy in a committee of directors or in the office of the auditor of the Board; or to approve the annual financial statements of the Board (s. 9 [2]). These powers are all the exclusive prerogative of the Board. The CEO of the Investment Board describes the relationship between the Board and management this way:

> The directors do not manage the CPP Investment Board on a day-to-day basis. The Board's goal is to make sure that the CPP Investment Board is managed competently, that the corporation acts with integrity, and that all efforts are focused on building long-term value to help pay future CPP pensions. Our directors approve

strategic plans, annual business plans and budgets, as well as investment and risk management policies and controls. Our Board, pursuant to its authority under our legislation, appoints the President and CEO . . . and approves his appointment of officers. This is a key element at keeping our organization at arm's length from governments and establishing the accountability of management to the Board. For its part, management is responsible for implementation of all Board approved strategies, plans and policies and is accountable to the Board for doing so.[15]

The 12-member board of directors was appointed in October 1998 and through the rest of that year to the middle of the next, interim investment policies were set, fund managers and a financial consultant were retained, and the President and CEO was recruited, assuming his office in September 1999. Early in 2000, the business plan was approved by the Board and the management team began to be recruited, with key executive appointments made through 2000 and 2001.

The Board's Organizational Culture: A Virtual Corporation with Transparency and Integrity

Good corporate governance requires a legislative framework, but ultimately rests on a vibrant organizational culture: a set of core values, beliefs, and practices shared by the directors and staff as they do their work. The culture of the Investment Board is shaped by several factors: the statutory duties and limits, of course, but also pension industry and financial market practices, public expectations, the people recruited to the Board and management, and the organization's relatively small size and recent establishment. Although the Investment Board is a young organization, a mature culture has already emerged out of its collective assumptions and aims for the implementation of its mandate and its interactions with public and private sector organizations. Beliefs about who and what the Board is as an organization, what it is trying to achieve and for whom, and what the environment is like, are all defining features of the organizational culture. The CEO and directors appear to be seeking a balance between rules and results, governance and growth, and principles and performance. They also need to strike a balance, as we will see in the next section, among the values of accountability and autonomy.

One deliberate choice informing the culture is to keep the number of staff low and the management expenses modest, especially in comparison to standard practices in the mutual fund industry. By keeping its staff small (less than 40), the Investment Board emulates private sector culture (and the recent public sector, in the age of downsizing), and retains flexibility as an organization. As well, a small, low-cost operation is meant to assure the public that their pension contributions are for the most part going into assets rather than administrative overheads. To achieve that, the Board has adopted the image of being a virtual corporation:

The CPP Investment Board is a virtual corporation with a small team of experienced professionals setting our operating and investment strategies and then retaining external organizations to help us to implement those strategies. We want to benefit by accessing and leveraging the best services available in the competitive marketplace rather than building a bureaucracy and expensive internal systems to do everything in-house ourselves. That way we can contain costs and focus on strategic investment decisions that can add significant long-term value.[16]

As a virtual corporation, the Board embraces a private market culture not only by staying small, but also with respect to investment rules and practices. The goal is to position the CPP Investment Board 'as a preferred investor for the top private equity managers and merchant banks in Canada and around the world.'[17] Since it is expected that about 20 years will elapse before investments begin to help pay for CPP pensions, the Board is 'a cash-rich investor' and has the ability to adopt a long-term time horizon for developing policies and making investment decisions. A sense of responsibility for the future is therefore part of the Board's culture.

The Board will, of course, meet all legislative and regulatory requirements, but beyond that, it also wants to be a leader with respect to ethical governance. In the words of the Board CEO, 'We intend to be a forthright public advocate of good governance because we accept the premise and the evidence that good governance policies and practices are a component in superior portfolio performance.'[18] The CEO also foresees the Board's being an advocate of 'proactive disclosure' and transparency of investment information. As the Senate Standing Committee observed, the Board was 'established at a time of high public cynicism about bureaucracy and governments at all levels. Thus, it is crucial that every aspect of the Board—the appointment of its directors, as well as all of its policies, procedures and methods of operation—be as transparent as possible.'[19]

Transparency entails openness, to be sure, but in addition it implies accessibility in a timely fashion by the general public to materials that are readily understandable, through regular reporting procedures and clear communications. Sections 50 and 51 of the legislation deal with public reporting provisions. To the federal minister of finance and the appropriate provincial ministers, the Board must provide quarterly financial statements within 45 days of the end of the quarterly period as well as an annual report on the operations of the Board within 90 days after the end of each financial year. The CPP Investment Board is the only pension fund in Canada required by law to produce such reports to ministers at both levels of government. The annual report includes the Board's auditor's report, statements of current and future Board objectives, and 'a certificate, signed by the director on the behalf of the board of directors, stating that the investments of the Board held during the year were in accordance with this Act and the Board's investment policies, standards and procedures' (s. 51 [3]). After receiving the annual report, the minister of finance is required to have it tabled before each house of Parliament within 15 days or, if the house is not sitting, at the beginning of its next session (s. 51 [2]).

The legislation further sets out requirements that 'the Board shall hold a public meeting once every two years in each participating province'. The purpose of this meeting is 'to discuss the Board's most recent annual report and to give interested persons an opportunity to comment on it'. One or more directors or officers of the Board are obliged, under the law, to attend each of these meetings and answer questions from the public, and make copies of the Board's most recent annual report available for distribution (s. 52). In 2001, the Board held its first series of bi-annual public meetings across the country in the capital of every province except Quebec (which administers the QPP). The Board Chair and CEO attended the meetings to explain the creation of the Board, its mandate, objectives, recent activities, and future priorities, and to discuss the annual report and give citizens a chance to ask questions and offer comments.

Beyond these legal requirements for transparency, which are quite extensive in themselves, the Board has adopted the practice of making public the quarterly financial statements provided to ministers, along with a summary of the CPP's public equities and private equity holdings, and the estimated market value of the government bonds and short-term securities it holds, updated quarterly. In May 2002, the Investment Board launched a new web site to implement a disclosure policy approved by the board of directors. The disclosure policy affirms that 'Canadians have the right to know why, how and where we invest their Canada Pension Plan money, who makes the investment decisions, what assets are owned on their behalf and how the investments are performing.'[20] While there are limits to disclosure, such as proposed investments and third-party confidences, the Board's practice does expand the scope of disclosure well beyond that provided by most other public and private sector corporations.

In the course of meeting its legal obligations and building trust with Canadians, the Board has devoted considerable time to establishing a working culture of integrity. The Canada Pension Plan Investment Board Act sets out conflict of interest provisions for both Board directors and officers that are stronger and more comprehensive than equivalent provisions in the Bank Act and the Canada Business Corporations Act.[21] The Investment Board has also developed codes of conduct, one for directors and another for management and employees, that address such issues as the confidentiality of third-party proprietary information, personal investments, and relations with suppliers. Each year all directors must submit signed, revised resumés noting any changes in their professional and financial relationships that might give rise to conflict. These submissions are reviewed by the governance committee of the board of directors. In addition, before directors may accept new directorships or other positions of authority in entities that may benefit them, they must notify the Board Chair. The Board has also established guidelines for officers concerning the disclosure of material inside information. They are required to submit monthly personal trading reports and annual statements of their securities holdings to the external auditor of the Board.

Whether an issue of ethical conduct or good governance is covered by legislation, regulations, or codes, the Investment Board has articulated three questions that directors and employees are expected to address: Is it legal? Is it in conflict with the best interests of the CPP beneficiaries and contributors? Will the action meet or exceed the standard of behaviour that might reasonably be expected of the CPP Investment Board by the Canadian public? These questions exemplify the culture of ethical governance the Board wishes to uphold.

Accountability Versus Autonomy

Interrelations between accountability and autonomy are a source of continuing tension in public administration: continuing, because in debates and situations that are never fully resolved governments need to strike some balance between holding an organization politically accountable and allowing it some degree of freedom of managerial action.

For the CPP Investment Board, accountability involves the duty to answer, explain, and justify to the federal government and nine participating provincial governments, through their finance ministers, and to Parliament, the exercise of public powers, the management and stewardship of public funds, and the pursuit of public policy objectives. Board directors and managers express a sense of accountability to the Canadian public, specifically to the 16 million CPP contributors and beneficiaries, and to younger Canadians, who will be drawing pensions based on the results of investment made by the Board over the next few decades.

In pension plan governance, fiduciary duty is central to accountability. In the Board's legislation, this concept is expressed in terms of a series of duties required of every director and officer of the Board: the duty of care, the duty to exercise one's relevant knowledge or special skill, and the duty to comply with the Act and the by-laws. In discharging their duty of care, for example, directors and officers are required to '(a) act honestly and in good faith with a view to the best interests of the Board; and (b) exercise the care, diligence and skill that a reasonably prudent person would exercise in comparable circumstances'.[22]

Other methods, expressed in the Act and Regulations, by which the Investment Board is held accountable to governments, Parliament, and the public include the following:

- every by-law made, amended, and repealed by the board of directors must be reported to the federal minister of finance and the provincial ministers within two weeks (s. 28);
- quarterly and annual financial statements must be submitted to federal and provincial ministers of finance (s. 39);
- internal audits of financial and management control and information systems and practices must be conducted;
- an annual auditor's report must be prepared in accordance with generally accepted auditing standards in Canada (s. 40, 41);
- an annual report must be prepared, containing a statement of the corporate governance practices of the board of directors, including the code of conduct, as well as information disclosing the total compensation awarded or paid to the directors and executive officers;

- a special audit of the Board or any of its subsidiaries may be conducted by an auditor appointed by the federal finance minister if considered necessary (s. 46);
- a special examination of the Board or any of its subsidiaries must be held at least once every six years, as decided by the minister of finance, to determine if the financial and management controls and information systems were 'maintained in a manner that provided reasonable assurance' that they safeguarded and controlled the Board's assets and that the Board's resources (human, financial, and physical) were managed economically, efficiently, and effectively (s. 47-49);
- public meetings must be held once every two years in each of the participating provinces (s. 52);
- the federal cabinet (Governor in Council) may make regulations, among other items, respecting the investments the Board may make. Any such regulation, however, 'has no force or effect until the appropriate provincial Minister of each of at least two thirds of the participating provinces having in total not less than two thirds of the population of all of the participating provinces has approved the regulation' (s. 53 [2]); and
- the minister of finance may, on giving the Board 30 days notice in writing, require a transfer of an amount from the Board to the CPP Account established under the Canada Pension Plan 'if the Minister considers that the transfer is necessary to meet any payment that is required to be made' under the CPP (s. 57).

Parliament plays a minor role in this system of accountability, and the provincial legislatures an even slighter part, one more piece of evidence of the dominance of the central government and of executive federalism in Canada.[23]

Autonomy customarily means operating at some distance from direct everyday control by government, and the rhetoric in relation to the Investment Board certainly reflects concern for that principle. CEO MacNaughton has gone so far to say that 'unless federal and provincial finance ministers and the Canadian public could be assured that the CPP Investment Board would be able to operate at arm's length from government, it would never have been born.' Public opinion remains strongly concerned about such political influence.[24] Autonomy is seen as critical to the ability of the Board to freely recruit well-qualified directors and management staff, and to develop an investment policy and then select investments as the Board and management see fit, governed by their duty of care rather than by partisan considerations in regard to one government or another. Some citizens may also fear that politicians would 'raid the CPP piggy bank' of growing assets and divert them to other political projects, a scenario that is expressly prohibited by the legislation.

Various checks and balances are in place to establish and maintain the relative autonomy of the Board so that it is free from direct daily governmental influence—so that, in effect, this public sector institution can operate like a private sector corporation. In addition to the fiduciary duties and the nomination process for Board directors outlined above, several devices exist for promoting autonomy while also promoting a private sector investment management ethos:

- the constitution of the Board specifies in the Act that it is not an agent of Her Majesty and that directors, officers, employees, and agents of the Board are not part of the public service of Canada (s. 3);
- the Investment Board, as a public program, is separate and distinct from the Canada Pension Plan. The administration, actuarial and policy review, setting of benefits and contribution rates, and appeals system associated with the CPP are the specific responsibility of other federal offices and departments;
- agents or employees of the federal or provincial governments, and members of the Senate or House of Commons or members of a provincial legislature are disqualified from being directors of the Investment Board (s. 9);
- the Access to Information Act, the Canada Corporations Act, the Financial Administration Act, and the Public Service Staff Relations Act, among other federal statutes, do not apply to the Board. This gives the Board, not the government, the authority to set budgets and to appoint an external auditor, the ability to recruit directors and professional investment managers, the power to formulate expansive disclosure policies, and the ability to determine compensation policies;
- the CEO is recruited by the board of directors, which, in turn, is responsible for pulling together the senior management team drawn from the private sector;
- the Board forges partnerships with private sector mutual fund and investment management firms nationally and internationally in order to implement the virtual corporation vision and the investment plans of the Board.

Symbolically as well as substantively, the Board's independence from government is also made apparent by the fact that the organization is located not in Ottawa but in downtown Toronto, in the heart of the country's main business and financial district.

TAKING ON THE MARKETS: STOCKING UP AND TAKING HITS

Under the Board's investment policy framework, categories of permitted investments include public equities (securities publicly traded on stock markets) in Canada, the United States, and elsewhere; private equities (securities not publicly traded), including venture capital and buyouts (investment in the purchase or takeover of a company); real assets, that is, real estate properties and capital-intensive infrastructure projects; nominal fixed income assets, which include cash and cash equivalents, such as short-term notes and treasury bills; and foreign currencies. The primary investment activity is overwhelmingly in public equities, with modest portions targeted for fixed income assets, private equities, and real assets. Investment in foreign currencies and foreign assets is limited by the federal government's 30 per cent foreign property rule, which applies to all pension funds and registered retirement savings plans. The federal government and participating provinces have set out quantitative limits to regulate the proportion of CPP assets the Board may direct to specific kinds of investments. These include no more than 10 per cent of the total book value of Board assets in the securities of any one person, two or more associated persons, or two or more affiliated corporations; no more than five per cent of the Board's assets in any one parcel of real property or Canadian resource property; no more than 15 per cent of Board assets in Canadian resource properties; and no more than 25 per cent of the Board's assets in real property and Canadian resource properties. The Investment Board is also prohibited from investing directly or indirectly in the securities of a corporation to which more than 30 per cent of the votes that may be cast to elect the directors of the corporation are attached.[25]

With these limitations, governments have set out some clear boundaries as to the potential power and influence of the CPP Investment Board within various sectors of the Canadian economy. Most Canadians, I think it is reasonable to suppose, would agree with the intent if not the specifics of such limits, and would regard these rules as a warranted exercise of political control.

In the most recent actuarial report on the current and projected financial status of the CPP, tabled in the House of Commons by the Finance Minister in December 2001, the Chief Actuary projected that the Investment Board will earn a long-term real rate of return of 4.25 per cent on the total portfolio. That is, presuming a certain asset mix, the return rate over and above the inflation rate for all the assets owned and/or controlled by the investment Board will be 4.25 per cent through the long term.[26] The Board itself tends to not make specific forecasts of investment returns, using instead the targets estimated by the Chief Actuary, while pointing out that yearly returns could vary extensively above or below this target.

Other noteworthy elements of the Board's investment policy framework include diversification, a move to active investing, a noncommittal position on ethical investing, and plans to expand investments in private markets:

- On the basis of the principle of diversification, the Board is supplementing the large existing asset base of government bonds, with their secure but modest returns, with equity investments in stock markets and private equities, which may be riskier but also promise higher returns over the long term. At present, the Board is only investing in equities to offset the dominance of the $30 billion in government bonds that the CPP holds. Diversification of the overall portfolio will increase the long-term value of funds and thus contribute to the financial sustainability of the Plan.[27]
- The Board is shifting from an entirely passive investment strategy to one that combines passive and active investing. Initially, the Board was limited, under regulations, to passive investing in Canadian and foreign public equities, which means replicating a stock index, such as the Toronto Stock Exchange 300 composite index or the Standard and Poor's 500 index of American stocks,

buying shares in exactly the same proportion as they are represented in the index. In August 2000, amended regulations took effect that let the Board actively manage up to half the assets it allocates to Canadian public equities. This allows the Board, through its managers and agents, to pick individual stocks with the aim of earning higher returns than the stock index. The Board is considering designing its own market indexes to better reflect its mandate and the broader economy.

- On the issue of ethical or social investing, CPP Investment Board policy says that the Board will 'consider as eligible for investment . . . (a) the securities of any issuer engaged in a business that is lawful in Canada; and (b) the securities of issuers in any country with which Canada maintains normal financial, trade and investment relations.' Thus, the Board will not invest in countries on which Canada has imposed financial, trade, or investment sanctions or restrictions. Endeavouring to take a neutral stance on the issue, the Board's policy states, on the one hand, that it will 'not give preference to or consider as ineligible for investment the securities of any issuer based on non-investment criteria', but, on the other hand, that it will 'generally support corporate policies and practices and shareholder resolutions that would result in the disclosure of information that would assist investors in assessing whether corporate behaviour was contributing to or detracting from long-term investment'. Considering social investment to be an idea that means different things to different people, the Board believes that it 'cannot reflect the divergent religious, economic, political, social and personal views of millions of Canadians in its investment decisions'.[28] The Board emphasizes that its fiduciary and statutory duties are to achieve a maximum rate of return without undue risk of loss, and that companies that act in a socially responsible manner tend to perform better over the long run. In this light, they do not see an inherent trade-off between social investing and investing in the best interests of the Plan members.

- While publicly traded securities in domestic and foreign stock markets form the heart of the Board's investment approach, in 2001 the Board announced that it plans to place up to 10 per cent of its assets, or $1.8 billion, in private market equities over the next five years. In the words of the Board's Vice President of Private Market Investments, 'Structured appropriately, private equities offer superior returns relative to public equities and fixed-income securities and provide some risk diversification to our portfolio. Our target for these investments is to exceed inflation by 8 per cent annually over a 10 year period.'[29] Venture capital to new companies, expansion capital to more established firms, and buyouts and acquisitions: pooled funds of this kind are the private equity investments that the CPP Investment Board is now making. In time, this may well mean that the Board will acquire ownership interests in real estate and a diverse range of natural resource projects and properties. The Board is applying its 'virtual corporation model' by forging partnerships with private market experts in North America and Europe. As of November 2002, the Board had pledged $4.9 billion, to be drawn over the next several years, to limited partnerships managed by 28 private equity firms. To date, $1.1 billion has been invested in private equities, compared with $15.8 billion in publicly traded equities on the stock markets. The move to private equities is seen as a way to offset recent instability in stock markets.[30]

The CPP Investment Board made its first investment of $12.1 million in the equity markets in March 1999. By March 2000, the cumulative total invested in the markets was $2.4 billion, growing to $7.2 billion in March 2001, then reaching $14.3 billion in March 2002 and $17.1 billion in June 2002. This stream of capital investments has altered the overall mix of assets available to the CPP. Fixed income, such as bonds, has gone from 86 per cent of consolidated assets in 2001 to 69 per cent in 2003, with equities rising correspondingly from 14 per cent to 31 per cent of the portfolio. The Board expects to receive between $6 billion and $8 billion each year in new cash, all of which will be invested in markets.

The performance of the assets managed by the Investment Board from 1999 to the latest quarter of 2002 is presented in Table 9.1. The Board has experienced a varied and challenging investment market, with both gains and losses, in its early years. To September 2002, the latest reporting period, the Board has an accumulated loss of $4.1 billion over the last two quarters, as a result of the severe volatility of equity markets in Canada, the United States, and elsewhere. Economic slowdowns, declines, and market uncertainties characterized many economies in the later part of 2001 and through 2002. To put the Board's performance in some comparative context, their results largely mirror the benchmark returns of the major stock

Table 9.1
Performance of CPP Investment Board Equities

Results/Year	1999	2000	2001	2002	2003*	Since Inception (Annualized)
Investment Income/(loss) ($ billions)	**	0.5	(0.8)	0.3	(4.1)	N/A
Portfolio Returns (%)	5.0	40.1	(9.4)	3.4	(20.5)	2.6
Benchmark Returns (%)	4.7	39.3	(17.8)	2.4	(20.7)	(0.8)
Assets ($ billions)	0.01	2.4	7.2	14.3	16.9	N/A

*2003 is year to date, April to September 2002.
**$200,000 for one month of investing.
Source: Canada Pension Plan Investment Board, 'Results', at web site http://www.cppib.ca/invest/results/index.htm

indexes in Canada and the Unites States—understandably so, since, as noted earlier, the Board engages in passive investing. Other large public pension funds, such as the Ontario Teachers Pension Plan and the Quebec Pension Plan, and related government investment funds, such as the Alberta Heritage Savings Trust Fund, have also experienced negative returns and actual declines in assets in recent years.

As the CPP Investment Board President and CEO remarked a short time ago, 'we have just come through one of the worst periods for equity markets in the last 100 years', a thorny situation to be sure, but one that presents a great opportunity for a cash-rich investor like the CPP Board to buy undervalued shares. 'We expect these wide swings in performance to continue as we methodically build a broadly based equity portfolio that will provide superior returns over the long term. We have 20 years before we are expected to provide income to the Canada Pension Plan to help pay pensions, so we are in a highly advantageous position as an equity buyer.'[31] While the Board's equity portfolio grows, quarterly gains (and losses) may amount to several billion dollars, which will present the Board with a public education challenge. The challenge is to reassure Canadians about the inevitable realities of market swings, with the associated opportunities, and the underlying logic of long-term and diversified investment in stocks and private equities as well as in bonds and guaranteed income certificates. Perhaps an effective example of this educational task is the point made by the CEO that the $4.1 billion loss does not mean cash gone forever, but rather a decline in the value of equities and shares held in major corporations, which, experience tells us, will recover and expand.[32]

TAKING STOCK: AN EXPANSIONIST DYNAMIC?

The CPP Investment Board was established in response to the perceived funding crisis of the Plan, which was looming a decade or so ahead. Reforms to the CPP in 1997 involved a combination of actions: (a) some program retrenchment on the benefit side, (b) a strong defence of the Plan itself by the public and interest groups, which was acknowledged by governments, and resulted in the maintenance of benefits for current pensioners, and (c) innovations to the financing, lending, and investing features of the Plan. It is these new departures on the fiscal side of the CPP, specifically the formation of the Investment Board, that has been our concern in this chapter. The mandate and operation of the Board does not signal a threatening break with the goals and methods of the CPP as a social insurance pension plan; rather it is supportive of them. For the Board, making a solid return on investments is serving the public purpose of maintaining this essential component in Canada's retirement income system. In short, the CPP fund is subject to fluctuations in market value, but over the long term it will be available for meeting pension obligations for today's younger workers.

Since its inception in 1966, the CPP's goals have been to provide a modest level of retirement pensions and supplementary benefits to working Canadians and their families, and to provide a source of capital to the participating provinces for financing public infrastructure projects and public services. With these latest reforms and the establishment of the Board, the Plan has added a third policy goal: that of providing a source of funds to invest in the private sector in Canada and internationally so as to promote capital accumulation. Thus, a major reason for creating the Investment Board was to ensure the long-term financial sustainability of this national social program. No doubt a wish to separate this investment function from direct political control and to draw in skilled business people as directors and financial managers were other motivations for the specific organizational form the Board has taken and the culture it has developed.

On the issue of the balance between accountability and autonomy, the emphasis for the Investment Board is on autonomy in relation to the political executives. A federal Crown corporation with its own enabling legislation, the Board belongs to the federal state and the nine participating provincial states. While it is definitely an instrument of public policy and part of Canada's public sector, the Board operates at a distance from these governments and is certainly not exclusively or even tightly controlled by them. Board directors are nominated and appointed by a unique process, and the CEO is appointed by the directors rather than by a minister. The auditor, in this case a private firm rather than the Office of the Auditor General of Canada, is also appointed by the board of directors.

Over the next decade, in the face of financial success by the Board and assets considerably exceeding $100 billion, we can expect more public interest in the expansion of CPP benefits and more policy debates about the subject than before. If the federal-provincial aspect of the CPP, with its divided jurisdiction, has insulated this pension scheme from pressures for expansion, then the market investment aspect might expose the CPP to pressures to liberalize benefits. While it has been argued in the past that executive federalism has been a conservative force in pension policy, equity capitalism may facilitate an expansionist dynamic leading to reforms.[33] With a growing pool of assets from market and private equity investments, it may be that the social policy aspects of the program will be less overshadowed by budgetary concerns. The success of the Board will elevate the political and financial feasibility of reformist ideas regarding more generous CPP benefits in the coming decades. Expanding the modest earnings-replacement rate of the CPP will become a more attractive idea to many and perhaps an easier 'sell' to governments. Pressure for public pension reform will be reinforced by the continued inadequate coverage of workers offered by private pension plans and the inability of many Canadians with low or modest incomes to take advantage of registered retirement savings plans. Any improvements to the pension plan would not necessarily require provinces to repay borrowings from the Plan earlier than scheduled; instead, such improvements could conceivably come from a surplus derived from strong real rates of return on CPP assets. Furthermore, a liberalization of CPP retirement or disability benefits could take pressure off such provincial programs as workers' compensation, social assistance, and related supplement programs for seniors and persons with disabilities. We may once again have a great pension debate in Canada.

NOTES

1 Senate of Canada, *The Governance Practices of Institutional Investors*, Report of the Standing Senate Committee on Banking, Trade and Commerce, Nov. 1998, Issue no. 40, Proceedings, p. 14.
2 The Hon. Paul Martin, *Budget Speech* (Ottawa: Department of Finance, 27 Feb. 1995), 20.
3 The Hon, Paul Martin, *Budget Speech* (Ottawa: Department of Finance, 6 Mar. 1996), 3, 12.
4 The Hon. Paul Martin, 'Notes for Remarks Before the Senate Standing Committee on Finance on Bill C-2' (Ottawa: Department of Finance, 28 Oct. 1997), 2–3.
5 For the first three-year period (1998–2001), provinces were guaranteed access to half of the new CPP funds that the Investment Board chose to invest in bonds. Since then, new CPP funds invested in provincial securities are limited to the share of provincial and municipal bonds held by other Canadian pension funds. Existing provincial bonds held under the CPP as of March 1997 could be rolled over for one additional 20-year term, although they are now subject to prevailing market interest rates.
6 The delay in the implementation of the governance and investment provisions was agreed to by the Finance Minister in response to a request by the Standing Senate Committee on Banking, Trade and Commerce to study these aspects of the legislation. Senate of Canada, *The Canada Pension Plan Investment Board: Getting It Right*, Report of the Standing Senate Committee on Banking, Trade and Commerce, Issue no. 16, Proceedings, 23 Apr. 1998. The Senators held hearings in Toronto, Halifax, Calgary, Vancouver, and Ottawa, and heard from several academics, a few think tanks, various pension funds, and Finance Canada officials. The Committee examined the issues of transparency and accountability, the appointment of directors, the audit function, conflict of interest, and the foreign property rule on investments.
7 Association of Canadian Pension Management, *Governance of Pension Plans* (Toronto, 1997), 4. See also Senate of Canada, *The Governance Practices of Institutional Investors*; Pension Investment Association of Canada, *Effective Pension Plan Governance* (Toronto, 1997); Office of the Superintendent of Financial Institutions, *Guidelines for Governance of Federally Regulated Pension Plans* (Ottawa, 1998).
8 John A. MacNaughton, 'Building Excellence in Governance, Management and Accountability in the Public Sector', Remarks to the CCAF-FCVI National Conference, 19 Mar. 2001, 8. Available at web site http://www.cppib.ca/media/031901J_SP.htm
9 See 'Great Expectations', *Report on Business Magazine, The Globe and Mail* [Toronto], Feb. 2002.
10 Canada Pension Plan Investment Board Act, 1997, sections 5 and 6.
11 Canada Pension Plan Investment Board, *Investment Statement* (Toronto, 10 Apr. 2002), 2.
12 John A. MacNaughton, 'Helping to Keep the Long-Term Pension Promise to Canadians', Keynote Address to the Canadian Association of Financial Planners, Montreal, 8 June 2001.

13 For more details on the qualifications and considerations used in the appointment process, see Department of Finance Canada, 'CPP Investment Board of Directors Announces' and 'The Canada Pension Plan Investment Board: Criteria for the Selection of Candidates for the Board of Directors', *News Release 98–108*, 28 Oct. 1998. Available at web site http://www.fin.gc.ca/news/98-108e.html

14 Department of Finance Canada, 'Directors of the Canada Pension Plan Investment Board: Biographical Sketches', *News Release 98–108*; 'New Appointments and Reappointments to the Canada Pension Plan Investment Board', *News Release 2001–030* (22 Mar. 2001). Available at web site http://www.fin.gc.ca/news.01/01-030e.html

15 MacNaughton, 'Building Excellence', 2. Available at web site http://www.cppib.ca.media/031901J_SP.htm

16 John A. MacNaughton, quoted in 'CPP Investment Board Retains External Expertise to Provide Key Services', CPP *Investment Board News Release* (21 Feb. 2002), 1. Available at web site http://www.cppib.ca/info/releases.

17 John A. MacNaughton, 'Helping to Keep the Long-Term Pension Promise to Canadians', *New Release*, 8 June 2001.

18 John A. MacNaughton, CPP *Investment Board News Release*, 4 May 2000, 1. Available at web site http://www.cppib.ca/info/releases.

19 Senate of Canada, *The Governance Practices of Institutional Investors*, 2.

20 'CPP Investment Board Announces Expansive Disclosure on Web Site,' CPP *Investment Board News Release*, 25 Apr. 2002, 1. Available at web site http://www.cppib.ca/info/releases. See also Rob Carrick, 'New Web Site Takes Mystery Out of CPP Investing', *The Globe and Mail* [Toronto], 16 May 2002, B22.

21 See *Discussion Paper on Conflicts of Interest* (Toronto: CPP Investment Board, Sept. 2002). Section 54 of the Canada Pension Plan Investment Act provides that 'every director, officer, employee, agent or auditor of the board who, in carrying out their duties, approves, prepares or concurs in any statement that contains false or deceptive information is guilty of an offence. On summary conviction, a person is liable of a fine up to $100,000 or imprisonment for up to one year, and for the corporate entity a fine of up to $500,000'.

22 Canada Pension Plan Investment Board Act, s. 14. For a fuller discussion of fiduciary duties in pension plans, see Pension Investment Association of Canada, *Effective Pension Plan Governance*, 4.

23 Parliament is guaranteed, under section 39 of the Act, to receive the annual reports of the Board, and under section 55 the affairs of the Board cannot be wound up unless Parliament provides. There is no statutory requirement to refer the annual reports to an appropriate committee in the House of Commons or the Senate, nor, of course, to the legislatures of the participating provinces. This issue was raised by academics and others at the time that Bill C-2 established the Board, but with no effect on government policy or public attention at the time. See the Standing Senate Committee, *The Canada Pension Plan Investment Board*.

24 MacNaughton, 'Building Excellence', 3. See also EKOS, *Public Opinion*, 100–1.

25 *Canada Pension Plan Investment Board Regulations*, P.C. 1999-731, 22 Apr. 1999, s. 11, 12, 13. Available at web site http://www.laws.justice.gc.ca/en/C-83/SOR-99-190/40914.htm.

26 Office of the Superintendent of Financial Institutions, Office of the Chief Actuary, *Eighteenth Actuarial Report on the Canada Pension Plan, as at 31 December 2000* (Ottawa: Public Works and Government Services Canada, 2001). Interestingly, inde-

pendent actuaries would have selected an assumed real rate of return on CPP assets about 0.5 to 0.75 per cent higher than that figure.

27 Over the 1996 to 2000 period, long-term Canadian bonds had a 3.5 per cent annual real rate of return, whereas Canadian stocks had a 5.2 per cent rate and American stocks a 7.4 per cent rate. Canadian Institute of Actuaries, *Report on Canadian Economic Statistics*, available at web site www.actuaries.ca.

28 Canada Pension Plan Investment Board, *Social Investing Policy*, 6 Mar. 2002, 1–2. Available at web site http://www.cppib.ca. Public survey research by EKOS has found that ethical investing 'is not novel to many Canadians' and 'that large numbers of Canadians are sympathetic to the idea', although the survey did not specifically probe public views on what the stance of the CPP Investment Board should be with respect to ethical or social investing. See EKOS, *Public Opinion*, 44–5. For further discussion and a position similar to the Board's, see the Standing Senate Committee reports, *The Canada Pension Plan Investment Board*, 24, and *The Governance Practices*, 26–7.

29 Mark Weisdorf, quoted in 'CPP Investment Board to Enhance Returns Through Private Equity Investments', *News Release*, Toronto, 26 June 2001, 1. Available at web site http:www.cppib/ca/media..

30 'CPP Investment Board Expands Investments to Offset Volatile Markets', *News Release*, 13 Nov. 2002. Available at web site http://www.cppib/ca/info/releases.

31 John A. MacNaughton, quoted in 'CPP Assets Report Loss During One of the Worst Equity Markets in a Century', CPP Investment Board *News Release*, 12 Nov. 2002, 1. Available at web site http://www.cppib/ca/info/releases. See also Carolyn Leitch, 'CPP Board Loses $4 Billion on Stocks', *The Globe and Mail* [Toronto], 13 Nov. 2002, B16.

32 John A. MacNaughton, *Remarks on Bill C-3 to the House of Commons Finance Committee*, 26 Nov. 2002, 12. Available at web site http://www.cppib/ca/news.

33 On the conservatism of federalism for pension reform, see Keith G. Banting, *The Welfare State and Canadian Federalism*, 2nd edn (Kingston and Montreal: McGill-Queen's University Press, 1987).

10

'Smart Money?' Government Spending on Student Financial Aid in Canada

ROSS FINNIE, SAUL SCHWARTZ, AND ERIC LASCELLES

INTRODUCTION[1]

The 1990s was a decade of significant change for student finances and student financial aid in Canada. Tuition fees rose sharply. Many provincial grant programs were replaced with loan programs. Various debt reduction measures were introduced in response to public concern about mounting levels of borrowing. The basic structure of the Canada Student Loans Program (CSLP) changed twice, and most provincial loan programs moved in tandem with it. Interest relief programs for those experiencing difficulties with the repayment of their loans after leaving school were expanded. The Canada Millennium Scholarship Foundation came into existence and injected substantial new resources into the system. Existing tax credits (and therefore tax expenditures) related to educational spending were increased, and new ones introduced.

Our goal here is, first, to estimate the amount of government spending, in the 2000/1 fiscal year, on student financial aid programs. Our definition of student financial aid includes not only the usual candidates, such as student loan and grant programs, but also some less obvious ones, such as the various tax credits available to students and their families.

The results are interesting, and perhaps surprising. For example, the tax expenditures generated by the recently enhanced tuition and educational expense credits and the newly introduced tax credit for student loan interest now constitute almost 40 per cent of all government spending on student financial aid. And even though federal and provincial student loan programs and other more traditional types of spending remain important, the structure of that spending has changed in some significant ways. At the same time, a substantial and growing proportion of direct student aid spending is not based on students' need.

We hope that our estimates will provide an empirical basis for policy discussions related to student financial aid. For example, tax credits are equally available to students and families of all income levels, but provide no assistance in the absence of a tax liability, so that very low-income individuals do not benefit. For those in greatest need, then, this form of spending to deliver financial assistance is a relatively blunt instrument. Is this the best way to spend money on student financial assistance? Our estimates provide an empirical basis for such discussions.

The two following sections will introduce the concepts underlying our spending estimates and describe the amounts involved in the various categories of spending used here. These categories are

- *student loan costs*, which include in-school interest subsidies, loan default costs, and means-tested post-schooling debt relief programs;
- *grants* of all types;
- *loan remission* programs, which reduce the amount of student loans that needs to be repaid, without regard to the individual's ability to do so;
- *tax expenditures*, which represent the reductions in government tax revenues associated with various tax credits available to students and their families.[2]

Spending is broken down by level of government—federal, provincial, and territorial—and by spending category. Our estimates are shown in Table 10.1.

In the final section, we set out our major findings and draw out various policy implications. This discussion is intended only to raise some of the relevant issues; it does not pretend to resolve them. It is worth repeating that the more modest goal of this chapter is to provide an empirical basis for policy discussions in the months and years to come, while raising some specific policy-related questions that stem directly from our findings.

UNDERLYING CONCEPTS

Any attempt to estimate government spending on post-secondary education must make various assumptions and adopt certain definitions. In this section, we discuss the ones we have chosen. At the same time, we acknowledge that others might choose different ones.

Table 10.1

Government Spending on Student Financial Aid 2000–2001
($millions, percentages in brackets)

	A CMSF as Provincial Spending*		B CMSF as Federal Spending*		
	Provinces	*Federal*	*Provinces*	*Federal*	*Total*
Loan Programs					
Default Costs	165.3	185.4	165.3	185.4	**350.7**
In-school Interest Subsidy	202.3	235.2	202.3	235.2	**437.5**
Interest Relief	45.5	107.4	45.5	107.4	**152.9**
Debt Reduction in Repayment	0.3	2.0	0.3	2.0	**2.3**
	413.4	**530.0**	**413.4**	**530.0**	**943.4**
	(19.1%)	(21.1%)	(22.0%)	(19.0%)	(20.2%)
Grants					
CMSF**	252.9	0.0	0.0	252.9	**252.9**
CESG**		301.0		301.0	**301.0**
Science		196.7		196.7	**196.7**
Aboriginal (PSSSP/UCEP)		288.0		288.0	**288.0**
CSG**		81.1		81.1	**81.1**
Provincial Programs	440.3		440.3		**440.3**
	693.2	**866.8**	**440.3**	**1119.7**	**1560.0**
	(32.1%)	(34.6%)	(23.4%)	(40.1%)	(33.4%)
Loan Remission					
CMSF**	31.3	0.0	0.0	31.3	**31.3**
Other	394.0	9.4	394.0	9.4	**403.4**
	425.3	**9.4**	**394.0**	**40.7**	**434.7**
	(19.7%)	(0.4%)	(21.0%)	(1.5%)	(9.3%)
Tax Expenditures					
RESP**		71.0		71.0	**71.0**
Tuition and Educ. Tax Credit		865.0		865.0	**865.0**
Student Loan Interest Credit		45.0		45.0	**45.0**
Other	630.0	119.9	630.0	119.9	**749.9**
	630.0	**1100.9**	**630.0**	**1100.9**	**1730.9**
	(29.1%)	(43.9%)	(33.6%)	(39.4%)	(37.1%)
Total	**2161.9**	**2507.1**	**1877.7**	**2791.3**	**4669.0**

Note:

*Canada Millenium Scholarship Foundation spending is recorded as provincial spending in Panel A (since spending decisions are made at the provincial level) and as federal spending in Panel B (since the money originated at the federal level).

**CMSF is Canada Millennium Scholarship Foundation; CESG is Canada Education Savings Grant; CSG is Canada Study Grant; RESP is Registered Education Savings Plan.

We want to estimate government spending in support of post-secondary education. There is, however, a fine line between post-secondary education and vocational training. We have adopted the expedient of defining post-secondary education as any schooling that would qualify students for a loan from the CSLP. Such a definition means that, in principle, we include expenditures on individuals who are

- enrolled in a public or private post-secondary institution that is accredited by the province for the purposes of the CSLP;
- enrolled in a program leading to a degree or certificate;
- studying at a level of intensity greater than one full-year course (20 per cent of a full-time load).

In practice, this definition leads us to exclude government spending on short vocational training programs, courses provided by social programs to help their clients learn about parenting or how to live with particular disabilities, and various other shorter and less formal programs. Note, however, that many conventional vocationally oriented programs are included, as long as they meet the above criteria. While these other forms of education might be of interest, adopting the CSLP definition seemed preferable to making our own distinctions between education and training, and then attempting to adjust the spending figures accordingly.

We count government *spending* on student financial aid, not what students or their families actually *receive*. For example, we calculate the costs associated with loan programs, such as the in-school interest subsidy and the losses due to default, but do not report the amount of lending itself. For grant programs, the amounts spent and received coincide, since each dollar of spending represents a dollar in students' pockets.[3] Administrative costs are not included.

This chapter thus addresses the question: 'What do governments spend on direct student financial aid?' rather than 'How many dollars do students receive?' or 'What is the benefit of the aid received?'

Governments can ease the financial burden on students in various ways. One very important way of doing so is to keep tuition low, and some provinces have maintained lower fees precisely in order to enhance accessibility to the post-secondary system. This money does not, however, go directly to students, and therefore does not constitute a direct form of support and is not counted here. Neither do we consider general spending on post-secondary education, including institutional grants, even though some of that money is spent on student assistance.

There are some types of government spending that might arguably be considered direct student financial aid but that is not counted as such in this chapter. For example, we do not count spending on student employment or 'work study' programs, because students must work for the money and might well have been hired in the absence of such programs. Another, perhaps more important 'debatable' category is the tax expenditure created by the federal and provincial sales tax (GST and PST/HST) that is not charged on tuition fees. Finally, consider the Ontario policy of requiring that institutions earmark 30 per cent of recent tuition fee increases for student financial aid, administered at the institutional level. In one sense, this represents government money spent on student financial aid, and should be counted as such. However, these funds effectively come from other students, and we do not count the amount spent as direct student aid.

Our analysis is limited to amounts spent on students (and their families) *because* they are students. We do not try to calculate spending on students net of what might have been spent had they not been students. For example, there are students who might have ended up collecting unemployment insurance benefits if they had not been in school. We cannot know, and do not attempt to unravel, such behavioural relationships. In short, we adopt an 'accounting' approach, as opposed to a 'counter-factual' approach.

We focus on identifying government spending on student financial aid in the 2000/1 fiscal year.[4] This period is current enough to be relevant, while sufficiently distant that the spending amounts are available in most cases. In some instances, data from other years were used because of the unavailability of 2000/1 data.

THE SPENDING CATEGORIES

Not surprisingly, there are many types of direct student financial aid, even when restricted in the ways just discussed. To give some order to the plethora of programs, we have divided them into the categories listed in the introduction. For each category, this section

- describes the spending category;
- lists recent policy and programmatic changes; and
- provides our estimates of the amounts spent in each category.

Student Loan Costs

Student loan costs, as defined here, consist of three principal elements: in-school interest subsidies; the costs of loan defaults; programs that provide help to borrowers in repayment.[5] We estimate that government spending on student loan programs, excluding administrative costs, was almost $1 billion in 2000/1 (Table 10.1).

The CSLP is the major provider of student loans at the federal level; in addition, each province has its own loan program, which is harmonized, to varying degrees, with the CSLP.[6] Since the beginning of the 1990s, student loans have been issued under four different regimes. Before 1995, private financial institutions issued student loans. Government agencies—both federal and provincial—guaranteed these loans by committing themselves to buying defaulted loans, at full value (including outstanding interest), from the lending institution.[7] From 1995 to 2000, instead of acting as guarantor the government paid the lenders a 5 per cent 'risk premium' on all loans going into repayment in a given year. In return, the banks assumed full responsibility for collection. When the 1995–2000 agreement ended, an interim arrangement was put into place whereby the government lent directly to students and assumed full responsibility for all new loans issued.[8] Since 2001, the government has issued student loans directly and assigned their management and collection to private companies brought into existence for this purpose. While these major changes in the delivery of student loans were going on, however, the other parameters of the loan system, such as the loan limits and the criteria for determining 'need', remained relatively constant.

In-school Interest Subsidies

In-school interest subsidies represent interest payments made on behalf of student borrowers while they are in school on a full-time basis.[9] These payments represent a substantial benefit to students, if a rarely acknowledged one, and comprise a significant share of the overall costs of student loan programs. The in-school interest subsidies for 2000/1 represent subsidies on all outstanding 'in-school' loans and thus correspond to loans issued in a number of different years.[10] In most cases, estimates of the interest subsidy costs were obtained directly from the CSLP and its provincial counterparts. For the CSLP, we used the amount reported to have been spent in 2000/1 for in-school interest subsidies—$235.2 million. With the exception of one large jurisdiction, all provinces and territories provided a comparable amount of spending on the in-school interest subsidy. By combining those amounts with an estimate for the missing province we were able to produce an estimate of provincial spending on in-school interest of $202.3 million.

Default Costs

Default costs arise when students do not meet their loan payments in the post-schooling period. These costs are surprisingly difficult to quantify, at least partly because loan default is a dynamic process, in which students can fail to make the required payments at any point in the payback period. Subsequent collection efforts can then extend over a number of years as loans are passed among various public authorities and collection agencies.[11]

The task is further complicated by the fact that four different lending regimes have been in place in recent years, and current loan portfolios include loans issued under each regime. More specifically, the FY 2000/1 default costs include

- the purchase of loans issued by private financial institutions under the pre-1995 regime, net of collection on these defaulted loans;
- the payment of the 5 per cent risk premium on loans issued under the 1995–2000 rules, as those loans come into repayment; and
- the allocation of money that must now, by rule, be set aside for future default costs on loans issued under both the interim and direct lending schemes in place since August 2000.

Because governments are paying for past and future loans at the same time, spending in any one year is not necessarily representative of any stable long-run situation. Our approach in estimating CSLP loan costs is, therefore, to use the set-asides for new lending, established under instructions from the Office of the Auditor General, and to ignore all losses, recoveries, and payments pertaining to loans issued in previous years.[12] This amount was $185.4 million, or 11.2 per cent of the value of loans issued in 2000/1.

Given the absence of comparable data for most of the provinces, and after experimenting with a variety of estimates, we decided, in the end, to use a very simple estimation technique. We estimated the provincial loan costs as 11.2 per cent of the value of provincial student loans disbursed in 2000/1.[13] Using that method, we estimate overall provincial default costs to be $165.3 million.

Interest Relief and Debt Reduction in Repayment
Interest relief and debt reduction in repayment programs help students deemed to be experiencing difficulties in meeting their post-schooling loan payments. Among the criteria for deciding whether or not a borrower is experiencing difficulty are the borrower's income and debt level. As a result, students with similar debt loads receive different levels of aid, depending on their income (that is, more aid goes to the lower-income students).

Interest relief programs were originally created for disadvantaged students (for example, students with disabilities or unemployed students). In 1997, the maximum period during which a borrower could use the CSLP Interest Relief program was extended to 30 months. Then, as part of the 'The Canadian Opportunities Strategy', announced in the 1998 budget speech, the Interest Relief program was made more generous. The maximum period of participation was increased to 54 months, and the income thresholds used to determine eligibility were raised by 9 per cent. Also, a new 'debt reduction in repayment' program was introduced, in which a specified amount of debt can be forgiven when an individual has faced a prolonged period of hardship. Most provinces have Interest Relief programs that are variants of the CSLP program.

Spending on these two types of programs is not very large, but represents an important form of support to needy individuals. Expenditures on the CSLP Interest Relief program were $107.4 million in 2000/1; the combined provincial spending was $45.5 million. Because the debt reduction in repayment programs are new and because they do not 'kick in' until borrowers have exhausted their eligibility for interest relief, very little was spent on these programs in 2000/1—$2.0 million by the CSLP and $0.3 million by the one province that reported spending in this category.

A combination of the sub-categories of student loan cost estimates—interest subsidies, default costs, and interest relief—yields a total federal expenditure estimate of $530.0 million and a combined provincial expenditure estimate of $413.4 million.

Grants

Grants are defined here in a straightforward manner—money given with no obligation to repay. Combining both federal and provincial grants, Table 10.1 indicates that more than $1.5 billion in grant aid was offered to Canadian students in 2000/1.

We include awards based on both need and merit. Some are available to the general population, while others are aimed at specific groups, such as students with disabilities, First Nations students, and women in certain doctoral programs. Also included are various provincial programs, the federal research granting agencies (including NSERC, SSHRC, CIHR), other federal agencies (such as CIDA), Canadian Education Savings Grants, and others.[14]

The Canadian Millennium Scholarship Foundation

An important new source of direct student financial aid is the Canadian Millennium Scholarships Foundation (CMSF). Created in 1998 as part of 'The Canadian Opportunities Strategy', the CMSF tries to increase access to post-secondary education by reducing student indebtedness. It began disbursing funds to students early in 2000, and will last for ten years. The initial CMSF endowment from the federal government was $2.5 billion, and its spending comes out of this capital and the return on this investment. CMSF spending amounted to $284.2 million in 2000/1.

The essence of the method of 'reducing student indebtedness', agreed between the CMSF and the provinces, was to allow each province to determine how much each student was eligible to borrow and then to use CMSF 'bursaries' to replace part of that potential borrowing with grants. In cases where the student never takes out the loan, this assistance might be called 'the *ex ante* substitution of grants for loans' and might therefore be counted as a 'grant'. A 'grant' of this type, however, does not usually result in more money being immediately available to students. Instead, the ultimate cost of education is reduced, because the amount borrowed is reduced. In other cases, CMSF spending takes the form of more traditional grants, including the 'excellence awards' and needs-based grants. Of the $284.2 million spent by the CMSF, we categorized $252.9 million as 'grant' spending.[15]

Federal Grant Programs

Apart from the CMSF, we identified four major federal grant programs. First, the Canada Education Savings Grant (CESG) program—yet another part of the 1998 Canadian Opportunities Strategy—provides a grant of 20 cents for each dollar deposited in an RESP, up to a maximum of $400 per year per beneficiary. In 2000/1, $301.0 million was spent on the CESG. Secondly, there is a substantial federal grant program—$288.0 million—for Aboriginal students.[16] 'Science grants' of $196.7 million form a third category; this category encompasses a variety of grants offered by federal government departments in support of post-secondary students.[17] Finally, the CSLP administers a grant program called 'Canada Study Grants', which provides aid to a number of specifically targeted groups; there are Canada Study Grants for 'students with dependents' and for 'women in doctoral studies'. Spending on Canada Study Grants in 2000/1 was $81.1 million.

If the $252.9 million in CMSF bursaries is included as federal spending, our overall estimate of federal grant spending is $1,119.7 million. If the CMSF bursaries are counted as provincial spending, the federal estimate falls to $866.8 million.

Provincial Grant Programs

In the early 1990s, some provinces, including Ontario, transformed existing grant programs into loan programs. Other provinces—Quebec, Alberta, and British Columbia—continued to offer substantial grant aid. In 2000/1, this overall pattern can still be seen. Excluding CMSF spending, Quebec gives out by far the largest amount of grants, followed by Alberta and British Columbia. Grant programs in Ontario and in the Maritime provinces are relatively small. Overall, we estimate that spending on provincial grants was $440.3 million, excluding CMSF awards. If CMSF awards are included in provincial spending, the estimate rises to $693.2 million.

Loan Remission

Loan remission represents the forgiveness of all or part of an existing student loan. Such aid is different from the *ex ante* substitution of grants for loans discussed above, in that the latter replaces loans with grants before the loans actually come to exist (or very soon thereafter). Loan remission is also different from interest relief and debt reduction in repayment programs in that the latter are available only to individuals judged to be experiencing difficulties with debt repayment, whereas loan remission is generally granted before repayment begins and is based only on the level of debt, with no regard to the individual's ability to repay.[18] Overall, we estimate that the provinces spent $394.0 million on loan remission, if we exclude CMSF awards that we categorize as debt remission, and $425.3 million if we include the CMSF awards.[19]

Loan remission programs take several different forms. Some provinces forgive a certain amount of debt when borrowing is above a specified threshold at the time of graduation. Others base the amount of remission on the amount borrowed within a one- or two-year period. Still others remit part of the outstanding loan for those who finish their studies in a timely fashion.

We define debt remission programs by their form and function and not necessarily by what they are called. A good case in point is the Ontario Student Opportunity Grant (OSOG) program, which repays, on behalf of the borrower, the amount by which Ontario Student Loans exceed $7,000 per year, as long as the student successfully completes the year of study. We classify OSOG as a debt remission program rather than a grant program.

Ontario's OSOG is by far the largest debt remission program, although the western provinces also spend substantial amounts. Quebec spends relatively little, but it should be noted that Quebec has much more generous grant programs and lower tuition for in-province students; this results in less debt, and therefore less debt to remit.

Tax Expenditures

The personal income tax system in Canada provides assistance to students and their families through various deductions, credits, exemptions, and deferrals. In general, these provisions result in 'tax expenditures', defined as 'the values of tax revenues forgone in order to achieve a variety of economic and social objectives'.[20] Tax expenditures can be viewed as 'direct spending programs delivered through the tax system', and those related to post-secondary education are in this sense little different from traditional direct student aid programs.[21] Table 10.1 indicates that tax expenditures on education-related credits are very substantial—$1,100.9 million in 2000/1 at the federal level and another $630.0 million at the provincial level.

By and large, Canadian tax expenditures originate in the federal income tax code. But because provincial taxes are linked directly to federal taxes, tax expenditures at the federal level also result in provincial tax expenditures. Quebec, having its own tax system, also has its own set of tax expenditures, and certain other provinces have their own education-related tax provisions in addition to those that derive from the federal system.

The most important tax expenditures related to post-secondary education are three non-refundable income tax credits related to tuition fees, education expenses, and student loan interest.

In 2000, the tuition tax credit allowed the deduction of 17 per cent of the amount paid for tuition fees and mandatory ancillary fees (such as those imposed for the use of libraries or laboratories) from the amount of tax payable.[22] These credits accrue to the students themselves, but unused credits, up to a maximum of $5,000, can be transferred to parents or grandparents, to spouses, or to the spouses' parents or grandparents. Students can also carry forward unused credits to future years and use them to reduce their future taxes.[23]

The education tax credit in 2000 similarly allowed for 17 per cent of a predefined amount for every month in which the taxpayer was a student. For the 2000 tax year, this amount was $200 per month (raised to $400 per month in 2001) for full-time students and $60 per month (raised to $120 per month in 2001) for part-time students. The same transfer and carry-forward provisions apply as for the tuition tax credit.[24]

The student loan interest tax credit was instituted in 1998 as another part of the Canadian Opportunities Strategy. In 2000, students who had consolidated their federal or provincial student loans and begun repayment were allowed a tax credit equal to 17 per cent (22 per cent in Quebec) of the interest paid. Again, this credit can be transferred or carried forward.

Two other important tax provisions apply to post-secondary students. First, grants of less than $3,000 do not need to be declared as income.[25] Second, the income generated by money invested in Registered Education Savings Plans (RESPs), up to certain maximums, is not taxable until it is withdrawn.[26] RESPs generate tax expenditures because (a) the income generated is taxed at a later point than it would normally be, and (b) the savings are taxable in the hands of the beneficiary (normally the student) rather than the person who made the investment (normally the parent), and thus typically at a lower rate.

We estimated the education-related tax expenditures reported above using three sources:

- federal tax expenditures were drawn from a 2001 Department of Finance publication;
- the related provincial expenditures were, for the most part, calculated using a method originally developed for similar purposes by David Perry of the Canadian Taxpayers Foundation;[27] and
- expenditures for Quebec and other particular provincial programs were drawn from provincial documents.

KEY FINDINGS AND CONCLUSIONS

In this section, we first highlight our four most important findings. We then discuss some of the policy implications and related conclusions that arise from those findings.

Four Key Findings

As the bottom rows of Table 10.1 show, total spending on direct financial assistance to post-secondary students and their families by all levels of government is estimated to have been just under $4.7 billion in 2000/1. This is a substantial sum, although whether it is enough or too much, or spent wisely, is open to discussion and debate.

The importance of tax expenditures is the first and perhaps the most dramatic of our findings. More than $1.7 billion—37.0 per cent of the combined federal-provincial total—was spent in this way, primarily through the tuition tax credit and the tax credit for educational expenses. Tax expenditures represented 43.7 per cent of federal spending and 29.1 per cent of provincial spending on direct aid to students. Furthermore, while we did not make comparable historical estimates, it is clear that these tax credits have grown substantially. Tuition fees rose sharply in the 1990s, and thus the amounts of the associated credits increased; the educational expense tax credit has been increased several times; and because higher past levels of borrowing lead to higher current interest payments, the tax expenditure associated with the student loan interest tax credit has also increased.

Secondly, the size and composition of spending on grants is perhaps surprising. Grants are the most traditional form of student financial aid, and this category still comprises an important share of spending—$1.6 billion, or approximately one-third of all spending. What is noteworthy, however, is the distribution of this spending between the federal and provincial levels and among the provinces. Recently created federal grant programs have quickly become an important part of overall spending and an even more important part of all spending on grants. The new federal programs include grants from the Canadian Millennium Scholarship Foundation (over $250 million) and the Canada Education Savings Grant (just over $300 million). Among the provinces, Alberta, Quebec, and British Columbia are notable for their relatively heavy grant spending. In the Maritime provinces and Ontario, on the other hand, aid in the form of grants is a relatively low percentage of overall spending.

Thirdly, debt remission programs have garnered a good deal of attention in recent years, after having been introduced in response to perceptions that student debt levels had risen too high. They represent about $435 million in spending, or 9.3 per cent of the overall total. A large portion of this spending occurred in Ontario, where the Ontario Student Opportunity Grant (OSOG) spent $280 million to reduce the maximum amount of borrowing for Ontario students to $7,000 per year. In addition, both British Columbia and Alberta directly fund substantial debt remission programs. Finally, some provinces, particularly the Maritime provinces, use funds from the Canada Millennium Scholarship Foundation to pay for newly created provincial debt remission programs.

Finally, we note that programs that reduce the amount of debt held by former students who are demonstrably having difficulty repaying their loans provide only a tiny part of direct aid to students, despite the existence of such programs in many jurisdictions. Provincial and federal interest relief programs, however, are also aimed at former students having trouble repaying their student loans, and these programs have grown in recent years.

Policy Implications

Direct financial aid to post-secondary students and their families can serve a number of policy objectives. First, needs-based financial aid increases access to higher education by providing qualified students with the immediate financial resources they need to pay tuition fees and support themselves while in school. Even for those able to pursue their studies somewhere in the post-secondary system without financial aid, such assistance can increase schooling options, making it possible to choose among different institutions, to reduce paid work while in school, or to study full-time rather than part-time.

Secondly, student financial aid in the form of merit scholarships and other targeted grants can reward academic excellence in secondary or post-secondary schools, provide incentives that increase the numbers of students in particular areas of study, or encourage post-secondary participation by particular groups of Canadians. The case for encouraging excellence is clear. The reasons for increasing participation in certain programs by certain groups is typically based on a perception that the social returns to the targeted areas of study are particularly high or that there are barriers to entry for certain groups.

Finally, student financial aid can advance more political objectives. It can, for example, be thought of as demonstrating the government's support for post-secondary education, thus sending a message that 'education matters', and thereby encouraging individuals to go on to higher studies. Financial aid can also provide a means for the federal government to play a role in post-secondary education, which is a provincial jurisdiction. In the Canadian context, student financial aid also represents a subsidy of post-secondary education for middle-class families.

Having established these three very general justifications for student financial aid, we now discuss each of our broad categories of spending in that context. The principal function of needs-based student loan programs is to remove financial barriers that stand in the way of going to school for those from lower- and middle-income families. Eligibility is restricted to potential students who are 'in need' as defined by the loan programs. Loans not only provide access to post-secondary education but they widen other education-related choices. Loans thus clearly further the first objective listed above.

Grant programs improve access and widen choice for needy students. They also reward academic excellence, encourage entry into certain programs by certain groups (female Ph.D. students in the sciences, for example), and provide aid to particular types of students (such as First Nation students or students with disabilities). Grant programs thus contribute to the first two objectives.

The contribution of debt remission programs is harder to determine, because the direct effect of such programs is to reduce the repayment obligations of those who have already made it into the system and completed some or all of their studies. To be sure, only those who were at some point judged to be needy are eligible for loans, and thus for debt remission. But student loan recipients who go on to financially remunerative careers after leaving school are eligible for remission even if they are able to repay their debts without any undue hardship. By contrast, interest relief and debt reduction in repayment are needs-based programs that target benefits to those who are in financial difficulty. Both debt remission and debt reduction in repayment programs might encourage access indirectly, by making it known to potential students that there are limits on prospective debt levels, and by reducing the long-run cost of schooling. The extent of these access effects is unknown.

Tax expenditures are the hardest form of spending to justify in terms of improving access and choice or as a way of targeting aid to particular groups. The basic education and tuition tax credits provide a benefit to all tax-paying families without regard to need. Lower-income families benefit from these credits only if they have sufficient tax liabilities to take advantage of them. At the same time, wealthy families whose children would go to school even if the tax credits did not exist also benefit. The student interest deduction suffers from the additional disadvantage that the benefits are received only in the post-schooling period, which means that access and choice are affected only to the extent that prospective students consider such future benefits in making their enrolment decisions. Tax expenditures are a very blunt instrument for achieving either of the two non-political goals of student financial aid.

Thus, in terms of providing access and choice to needy students, the most crucial forms of support are student loans and needs-based grants. It is therefore interesting to observe that such needs-based spending represents only a little over half (53.5

per cent) of all spending on student financial aid. This is, furthermore, an upper bound on the amount of true needs-based aid, since that percentage includes merit scholarships, other non-needs based awards, and some forms of debt remission. Those who believe that the primary purpose of student financial aid is to foster access and choice would, therefore, likely support a shift of spending toward these needs-based programs, especially at a time when education costs have risen and needs-based loan and grant programs have not generally kept pace.[28]

As for debt remission, these programs lack any sensitivity to the borrower's actual debt burden (that is, the amount of borrowing relative to the individual's capacity to repay), such as exists in the interest relief and debt reduction in repayment elements of loan programs, and hence they do not relieve debt loads where they are truly heaviest. We believe that a combination of needs-based grants and loan programs with substantial interest and debt relief elements would do a better job of improving access and providing effective relief to those burdened with excessive debt loads than debt remission does. And with debt remission programs comprising 9.3 per cent of all spending on student financial support, a shift to needs-based grant and loan programs could make an important difference in terms of access and choice.

Regarding the tax expenditure component of spending on students and their families, the amounts are very substantial and exceed the spending on loan programs in every jurisdiction. Yet this spending is the least justifiable in terms of the traditional goals of helping students overcome financial barriers that stand in the way of their studies. That said, a few of the tax expenditures might make sense. Examples include the exemption of scholarship income from taxation, and perhaps the basic education and tuition credits as they apply to students themselves (that is, before being carried forward or transferred to students' parents). But allowing the transfer of such credits to wealthy parents of students or to other eligible credit recipients makes much less sense. Nor does permitting the deductibility of interest on student loans, no matter what the individual's income level. Why not simply provide interest relief and debt reduction in repayment for those with debt burdens thought to be overly burdensome?

Our view is that the most important goal of student financial aid is to improve access and choice. Perhaps not surprisingly, we believe that current spending on student financial assistance could be better targeted—less on tax expenditures and debt remission, and more on loans (including interest relief and debt reduction in repayment) and grants. We recognize, however, that not all readers will share our view. Moreover, we know that political factors influence the design of social programs, and may have influenced the current structure of student aid programs. Even so, we hope that in providing estimates of the levels of the various types of government spending on post-secondary students and their families, this chapter will inspire and inform discussions regarding how existing moneys could be spent differently, or whether overall spending should be adjusted.

NOTES

1 This chapter is based on research carried out for the Council of Ministers of Education Canada. The results reported here summarize a more detailed analysis that may be published at a later date.

2 Another category of direct student aid is student financial assistance delivered through the nation's social programs. Because of the empirical and conceptual difficulties we encountered in measuring these amounts, we are unable to provide any plausible estimates of the amounts spent in this category. Several small programs that were difficult to classify in any of the four basic categories are also excluded. On the basis of our preliminary investigations, we believe that the omitted spending does not affect the thrust of the paper.

3 In the case of spending by the Canada Millennium Scholarship Foundation (CMSF), we measure disbursements, even though this does not represent current 'spending' in quite the same way as other spending does. Rather than coming out of current budgets, the CMSF programs are financed by a $2.5 billion endowment, and spending comes out of a combination of interest and a drawing down of the capital. The true cost to the government is, therefore, the opportunity cost of that money—the interest that it could have earned (or the amount of interest that could have been saved were that money put toward the national debt).

4 In fact, we were sometimes provided estimates for '2000/1' when it was not clear whether the information was for the fiscal year or for the calendar year. Other spending, such as that related to tax expenditures, is explicitly based on the calendar year. Moreover, different institutions define their fiscal years differently.

5 Together these components of what we call 'student loan costs' correspond roughly to the US definition of the 'subsidy expense' of a government loan program. See 'Accounting for Direct Loans and Loan Guarantees' (http://www.fasab.gov/codifica.htm, viewed 21 June 2002). These accounting standards, contained in the Statement of Federal Financial Accounting Standards No. 2, must be applied by *all* US government loan programs, including student loan programs. There are no equivalent standards in Canada.

6 'Alternative payments' are made to Quebec, the Northwest Territories, and Nunavut to run their own programs in lieu of the federal program. We count these payments as provincial/territorial spending, rather than federal spending.

7 In the era when governments guaranteed student loans, a loan 'default' did not mean that the loan was written off. 'Default' meant that the government purchased the loan from the bank and took over the responsibility for any further collections.

8 In this short interim period, students borrowed through private lending institutions, as before.

9 Until 1994, the interest subsidy payments on CSLP loans were made while the student was in full-time study and for a six-month grace period after the end of full-time study; beginning on 31 July 1994, the student was responsible for any interest that accrued after the end of full-time study, even though no payments had to be made for the first six months after leaving school.

10 In general, the 'interest subsidy' would include not only the payments made on behalf of students while they are in school but also the charging of an interest rate less than the appropriate discount rate. Because of the government guarantees,

lower-than-market interest rates were charged on student loans, creating this other kind of interest subsidy. Nonetheless, we ignore that kind of interest subsidy.

11 R. Finnie and S. Schwartz, 'Student Loans in Canada: Past, Present and Future' (Toronto: C.D. Howe Institute, 1996).

12 We thus employ a particular definition of 'government spending on loan default' that does not measure actual net payments in FY 2000/01. This approach was adopted because these current set-asides seem to be the best representation of the relevant loan loss costs in which we are interested.

13 A complication is that the total amount of loans disbursed had to be estimated for four provinces, including Ontario and British Columbia.

14 We do not generally include grants, scholarships, or bursaries given to students by particular institutions in this spending, principally because the amount of government funding going into such programs cannot generally be calculated. In some cases, a significant share comes from tuition fees and therefore does not represent government spending per se, but rather a transfer from one set of students to another. In Ontario, for example, 30 per cent of the fee increases instituted since the late 1990s have been earmarked for institution-based student aid, and this source now comprises a sizable share of this assistance. The acronyms in the text stand for the Natural Sciences and Engineering Research Council (NSERC); the Social Science and Humanities Research Council (SSHRC); Canadian Institutes of Health Research (CIHR); and the Canadian International Development Agency (CIDA).

15 As part of the agreements between the provinces and the CMSF, the provinces agreed to 're-invest' some of the savings created by the CMSF spending. The actual extent of that reinvestment is unclear. To the (unknown) extent that the savings were re-invested in direct student aid, the re-investment will be reflected in our provincial estimates.

16 Grants to Aboriginal students are provided by the Department of Indian and Northern Affairs through its Post-Secondary Student Support Plan (PSSSP) and through the University and College Entrance Preparation (UCEP) program.

17 The grants to students studying technology and natural sciences include grants made through the granting councils and by various government departments. Our estimate of spending on 'science grants' originates in the Federal Science Expenditures and Personnel survey that is conducted annually by the Science, Innovation and Electronic Information Division (SIEID) of Statistics Canada. Spending included in the $196.7 million figure was restricted to programs falling into a category called Education Support in the survey. This category represents 'grants to individuals or institutions on behalf of individuals which are intended to support the post-secondary education of students in technology and the natural sciences.'

18 Because only individuals holding loans can benefit from debt remission, and because loan remission programs are restricted to individuals who met the need criteria of the loan programs at the time they applied, there is still an element of need in determining who receives debt remission. However, *current* need is not considered.

19 The federal government, which does not have its own debt remission program, spends money on remission only indirectly, through the CMSF.

20 'Tax Expenditures and Evaluations 2001', 7. This document contains the latest estimates of tax expenditures and appears at www.fin.gc.ca/taxexp/2001/taxexp01_1e.html#_Toc519392243 (viewed 9 Dec. 2001).

21 'Tax Expenditures and Evaluations 2000', 48, http://www.fin.gc.ca/toce/2000/taxexp_e.html (viewed 18 Nov. 2001).

22 The rate on this tax credit was reduced to 16 per cent for the 2001 tax year.

23 In Quebec, the tuition tax credit consisted of 22 per cent of the amount paid for tuition; the Quebec credit could be carried forward in the same way as the federal credit but could not be transferred.

24 In Quebec, there is no equivalent to the education tax credit, but parents or guardians of students are eligible for a 22 per cent tax credit on $1,650 if the dependent is in school for 3 to 5 months, and $3,300 if the dependent is in school for 6 months or more.

25 In Quebec, the entire amount of scholarships and bursaries was deductible starting in 2001.

26 Since 1998, the Canada Education Savings Grant (CESG) program has provided a grant of 20 cents for each dollar deposited in an RESP, up to a maximum of $400 per year per beneficiary. These grants must be deposited in an RESP and the earnings on them generate a tax expenditure. We count the actual amount of the CESG (as opposed to the earnings it generates within the RESP) as a grant.

27 David B. Perry, 'Fiscal Figures: Federal and Provincial Tax Expenditures', *Canadian Tax Journal* 46, 1 (1998).

28 Fred Hemingway identifies various kinds of unmet need in the current student financial aid system and discusses how current programs could be modified to better reflect students' resources and financial requirements. There is, therefore, ample scope to increase needs-based spending in a way that could widen students' post-secondary choices. See Fred Hemingway, 'Assessing Canada's Need Assessment Policies: Focus on Student Aid', Canadian Millennium Scholarship Foundation Research Paper Series, 2002.

11

Ottawa's Imaginary Innovation Strategy: Progress or Drift?

JOHN DE LA MOTHE

Composing a major policy document with a multi-departmental team is always a daunting task, particularly in these turbulent, often contradictory times, in which globalization, interdependence, knowledge, and security issues intersect. Writing an Innovation Strategy amid the shuffling of three secretaries of state for science and three industry ministers—all vying for leadership at the time—must have been difficult. One minister, John Manley, declined the invitation from the Privy Council Office (PCO) to undertake the exercise.[1] Another minister, Brian Tobin, wishing to retreat to traditional (that is, archaic) forms of industrial policy, did not want the task.[2] The third and current minister, Allan Rock, did not want to engage with it.[3] In addition, there was no clear direction from the central agencies. Under the circumstances, the drafters are to be congratulated for having generated any kind of document at all. But the results of their efforts should not go uninspected.

In February 2002, the government of Canada released what it called an 'Innovation Strategy'. This was followed by a nine-month 'engagement' process[4] of 'key stakeholders' in a series of more than 100 regional, sectoral, youth, and Aboriginal meetings across the country. The National Summit was held on 18–19 November 2002. The engagement process was managed by a secretariat, dropped into place in Industry Canada after the strategy document was written and with few, if any, connections to the writing team, the Council of Science and Technology Advisors

(CSTA), or the Advisory Council on Science and Technology (ACST). This process was preceded by an even longer, often delayed process of trying to write a cohesive, collective paper involving federal departments and agencies, but led by Industry Canada (IC), Human Resources Development Canada (HRDC), and, lurking in the penumbra, the Privy Council Office (PCO). Astute observers looked forward to this unified approach, given that one of the key commitments of the 1994–6 Program Review exercise was to improve 'horizontal coordination' and to demonstrate greater transparency. The idea of a unified paper jointly penned by major departments seemed a hopeful demonstration of those 1996 principles. Many were disappointed when what started off in the public eye as a White Paper slid into being something between a strategy, an agenda, and a consultation.

Alas, and perhaps not unexpectedly, IC and HRDC could not agree on content or approach. The joint paper was abandoned and eventually each department produced its own separate paper. Sensitivities ran so high that when speculative op-ed pieces based on no direct knowledge, only expectations, appeared in various newspapers or industry publications, ADMs railed against staff in briefing meetings and forbad discussion of any developments with anyone outside the department.[5] Insiders estimate that the process, excluding staff time, cost roughly $15 million. Once the dust had fallen, this 'Innovation Strategy' demonstrated a remarkable discontinuity with more progressive science, technology, and innovation policy documents produced by this government between 1993 and 2000. This chapter will show that the entire process has not resulted in anything resembling a strategy, an agenda, or a consultation. Whereas the 1993 to 2000 period could reasonably be labelled a period of 'progress' in science, technology, and innovation policy, this most recent exercise must be typified as a soon-to-be-forgotten period of mere drift, in a sea of innovation-based activities, both within and outside government.

ADRIFT IN A SEA OF INNOVATION EXERCISES

At one level, it would be easy to summarily dismiss the recent Innovation Strategy. After all, in 2001–2 alone, numerous groups undertook innovation strategy and consultation exercises. In April 2002, for example, the Information Technology Association of Canada (ITAC) asked the Public Policy Forum (PPF) to design and host a roundtable on innovation, consisting of interviews and a meeting of high-level officials. This event took place on 27 May, and it resulted in a Summary Report, *Canada's Innovation Agenda: Where Are We Going?*[6] The challenges highlighted by this exercise focused on R&D, commercialization of research, skills, regulation, and the culture of innovation in Canada.

On 7–8 October 2002, the Conference Board of Canada organized, on behalf of the TD Bank Financial Group, the 'TD Forum on Canada's Standard of Living'. This high-level event, held in Ottawa and moderated by former Ontario Premier Bob Rae, grew out of a number of speeches given by A. Charles Baillie, then Chairman and CEO of the TD Bank Financial Group. The first high-profile speech was delivered before the Canadian Club in Toronto on 26 February 2001. In that speech Baillie suggested a number of initiatives to advance and protect Canada's distinctive way of life, which included tax and regulatory reform, but focused upon education, science, technology, and innovation. Subsequent speeches were given, notably 'Smart Nationalism: An Agenda for Canada's Future' (delivered to the Toronto Board of Trade on 17 December 2001) and 'Brave New Canada' (delivered to the Canadian Club of Ottawa on 19 March 2002). The theme of innovation was presented throughout. In preparation for the TD Forum, 50 papers were commissioned. Thirty-one (62 per cent) dealt directly with innovation. Although admittedly broader in focus than the ITAC/PPF Forum, the Conference Board/TD Bank Forum squarely addressed leadership and attitudes, human capital, making government a positive force for change, and bringing Canada's cities into the mix. All papers were sophisticated and clearly addressed the participants with the seriousness appropriate to their authority and responsibilities; these participants included the Canadian Council of Chief Executives, CAE Inc., the Canadian ambassador to the OECD, university professors and presidents, and representatives of social, first nations, and environmental groups. The Department of Finance and IC were represented—by senior officials—while HRDC was not.

The inclusion of cities as a focus of innovation is critically important,[7] but it is also politically interesting given that the then minister of finance, Paul Martin, referred to the importance of innovation in cities when speaking to the Canadian Advanced Technology Alliance (CATA) in 2001. Mr Martin had then included—and continues to include—discussions of cities as generators of economic growth in his various speeches to business groups and community leaders. As a result, CATA, with the assistance of the consulting firms KPMG and Ipsos-NPD, designed and is in the midst of organizing a series of TechAction Town Meetings. These innovation meetings, hosted in the town hall by the mayor of each city involved and attended by 50 to 150 local leaders from business, finance, universities, national laboratories, and volunteer organizations, were designed to stimulate focus upon the themes of innovation and the knowledge economy at the local level. They have taken place in St. John's, Halifax, Montreal, Ottawa, Toronto, Markham, Richmond Hill, Calgary, and Vancouver. Each meeting was preceded by a targeted survey to a larger audience of local leaders. A notice was then published in the main local newspaper inviting interested groups or individuals to submit written statements of their views concerning the viability of their city and their vision of its future. These presentations were summarized at the Town Hall Meeting, which was facilitated by a broadcast journalist, and the audience then took part in discussions, which were structured around four themes: leadership, access to—and quality of—capital, infrastructure, and people. These were then mapped onto a diamond, each corner of which was assigned an imaginary 'perfect city score' of 5, so that participants could visualize where they themselves saw their city—today and in the future. The outcome was a three-dimensional pyramid, designed with input by the manufacturing branch of IC as something called an 'Innovation Index'.[8]

And, of course, aside from the high-level innovation-focused activities already noted above, a real smorgasbord of innovation discussions were generated by telecom and photonics industrial associations, the National Research Council, and individuals.[9]

Thus, given the cacophony of the crosstown traffic on the theme of innovation, it is easy to see why the government's Innovation Strategy, in spite of the expectations it raised, sank beneath the din of other policy and political chatter. Yet anyone with a historical perspective could have predicted the disillusionment. This Innovation Strategy is the eighteenth major science, technology, and innovation policy paper or review in 24 years. Hence, to many 'old policy hacks' it was just another case of déja vu.[10]

But to take such a cynical view is not only to succumb to superficiality; more importantly, it is to fail to appreciate the complexity of policy-making, analytically

Table 11.1

**Major Government Science, Technology, and
Innovation Reports or Reviews Since 1978***

1978	*Strengthening R&D in Canada*, Ministry of State for Science and Technology
1979	*Forging the Links: A Technology Policy for Canada*, Science Council of Canada
1983	*A Technology Policy for Canada*, Government of Canada
1984	*Royal Commission on the Economic Union and Development Prospects for Canada*
1984	*Government Support for Technological Advancement*, Senate Standing Committee
1984	*Task Force on Federal Policies and Programs for Technological Development* (Wright Report)
1985	*Science, Technology and Economic Development*, Ministry of State for Science and Technology
1986	*National Forum on Science and Technology Policy*, Government of Canada
1987	*A National Science Policy*, Government of Canada
1987	*InnovAction: The Canadian Strategy for Science and Technology*, Government of Canada
1987	*A Discussion Paper on Canada's R&D Effort*, The Council of Science and Technology Ministers
1988	*The National Conference on Technology and Innovation*
1990	*Canada Must Compete*, House of Commons Standing Committee on Industry, Science, Technology, Regional and Northern Development
1991	*Canada at the Crossroads* (Porter Report)
1991	*Reaching For Tomorrow: Science and Technology Policy in Canada*, Science Council of Canada
1992	*Inventing Our Future: An Action Plan for Canada's Prosperity* (The Prosperity Initiative)
1996	*Science and Technology for the New Century*

*This list does not include the numerous provincial reports, the OECD review of the western provinces, NABST-ACST-CSTA Reports, or Science Council reports.

and in reality—particularly in the interconnected realms of education, science, technology, and innovation. Those who subscribe to such a perspective seem to be in a hurry; they conceive of policy-making as straightforward—without compromises or politics—and they want report recommendations to be implemented swiftly. Those holding such simplistic views should be pleased that innovation, which is of critical importance to the nation's economy and its standard of living, and which is not a homogeneous activity but displays differing characteristics in different sectors, is being talked about so much by so many leaders and groups across so many sectors. This in itself is success of a kind. People are 'getting it', and this in itself bodes well for Canada's competitive future.

THE PROGRESSIVE LIBERAL RECORD
ON INNOVATION: 1993–2001

To be sure, there is a longstanding culture of complaint in Canada. It has long been argued that Canada is 'losing the technological race', that it has an 'innovation gap', and that although its contributions to research and knowledge are world-class, it is monumentally poor at bringing these ideas to market.[11] Another longstanding member of this family of complaints is that Canada is a laggard at using new technologies to improve its productivity, a key element in achieving sustained economic growth.[12] By now fading somewhat in popular discourse, given the vibrant dynamics of integration and globalization, are the 'branch-plant economy' arguments and the debates regarding the ownership of multinational firms.[13] And yet they still resonate, especially given that the distribution of industrial R&D performers has not been dramatically broadened or deepened. Even today, Canada only has one firm, Nortel, that makes the ranks of the world's top 150 R&D performers.[14] Moreover, the complaint has long been heard that Canada's gross expenditure on R&D as a percentage of gross domestic product (GERD/GDP), which continually appeared near the bottom of the G-7 GERD/GDP numbers, had 'flat-lined'.[15]

This latter complaint is interesting. In 1984, the new Conservative government made a commitment to double our GERD/GDP ratio to about 2.8 per cent in order to rival Japan, Germany, and the United States. This was, of course, a foolish ambition, and it revealed a profound lack of understanding of what it would take to achieve this goal. Alas, more recently someone in Canada's central agencies—apparently with no knowledge of economics, innovation, or history—convinced the Prime Minister's Office and the Governor General's Office to make a commitment, in 2001, to move Canada from fifteenth to fifth in world performance of R&D. This was previewed by Paul Martin on 14 September 2000 in a speech to the Toronto Board of Trade, and it became policy in the Speech from the Throne in 2002. Statistics Canada and others quickly—if quietly—came out with an assessment of what this would mean, to cite a few examples, in terms of numbers of new Ph.D.s, new professors to fill the accelerating retirement roles, new firms conducting R&D, and new investments; it showed, in other words, that the goal was really an illusion. Indeed, it has been estimated that in order to go from fifteenth to fifth, Canada would have to increase its existing (2001) annual expenditure of $20.9 billion on R&D by *$25 billion annually*. Clearly this policy goal was intended as a political challenge to industry, universities, and communities, but it cannot be achieved using traditional instruments of fiscal or industrial policy. Moreover, it raised the question why, whereas once, in the 1980s, we benchmarked ourselves against the Triad, we were taking the recent impressive slope of growth of Denmark and Ireland as a challenge to Canada's performance and its markets (despite the remarkably low scale and scope of those countries). The assessment should have been based instead on an analysis of Canada's industrial structure and the needs of Canadians. Such an assessment might have led to the development of a unique vision of how science, technology, and innovation could advance Canadian society.

Another strange commitment in the Innovation Strategy was to create 10 new innovation clusters. Of course clusters have been noted as foci of valuable economic growth since at least Marshall's work in 1906. More recent analyses of clusters include those by Michael Porter, Philip Cooke, Zoltan Acs, and Canada's own Innovation Systems Research Network, which is anchored in Toronto but which includes more than 40 researchers in and around Vancouver, Calgary, Ottawa, Saint John, and Saint Foy. The point here is that a government cannot 'create' new clusters. This is not a Kevin Costner film in which 'if you build it they will come'. Recent world economic history is riddled with examples of governments trying to create clusters—think of Dresden, Germany and its Infineon Fab Lab, or the numerous empty science parks from New Haven to the University of Illinois at Chicago. Clusters cannot be simply inflated in economically distressed regions like so many balloons. To think that they can demonstrates a lack of understanding of economic and innovation dynamics and an attraction to an antiquated form of industrial policy.

But were suggestions of this kind in the last decade a failure of policy in the larger sense? I think not. It can be documented that since 1993—indeed, the period probably began in 1986—Canada's relative innovative performance has improved across a wide variety of fronts. For example, since 1992, R&D intensity in Canada (as measured by its GERD/GDP) has risen from 1.5 per cent to 1.9 per cent. Despite still ranking fourteenth in the OECD, Canada experienced the fastest growth in R&D intensity over the 1981–2000 period (an increase of 9.1 per cent for 2001 over 2000).[16] The performance of R&D has seen a healthy rise in the business and higher education sectors, while it has stayed (appropriately) flat in the government sector.[17] In patenting, Canada achieved the fastest rate of growth in the G7 in terms of external patent applications (20 per cent annually over the 1981–98 period), with the greatest concentration in biotechnology and computer-related fields. (Yet, patents in mechanical and civil engineering still account for the largest share of applications filed in the 1990s.)

The list of positive shifts in the innovation-economy dynamic is indeed a long and impressive one. There are, to be sure, still weaknesses—regarding, for example, the heavy concentration of industrial R&D in telecommunications, information and computer technologies (ICT), and biotechnology, the relatively low production of highly trained research personnel, and insufficient access to the full spectrum of quality capital (from angel financing, through venture capital, equity, and loans). But in keeping with the government's commitment, set out in its 1993 'Red Book' and its 1994 *Jobs and Growth Agenda: Building a More Innovative Economy*,[18] the Liberal government has invested heavily in knowledge and innovation. Their goal and strategy was clearly stated: '[increasing] our capacity to create new knowledge; seizing the transformative power of new technologies; and bringing our ideas to market more quickly than ever before' (1). In order to realize this demanding challenge, not only has the government invested in knowledge, it has itself become a strategic innovator—re-jigging the ways it does business (as through Alternative Service Delivery), innovating institutionally (by creating more responsive bodies, such as the Canadian Institutes for Health Research and the Canadian Foundation for Innovation), and innovating in terms of program designs (as in SSHRC's Initiative on the New Economy, or its Community-University Research Alliances). A partial list of examples and investments is given in Table 11.2.

The Value of a Framework

The impressive progress made by the government since 1993 was not a mere happenstance or a case of serendipity. It shows strong evidence of a framework that was, over time, utilized by major departments and agencies. Although the results have not been uniform in all areas of policy, the innovation systems framework has proven to be both robust analytically and effective in action. Leading agents in the promulgation of 'innovation systems' between 1993 and 2000 must include the Prime Minister's Office (particularly under the policy advice of Chaviva Hosek), backbenchers (particularly John Godfrey), the National Research Council (particularly supported by the foresight and strategic planning activities of Jack Smith), and the Micro Economic Analysis Group, formerly under Denis Gauthier (who is now ADM at Health Canada) and Alan Nymark (then ADM at Industry Canada, now DM at Environment Canada).

In a nutshell, the history of the federal government's adoption of the innovation system framework can be traced back to 1988, when the International Federation of Institutes for Advanced Study (IFIAS) held a congress at Niagara on the Lake, which was attended by many civil servants, to release the magisterial *Economic Theory and Technical Change*, edited by Giovanni Dosi, Chris Freeman, Luc Soete, Gerry Silverberg, and Dick Nelson. This tome included essays on innovation systems. A related event was the publication in 1992 of *National Systems of Innovation*, edited by B.Ä. Lundvall, and the culmination of the OECD's Technology-Economy Program (TEP) (1989–90), which was hosted by Canada in Montreal at the Ritz Carleton Hotel.

Analytically, the innovation systems approach is more evolutionary or neo-Schumpeterian than neo-classical. It eschews linear assumptions concerning R&D investments (inputs) and outcomes. It understands the interdependencies between producers of knowledge on the one hand and the processes of diffusion, identification, and adoption of knowledge on the other. Unlike traditional conceptions of the

Table 11.2
Recent Federal Investment in S&T and Innovation

Program	Funding $ millions
Canada Research Chairs	900
National Sciences and Engineering Council (NSERC)*	536
Social Sciences and Humanities Research Council (SSHRC)*	189
Canadian Institutes for Health Research (formerly MRC)*	767
Networks of Excellence*	120
National Research Council (NRC)*	389
Canadian Foundation for Innovation (CFI)	3,150
Genome Canada	300
Biotechnology R&D*	165
Trudeau Fellowships	125
Connectedness Agenda*	346
Government on-Line	600
CA*Net 4	110
SchoolNet and Community Access	40
Sustainable Development Technology Fund	100
Canada's National Research and Innovation Network	110
PRECARN (Pre-Competitive Applied Research Network)	20

*Values are for increased funding in budgets prior to 2001 and their outlays over the period 1998/9 to 2002/3; for the other programs they represent the total endowment announced to date. See below for the decisions in Budget 2001.
Source: 'The Budget Plan 2001', Table 6.2, 124; and other sources provided by Industry Canada.

factors of production (capital and labour), it understands that knowledge is the central resource of advanced economies. Moreover, knowledge—unlike physical resources like trees and oil—do not lose value with repeated and shared (distributed) use. What is old to one firm may be new to others, and may thus lead to new jobs, productivity, and growth.

Instead of rational actors who have perfect information (as expressed in prices) and whose competition is in perfect supply-demand equilibrium, the central elements of the innovation systems approach are interaction, co-evolution, value flows, institutional adaptation, knowledge creation and sharing (science, technology, and innovation), networks, partnerships, alliances, and institutional learning. All these new factors of production change the nature of governance and policy.[19]

This framework has been effectively present in all of the Liberal government's policy documents, speeches from the throne, and electoral documents, starting with

'The Red Book' in 1993. However, with the new Innovation Strategy, no framework is evident. There seems to have been no White Paper (such as was first announced), no strategy, no agenda, and no meaningful consultation.

WHERE HAVE ALL THE FRAMEWORKS GONE?

When the Innovation Strategy was first made public, the Government was said to be preparing a White Paper on Innovation.[20] To those familiar with the machinery of government, a White Paper is a statement of government intentions or policies. It usually includes draft legislation. White Papers are often used by governments to declare policies and to get public reaction before final legislation is presented to Parliament. The discussion that arises from publication of draft legislation in a White Paper enables a government to spot possible flaws or unintended results, and thus to improve the legislation.[21] Since there is no legislation attached to the Innovation Strategy, this clearly is not a White Paper.

We should now ask if this exercise could be described as a strategy. A 'strategy' is a plan—a tactic or line of attack. It requires a vision of where an organization (or a nation) is, where it wishes to go, *and how it plans to get there*. This involves not just cheerleading but also a notion of who is to do what. If a strategy is to be effective or successful, it must include, in addition to a vision, the possibility of the emergence of adaptive strategies. Every competent manager knows that he must be prepared to respond to a changing environment; he must be prepared for the emergence of new strategic possibilities—the offspring of the intended strategy, and moving in the same direction and with the same intent, but in response to differing circumstances. This innovation paper is not a strategy. It is neither visionary nor is it very adaptive.

Well then, is it an agenda? An agenda typically involves a schedule—a plan or a set of benchmarks. In this case, the only schedules are illusory. Fifteenth to five in seven years? This has been shown not to be a viable target. Every other target in these documents—which amounts to nothing more than that Canada should become more innovative—has either been achieved already or is as fluffy as the down on a cygnet's back. The Innovation Strategy is not an agenda.

Is it a consultation exercise? Consultation is a very interesting thing. As Arnstein pointed out in 1969 (Figure 11.1), there are at least eight levels of participation in any consultative process, ranging from power to tokenism to non-participation. In the case of the Innovation Strategy, and even though there were more than 100 people involved in the meetings, no one could reasonably argue that anything higher than a level 3 consultation—'informing'—occurred. But what information was offered? That innovation is important? The audiences already knew that. Was it level 4—'consultation'? Not likely, since the evening before the National Summit, at which delegates were to break into groups to arrive at recommendations, officials prepared a set of recommendations for circulation the day of the Summit: so there was no consultation. The entire Innovation Strategy exercise, then, drops almost to level 1, 'manipulation'. Is this assessment fair? Let's look.

Figure 11.1
Eight Levels of Participation in Consultation

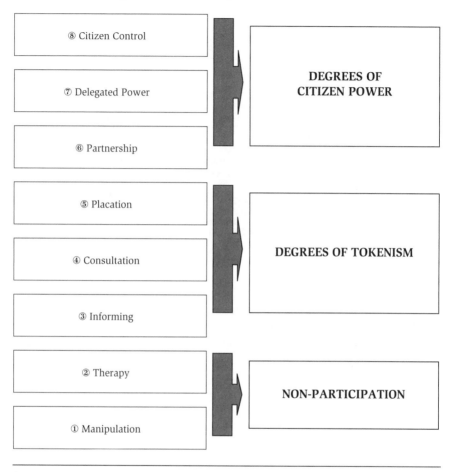

Source: S.R. Arnstein, 'A Ladder of Public Participation', *The Journal of American Institute of Planners* (July 1969), 216–24.

THE WEAKNESS OF THE INNOVATION STRATEGY

A study of the Innovation Strategy exercise and the associated set of documents reveals weaknesses at many levels.[22]

Intent
It is well known that the PCO was the driving political force behind the Innovation Strategy exercise. But at no point during the 18 months was its purpose or its desired outcome made clear, even to the members of the Engagement Secretariat.

Political Disconnect

From the civil service point of view, as noted at the outset, this was a difficult project to deliver, in part because of the involvement of a central agency, but also because of the rapid rotation of ministers at Industry Canada. As a result, the writing team suffered from a lack of political engagement and direction.

Politics and Leadership

The exercise also suffered from being used as a veil behind which certain ministers attempted to forward their leadership ambitions, and thus distracted attention from the serious task of creating an innovation policy. Members of the Engagement Secretariat, noting that the ministers were not interested in the regional and national summits, were dismissive about the role of senior officials in the process (see note 3, above). Indeed, cynics were pleased when Ministers Rock and Stewart stayed for the entire National Summit, working the corridors. Two independent observers saw Ms Stewart, closely followed by a hired photographer, spending several minutes positioning herself near a reluctant gentleman in a wheelchair for a photo-opportunity.

Invitations and Enquiries

Several innovation specialists interviewed for this chapter, despite numerous attempts to find out how to get an invitation to the many regional summits, were stonewalled by IC. The author of this chapter, for example, received his invitation to the Ottawa meeting only four days in advance, without any details, agenda, or other materials. Moreover, after this author had called Minister Rock's office seven times to ask how many meetings there would be in total, he was asked, 'Who are you and why do you want to know?' Only one official of the Engagement Secretariat was forthcoming with this basic information. Thus the Innovation Strategy exercise was kept been in a locked box, and its officials, aware that it was a straw dog, seemed resentful and fearful about outside interest.

Access

Access was also a problem. Although an IC press release for the National Summit dated 13 November 2002 boasted that it had received input from 10,000 Canadians, journalists had tremendous difficulty in getting invited and were barred from the breakout groups. Only when Mark Henderson of Re$earch Money and Wayne Kondro of Science cornered Minister Rock in the hallway was the matter resolved. This mode of defensive bureaucratic behaviour ensured that there was no media interest and, therefore, no coverage.

Analytic Capacity

There are many IC analysts who know about the new economy, but they were not involved. Given 'input' from 10,000 Canadians and written submissions from more than 150 groups and individuals (according to the IC website), the Engagement Secretariat, which will have been dissolved by the time this chapter is published, has neither the expertise nor the capacity to develop an adequate analysis or synthesis. Not that this is their fault, but given their ahistoric view of innovation policies, programs, and reviews, compounded by a lack of any obvious capacity in evolutionary economic analysis, the sum substantive gain from this exercise will be nil at the most, mere rhetorical window-dressing ('In 2002 we conducted. . . .').

Disengagement

Before the National Summit was over, members of the Engagement Secretariat (called by insiders 'the Estrangement Secretariat') were vocally anticipating winding down the 'job' within four weeks and getting on to other work. They viewed their jobs as making meetings happen, not advancing innovation in Canada. Unfortunately for them, this timeline was extended by two months.

Discontinuity

The strange thing about this Innovation Strategy exercise is the unmistakable sense that the authors were completely unaware of the developments of the past eight years, as presented in the literature and in policy papers. The *Jobs and Growth Agenda: Building a More Innovative Economy* document was extremely articulate. It was up to date conceptually and analytically. So too was *Investing in Excellence, 1996–2001*.[23] These were world-class publications—complete with agendas and strategies. But the Innovation Strategy documents show no connection with these earlier documents, no continuity with the government's previous success in innovation under Ministers Manley and Martin, DM Kevin Lynch, previous ADM at Industry Allan Nymark, Arthur Carty at the NRC, and others. The Innovation Strategy documents are fragmented, with no overarching economic theory, no deliberate purpose—aside from saying that 'innovation is important'. They say nothing about the new governance, about who should do what, about what responsibilities various sectors should take on. They have nothing to say about such key questions.

Consultation?

This exercise cannot be seriously taken as a consultation exercise. 'Consultation' means asking questions for which the government needs answers; it implies that the government is in need of suggestions from the interested communities and that it is willing to incorporate these suggestions when it is forging solutions. By writing conclusions before break-out sessions were finished, and by framing issues in the broadest and most obvious terms (skills, innovation environment, local sources of innovation, and the like), the government was able to do whatever it wanted, and then declare that its policies emerged from a 'consultation'. As Arnstein points out, consultation can involve partnerships, delegated powers, or citizen control. Less effectively, it can involve mere placation (which assumes that there are expectations) or informing (which assumes that there is an intended message). This is tokenism. Or, if a government wants the community to go in a certain direction or act in a certain way, it can use therapy or manipulation, and call that 'consultation'.

When you come right down to it, in this exercise government officials have shown no leadership.

Coordination

It was unfortunate that HRDC and IC could not see their way clear to write a visionary joint paper. Territorial and political rivalries apparently still hold sway. Innovation (knowledge, learning, research, development, science) does not.

Passive Verbs

Even a casual student of strategy would know that the language of effective strategies involves achievable goals, benchmarks, and vision. *Achieving Excellence* is so full of passive verbs that readers are left stunned when it comes to knowing what they are to do. We are told on page 17 that we are 'top' in labour markets (meaning what? measured how?). We must make 'the right policy choices' and keep businesses 'moving in the right direction' (18). 'It is time for Canada to adopt a true culture of opportunity' (23). We must 'use knowledge strategically' (33) (meaning what?). 'Ensure the supply of people who create and use knowledge' (33) (how?). 'Implement the new *Immigration and Refugee Protection Act and Regulation*' (60) (this at a time when the government is trying to send immigrants to rural communities, keep them out because of homeland security, etc.). 'Increase the admission to Master's and PhD students at Canadian universities by an average of 5 per cent per year' (60). (So is the government planning to undermine the criteria of excellence at individual universities?) 'Over the next five years, increase the number of adults pursuing learning opportunities by 1 million' (60) (how? and how would it be measured?). Look at the language ('Ensure . . . promote . . . address . . . improve . . . encourage . . . support . . .'): foggy and imprecise. It is a far cry from the 1993–2000 period of progress.

CONCLUSIONS

Innovation is centrally important to the future of Canada. Many parts of government are being innovative, thoughtful, and entrepreneurial, and many are attentive to what has been done already, and why. However, the Liberals' 2002 Innovation Strategy exercise was full of flaws. Most importantly, it lacked content, and as an exercise it was fraught with confusion. Nothing is more demoralizing or ineffective.

The chapter has shown that the 'Innovation Strategy' demonstrated a remarkable discontinuity with more progressive science, technology, and innovation policy documents produced by the Chrétien governments between 1993 and 2000. To a much greater extent than the Innovation Strategy, these earlier documents were informed by a framework. My conclusion is that the process has produced nothing resembling a strategy, an agenda, or a consultation. Whereas the 1993 to 2000 period could reasonably be labelled a period of 'progress' in the area of science, technology, and innovation policy, this most recent exercise must be characterized as a soon-to-be-forgotten period of mere drift amid a sea of innovation-based activities, both within and outside government.

NOTES

The research assistance of Jessica Vinograd and Tyler Chamberlin is greatly appreciated, as are the contributions of more than 20 federal government employees who agreed to be anonymously interviewed for this chapter, as well as numerous participants at various regional meetings, including the National Summit.

1 Interviews reveal that Minister Manley declined because he had already delivered the S&T Review in 1996 and wished to see the Report built upon and implemented.
2 Recall that one of Brian Tobin's moves in his short stint as minister of industry was to subsidize the dying shipbuilding industry in Newfoundland.
3 Senior members of Industry Canada, when asked in an interview if the minister or deputy minister would be attending many of the regional summits, responded, 'Why would he bother? This innovation stuff gets so old so fast'.
4 May to October 2002.
5 This was reported by numerous interviewees.
6 Public Policy Forum, 13 June 2002.
7 See, for example, Richard Florida, *The Rise of the Creative Class* (New York: Basic Books, 2002) and John de la Mothe and Gilles Paquet, eds, *Local and Regional Systems of Innovation* (Boston: Kluwer, 1997).
8 For a fuller discussion of the CATA exercise, see John de la Mothe, 'Constructing Advantage Through Community-Based Knowledge Transfer', *Journal of Technology Transfer* (June 2003); John de la Mothe and Geoff Mallory, 'The Role of Local Knowledge and the Strategy of Constructed Advantage: The Role of Community Alliances', *International Journal of Technology Management* (2003, in press); John de la Mothe and Geoff Mallory, 'Industry-Government Relations in a Knowledge Based Economy: The Role of Constructed Advantage', paper given at the 7th International Congress on International Business, Bangkok, 9 Jan. 2003.
9 For example, Charles M. Gastle, 'Innovation and Entropy Within the Global Economy: Accelerating the "Red Queen Game"', prepared for ITAC, 2002; Everett Anstey, Chair of the Board, President, and CEO of Sun Microsystems, 'Creating a Culture for Innovation', Ottawa, 24 Oct. 2002; Jocelyn Ghent-Mallett, 'Silicon Valley North: The Formation of the Ottawa Innovation Cluster', prepared for ITAC, 2002; and Canadian Federation of Business School Deans, 'Canadian Business Schools and the Innovation Agenda', Nov. 2002.
10 See Roger Voyer, 'Thirty Years of Canadian Science Policy: From 1.5 to 1.5', *Science and Public Policy* 26, 4 (1999), 277–82.
11 J.J. Brown, *Ideas in Exile* (Toronto: McClelland and Stewart, 1967).
12 See, for example, the series on 'Competitiveness' in *The Financial Post*, especially Roger Martin, 'Productivity Gets Rolling', 17 June 2002, FP9.
13 Arthur J. Cordell and James M. Gilmour, *Innovation in a Cold Climate* (Ottawa: Science Council of Canada, 1971); Arthur J. Cordell, *The Multinational Firm, Foreign Direct Investment and Canadian Science Policy* (Ottawa: Science Council of Canada, 1971); John N.H. Britton and James M. Gilmour, *The Weakest Link: A Technological*

Perspective on Canadian Industrial Underdevelopment (Ottawa: Science Council of Canada, 1972).

14 'Top 150 R&D Survey', *Technology Review* (Dec. 2002).

15 For examples of this perspective see Voyer, 'Thirty Years of Canadian Science Policy'.

16 Statistics Canada, 'Science Statistics Service Bulletin', Catalogue 88---1-XIB / ISSN 1209-1278, 25, 8 (Nov. 2001), 1; Industry Canada, 'Trends in R&D, Patents and Other Measures of Innovation', Micro-Economics Policy Analysis Branch, Industry Canada, Oct. 2002.

17 I say 'appropriately', because in the early to mid-1980s, the government performed more than half of Canada's R&D—a much higher proportion than in other leading countries.

18 This document and its summary were released by Industry Canada in November 1994. Many of these issues were laid out in the Mulroney government's 1984 strategy, *A New Direction for Canada: An Agenda for Economic Renewal*, presented by the Hon. Michael Wilson, Minister of Finance, 8 Nov. 1984.

19 See John de la Mothe and Albert N. Link, eds, *Networks, Alliances and Partnerships in the Innovation Process* (Boston: Kluwer, 2002).

20 Some interviewees suggested that perhaps the term 'white paper' was used inadvertently by a civil servant when talking to a journalist. Nonetheless, the term stuck for several months, and no official corrected it.

21 David Crane, *The Canadian Dictionary of Business and Economics* (Toronto: Stoddart, 1993), 678.

22 Here we are using as source material *Achieving Excellence: Investing in People, Knowledge and Opportunity. Canada's Innovation Strategy*, 2001; *National Summit on Innovation and Learning: Programme*, 2002; *National Summit on Innovation and Learning Discussion Guide*, 2002.

23 Canada, *Investing in Excellence 1996–2001* (Ottawa: Public Works and Government Services Canada, 2002).

12

Dancing Around the Digital Divide: The Fight for a Federal Broadband Access Policy

RICHARD J. SCHULTZ

Other chapters in this volume, notably those by Allan Tupper and Michael Prince, suggest that, in at least the university and pension policy sectors, the Chrétien government has shown considerable continuity, vigour, and, indeed, successful performance. Continuity, vigour, and success are not terms that could be employed to describe the development and implementation of federal high-speed Internet broadband access policy. Despite the importance given to this issue both in the Liberals' election campaign of 2000 and subsequently in the Speech from the Throne of January 2001, attempts to articulate and develop a policy have been characterized by a vast 'performance deficit', to reformulate a phrase much in use to describe the Chrétien years. Although the objective of reducing the so-called 'digital divide' that exists between those with and those without access to modern efficient Internet services is admirable, progress has been halting at best, at times overly ambitious, and poorly defended. Rather than remaining true to the original objective of achieving 'the critical goal of making broadband access widely available to citizens, businesses and public institutions and to all communities in Canada by 2004', which according to official estimates would have cost between $1.85 and $4.6 billion, in September 2002 the government announced a radically scaled-down, much more modest funding program of $105 million for pilot programs for rural and remote communities.[1]

The broadband access question has been embroiled, perhaps more than any other policy issue, in the political disarray and turmoil surrounding the internecine warfare of the leadership race, initially unofficial and now official, to succeed Jean Chrétien as leader of the Liberal party and as prime minister. The conflicts over this policy not only caused an unprecedented public trashing of a high-profile, government-appointed task force, but, more importantly, played a role in the resignation of an important minister in the Chrétien government, Brian Tobin, the Industry Canada minister and, most significantly, in the apparent termination of his leadership ambitions. It may also have cost one of the senior civil servants involved in the intra-governmental struggles a promotion to Clerk of the Privy Council.

The purpose of this chapter is to describe and analyse the political, bureaucratic, and interest group—corporate and consumer—processes that resulted in what can charitably be described as a two-year policy debacle. In this first section, I outline the background of the digital divide and broadband access issue and describe some of the major ideas and the interests, public and private, that catalysed the search for a public policy to address this wide-ranging issue. The next section analyses the development of the proposed policy as articulated by the National Broadband Task Force, created to advise the government on how to attain its Throne Speech objective. The third and final section examines the political conflicts that produced a radically different outcome than that favoured by the Task Force and its corporate, political, and bureaucratic advocates.

THE EMERGENCE OF THE ISSUE

Before turning to a discussion of the development of Canadian policy for high-speed broadband access, it is important to discuss aspects of the larger context in which the presumed need for such a policy occurs. Much has been written of the power of the information technology/communications revolution, of which the Internet is perhaps the most visible component. The impact of this revolution, it is said, will surely rival that of the agricultural and industrial revolutions that preceded it. It will lead to 'the death of distance' and the radical transformation of the firm, markets, national and international economies, governance, and social relationships.[2] It is indisputable, notwithstanding the hype that surrounds discussions of this revolution, that, as Cairncross notes, the emerging radical changes and future developments in information technologies and communications 'will change the world'. But she then goes on to add an important caveat: 'How they will change it is a mystery.'[3] To underscore the importance of her point she quotes the former chairman of AT&T, who in 1995 stated,

One could reasonably expect the chairman of AT&T to know what his corporation will be in ten years from now. He doesn't. One could, within reason, expect the chairman of AT&T to be able to predict how technology will transform his business a decade hence. He can't. At the least he should know who his major competitors will be in 2005. Stumped again. But here is what he does know: something startling, intriguing, and profound is afoot.[4]

The central point is that corporate and public policy-makers must be careful not to be swept away by the hype, and the special pleading that inevitably accompanies such hype, and should be extremely cautious and circumspect as they develop policies to take advantage of the information revolution. In stable times, the governmental record, in Canada and elsewhere, with respect to developing effective industrial policies and picking industrial winners is not a particularly enviable one. In revolutionary times, the pitfalls are dramatically multiplied. We simply do not know how economies in general, or specific sectors, will be linked to the information revolution. Nor can we realistically predict which individual corporations will successfully ride the revolutionary waves. As Peter Pitsch, drawing on the work of Hayek, has emphasized, in such turbulent and complex times it is vitally important that governmental policy-makers be extremely cautious, and 'take our ignorance more seriously.'[5] This point is also emphasized by Cohen and his colleagues in their discussion of the future emergence of what they label the e-conomy:

> In the real world, technology uptake and utilization by businesses, governments, and consumers is nearly unpredictable. Uses emerge within a process of search and experimentation—and may well be something we do not expect. Economic historian Paul David points out that it took nearly half a century for business users to figure out the possibilities for increased efficiency through factory reorganization opened up by the electric motor. Finding the most valued uses for the next wave of computer and communications technology may not take quite as long, but it will take time and probably a longer time than many expect.[6]

In short, experimentation, combined with acceptance of the inevitable 'roadkill along the way', is the realistic prescription for policy-makers. Given that Canada ranks first in the G7 countries for both telephone and cable penetration, it is surely no surprise that Canadians have vigorously embraced the Internet. A Conference Board study of national connectivity, based on a 'connectedness index' of factors that included price, availability, reach, and use, found that by 2000 Canada ranked second, behind the United States, as the most connected country in the world. We also ranked first in Internet usage in 2000, according to the Internet Industry Almanac.[7]

Despite the popularity of the Internet, there is concern in Canada, as in other countries, that access to the Internet is not equally available to all segments of society—that there is a so-called 'digital divide'. It should be underlined, of course, that any differential in access that does exist is not limited to the Internet. As Andrew Reddick of the Public Interest Advocacy Centre (PIAC) has noted, drawing on polling data from the Ekos organization, 'beyond the Internet and computers, differential levels of access also exist in other communications technologies. These include standard services such as cable television, and newer services such as cellular or PCS phones, telephone banking and satellite television.'[8]

As Reddick astutely notes, we need a much more subtle discussion and analysis of differential access, because it is not one-dimensional, as some would have it. Unequal access comes in many forms. One dimension is regional, in that individuals in urban areas are more likely to have access to the Internet than those in rural and remote communities. Another dimension is income, with high- and middle-income households more likely to have access than their low-income counterparts. Other factors shaping the digital divide are education levels and age: more educated and younger Canadians are more likely to have Internet access than less educated or older Canadians. Despite the different Internet penetration rates across these dimensions, recent research by Statistics Canada, according to Reddick, 'noted that there was a trend of higher overall rates of growth in access in the less-connected subgroups; a pattern which, if it holds, could lessen the divide over time.'[9]

With respect to the development of public policy initiatives to ameliorate the inequalities in Internet access that may exist, Reddick, although recognizing that such initiatives are both necessary and worthwhile, offers two cautionary comments. One is that we should not let our enthusiasm about the Internet be 'divorced from a serious consideration of how it is situated in our broader social and economic relations.' If we do so, he argues, there is a risk that public policy will be based on 'unfounded assumptions and expectations about the likelihood of Canadians, regardless of social class, being ubiquitously connected from home, and when this will happen.' He compares the situation to cable penetration, which has been widely available to Canadians for more than thirty years, yet 'there still exists substantial differences in cable subscribership based on social class and geographical location.' He points out that there are wide differences with respect to cable penetration between upper-income Canadians (83 per cent) and lower-income Canadians (64.7 per cent), and that regional availability and economic disadvantage, not simply rural technological factors, explain the differential penetration rates.[10] The comparison with cable systems should be kept in mind, because, as we will discuss below, the cable industry has been one of the primary advocates for a national broadband access policy.

Reddick offers a more general cautionary point that is worth quoting at length. He contends that we should move

beyond a simplistic notion of a divide between 'have' and 'have-nots,' conveying a pejorative view of first- and second-class information society citizens. It may be true that those not connected are already, or will be, disadvantaged in some way. And this is arguably the case with many who could realize a benefit through access . . . but are unable to because of a real barrier to access. However, it is also necessary to give the public its due, and recognize that one does not 'fail the test' by not being online! Of the approximately 50 percent of Canadians that are not connected, about half see no value, use or purpose in the Internet for them. . . . [T]hey should not be construed or treated *a priori* as second-class citizens, or simply be categorized with the others not online as being socially or economically disadvantaged.[11]

The Canadian government, reflecting prior concerns about the mythically powerful, if historically misconstrued concept of universal service in telecommunications, has for most of the past decade undertaken steps to address the digital divide.[12] On the one hand, the Canadian Radio-television and Telecommunications Commission (CRTC) began an investigation in 1997 into the cost of telephone service in remote, rural regions of Canada and in the Canadian far north. The Commission noted that 97 per cent of the over 18 million telephone lines in Canada are already connected to a digital switch that permits low-speed connection to the Internet without incurring long-distance charges. It also concluded that there were lower levels of service in what it defined as high-cost areas, and, as a result, it established a 'basic service objective' for local exchange carriers in those areas. For our purposes, the most significant part of that objective was that such service must include 'individual line service with touch-tone dialling, provided with capability to connect via low speed data transmission to the Internet at local rates'.[13] The Commission noted that, assuming that the existing service improvement plans of the individual telephone companies would be completed in the near future, only 7,700 currently served customers, out of 18 million telephone lines, would lack access to the Internet. In other words, in the very near future there will be no technical barrier to access to the Internet for all but an extremely small proportion of Canadian telephone subscribers, at least in terms of low-speed access.

For its part, Industry Canada established a number of programs by which it has aggressively, and very successfully, pursued a strategy of 'Connecting Canadians' to the Internet. One has been SchoolNet, launched in 1993, the objective of which has been to provide more than 250,000 computers, donated by government and the private sector, to schools and libraries across Canada.[14] A second initiative is the Community Access Program, the objective of which is to establish up to 10,000 affordable public access Internet sites in both rural and urban communities throughout Canada. This program operates through partnerships with provinces, municipalities, and non-profit community groups, and is well on its way to meeting its objective, with new sites being opened regularly.[15]

Given the relative success of existing public initiatives in narrowing any digital divide that may exist in Canada, what accounts for the demand for a new Internet access policy? Such a question is made all the more pertinent by Reddick's observations, and his supporting evidence, that 'the general public . . . in the context of their everyday lives did not find the lack of Internet access from home to be problematic', and that 'a slight majority of non-users from all segments with the exception of upper-income households would not have the Internet at home if they had a choice'.[16] The answer is simply that the idea of the digital divide, particularly to high-speed broadband service, has been embraced and championed by public and private sector interests that have the most to gain from persuading the government of Canada to undertake a new spending initiative. Although the concept of the digital divide is less than a decade old, the current policy dispute is over the adoption of a new definition of that divide. Specifically, the objective now is to define the digital divide as the gap between those who have access to high-speed 'always-on' broadband service and those who do not. High-speed broadband, it is claimed, will be the linchpin for the full development of the information revolution. As we shall see, the price tag to remove the new digital divide is extremely high, and it is this price tag that became a central element in the conflict that followed the publication of the Report of the National Broadband Task Force.

The original advocates for a broadband initiative were from the Telecommunications branch of Industry Canada. The department had been successful in persuading the Prime Minister and his advisors to establish the program of 'connecting Canadians' as a priority in the 1997 Speech from the Throne, in which the government announced its objective of making Canada the most connected nation in the world by 2000, a target that was reached. Subsequently, for the election campaign of 2000, the Minister of Industry Canada, John Manley, with the approval of the Prime Minister, committed the government to a new and more ambitious goal, making high-speed broadband access available to all Canadian communities by 2004.

The immediate interests of federal officials in gaining political approval and commitment to such a goal were obvious. Almost from the time the CRTC was created in 1968, the broadcasting directorate in the Department of Communications was unhappy to be playing second fiddle to that agency, which had emerged as an energetic policy-maker as well as a regulatory agency, and which was perfectly capable of defending its turf against challengers such as the Department. After the responsibility for telecommunications was transferred to the CRTC in 1976, both the broadcasting section and the telecommunications section watched enviously as the CRTC put its imprint on both sectors without any significant input from the Department.[17] In fact, the failure of the attempt by the telecommunications branch in 1992 to become the primary decision-maker in the telecommunications sector through new telecommunications legislation contributed to the disbanding of the Department of Communications shortly thereafter; in 1993, responsibilities for telecommunications were transferred to Industry Canada and those for broadcasting to Canadian Heritage.

Notwithstanding the government's embrace of the objective of high-speed access, the policy needed private sector champions if it were to progress from an objective to a full-blown program. Three such champions were ready at hand, the information technology firms, the cable television industry, and the telephone industry—or, more specifically, the incumbent telephone companies. New telecom entrants, as we shall see, played a much more modest role in the process. The information technology firms, like the telecommunications industry generally in Canada, had been adversely affected by the world-wide telecommunications crash, as witnessed, for example, by the significant decline in the fortunes of Nortel Networks and J.D.S. Uniphase, and the bursting of the dot.com bubble.[18]

In addition, there were uniquely Canadian reasons for creating a public push for an expansion of broadband capacity. The cable industry's support for such a program, for instance, was obvious. For the first time in the history of the industry it was losing significant market share as a result of the emergence of a competitor, the direct-to-home satellite systems, which included both the authorized Canadian service providers, Bell ExpressVu and Star Choice, and the unauthorized grey- and black-market American systems. Another important factor was that the industry, especially the three largest players, who provide approximately 70 per cent of cable services in Canada, was facing a significant cash crunch because of the high investment costs that were being incurred both to provide digital television services and to meet current demands for high-speed broadband access. Access to public funds to assist in the deployment and extension of the cable system would both provide important relief for the cable companies and help the industry maintain its competitive position in both Internet services and broadcasting distribution.

Although the primary Internet competitors for the incumbent telephone companies were the cable companies, the latter also recognized that both Internet service providers shared a common fundamental interest in having the federal government undertake a large-scale infrastructure investment program. For their part, the incumbent telephone companies, especially the two largest, Bell Canada and Telus, were suffering financially as a result of both the intense competition in the telephone industry that had occurred since 1992 and expensive acquisitions or investments. In the latter half of the 1990s, the incumbent telephone companies and the new entrants had become engaged in a costly, apparently interminable price war, which had seen substantial growth in demand, significant loss of market share for the incumbents, and a decrease in profit margins for all players.[19]

The two largest telephone companies—or, in the case of Bell Canada, its parent, BCE, which depends on Bell for most of its revenue—had made costly investments and acquisitions that were placing great strains on them. The $6.6 billion that Telus paid for Clearnet, a wireless service provider, when added to other factors, left it with an onerous $8 billion debt load. BCE was also suffering as a result of the premium it had paid to acquire control of Teleglobe, which subsequently had to be written off when it went bankrupt. In addition, BCE had made costly international investments through its subsidiary BCI, which had to be written off when the latter went out of business. Given that neither telephone company faced much competition in the residential markets, and high-speed access was the fastest growing segment of the Internet market, their interest in having the federal government significantly subsidize the growth of that market segment was clear and obvious.

CHOREOGRAPHING THE DANCE:
THE NATIONAL BROADBAND TASK FORCE

On 11 January 2001, the terms of reference and membership of the Broadband Task Force were announced. Underscoring the importance apparently placed on the attainment of its election promise, the government included in the Speech from the Throne, delivered later that month, as part of its 'innovation strategy', a commitment 'to work with the private sector to determine the best ways to make broadband internet access available to all communities in Canada by the year 2004.'[20] To meet this objective, the Task Force was asked to 'examine and report on the situation in a number of communities representing the full range of circumstances in Canada with respect to number of households, distance from existing high-speed infrastructure, institutional needs, existing local infrastructure and infrastructure soon to be available.' More specifically, the Task Force was, among other matters, to advise the minister on

- the types, characteristics and needs of communities which without government involvement will not likely be served by high-speed broadband Internet access by the private sector by 2004; . . .
- the models and contractual arrangements which the government might use which are neutral with respect to technologies and maximize the role and risk-taking of the private sector; and
- whether or not pilot projects would be useful to provide both the private sector and the Government of Canada with insights and experience that would usefully inform an approach to a broader effort and, if so, what aspects the pilots should test.[21]

Given that the Task Force was set up to seek advice from 'stakeholders', the membership was not particularly surprising. It consisted of a Chair and 33 members and included representatives of the telephone and cable industries, high technology communications firms, and consumers. It also included a number of 'participating associations' representing, among others, the cable television, private broadcasting, and the wireless telecommunications industries and Internet service providers. Two aspects of the membership are worth noting. First, the largest single component, almost one-third, came from the cable and telephone firms. Secondly—reflecting the importance that these firms obviously placed on the initiative—the membership included some of the most senior executives of the dominant telephone (Bell Canada and its affiliate, Aliant, and Telus) and cable (Rogers, Shaw, Cogeco) companies. It also included representatives from the new telephone entrants, AT&T, Call-Net, and Microcell. In addition, the members were supported by officials from their individual firms. The staff of the Task Force was drawn exclusively from Industry Canada, although other departments and agencies, such as Finance, DIAND, the PCO, and the CRTC sent observers to the meetings.

The telephone and cable industry representatives and the Industry Canada officials clearly dominated the work of the Task Force—as reflected in the Report, which was issued less than six months after the Task Force was created. For their part, the representatives of the new telephone entrants were there to keep a watching brief on what the incumbent firms were requesting and, more importantly, to exchange their support for the recommendation that a program to subsidize broad-band access be instituted for a recommendation unrelated to the mandate of the Task Force. The new entrants, along with the cable representatives, wanted the Task Force to recommend that the current foreign ownership restrictions in the telecommunications sector be removed or reduced significantly.[22] From their perspective the Task Force was extremely dysfunctional, because of the longstanding and wide-ranging conflicts, unrelated to broadband deployment, between themselves and the incumbent telephone companies. Their apprehensions that the Task Force might become largely a vehicle to advance the interests of the latter were reinforced when, at the very last minute, after the Task Force had agreed to the major recommendations, Michael Sabia, President of BCE, Bell Canada's parent company, intervened to persuade officials in Industry Canada to change the final draft of the Report so that it recommended not that the restrictions be lifted, but instead only that the federal government 'conduct an urgent review' of such restrictions.[23]

The influence of the incumbent telephone companies, the cable industry, and Industry Canada officials was obvious in the major recommendations of the Task Force. The telephone companies and the Canadian Cable Television Association provided the basic information for the Task Force on the existing gaps in the availability of high-speed broadband services, and the funding program at the heart of the Task Force's Report reflected their 'wish list'. The Task Force concluded that the government's stated objective could not be met unless it embarked on the following priorities:

- a plan to build a broadband transport link from the national broadband network to a point of presence within the community;
- a plan to connect public institutions in the community (e.g. learning and health care centres, and local provincial and federal services) to the broadband network; and
- a plan to offer local businesses and residents the opportunity to connect to the broadband network from their place of business or residence.[24]

To fulfill these priorities, the Task Force set out a series of estimates that ranged from slightly more than $2.7 billion to $4.5 billion, based on the following distribution of costs:

- Transport to unserved communities $1.3 to $1.9B
  (depending on mix of technologies)
- Connecting public institutions $500 to $600M
- Connecting businesses and residences $900M to $2B
  (depending on mix of technologies and take-up)
- Funding to community champions $50 to $70M[25]

Few public reports have received the near universal condemnation that greeted the publication of the Task Force Report. Although perhaps unfairly, but not surprisingly, most commentators concentrated on the upper-end estimated price tag of $4.6 billion.[26] It can be argued that the Report, and not simply the projected cost, was fundamentally flawed in a number of ways.

In the first place, the Task Force appears to have radically extended its mandate. It was asked by the Minister to advise on plans to provide Internet access to communities, yet its estimates, especially at the high end, included the cost of linking up businesses and residences. The recommendation was advanced to support what it labelled as an 'overarching principle', namely that 'as a matter of urgency . . . all Canadians should have access to broadband network services.'[27] Furthermore, it advanced the principle that 'all communities, institutions, businesses and individuals in Canada should have equitable and affordable access to broadband services and to the widest possible range of content and service providers.'[28] One problem with the Task Force's treatment of this principle, though, is that it failed to justify it: all it did was invoke it, without providing any guidance as to what constituted 'equitable and affordable access'. The Task Force appears to have been unaware of, or chose to ignore, the report by Andrew Reddick of the Public Interest Advocacy Centre, cited earlier, which discusses both the lack of interest on the part of many, and the fact that one of several reasons that there are many urban poor who lack access is the cost of computer equipment and training. This is particularly surprising in that Industry Canada, along with Human Resources Development Canada, commissioned Reddick's study only the year before the Task Force reported.[29]

A second fundamental problem with the Report is that it failed to specify which part of the funding would come from the federal government and which would be provided by the private sector. The impression was given that, for all the talk of a private sector-public sector partnership, the federal government would bear the greatest burden. And a closely related impression was that the program would amount to a large windfall for the traditional telephone and cable companies.

Notwithstanding the claim by the Task Force that its approach, which was said to be technologically neutral, would 'enhance effective competition', the suggested cost figures cited above appeared to be based on cable and telephone deployment. Wireless and satellite deployment, which would cost significantly less than either fibre optics or coaxial cable according to the Task Force's own calculations, while of course mentioned as possibilities, did not appear to be part of the preferred deployment plan.[30] In other words, the Task Force appears to have decided, contrary to the arguments cited in the first part of this paper, that the companies with the most effective technologies for providing high-speed Internet access were precisely those that were now providing such service—that is, primarily the telephone and cable companies. This presumption is reinforced by the fact that the Task Force recommended that the CRTC 'should ensure that its decisions, in matters affecting revenues, should reflect the particularly heavy demands and challenges facing facilities providers in terms of capital generation and capital recovery.'[31] Not only does this appear to justify a novel form of hidden cross-subsidization through the rate-setting process, at a time when the CRTC has been attempting to remove such cross-subsidies, especially from telecommunications rates, but it fails to acknowledge that the only facilities-providers now subject to some form of CRTC rate-setting, which is the avenue for capital generation and recovery, are the incumbent telephone and cable companies.

What makes this bias in favour of existing service providers even more questionable is the definition of broadband offered by the Task Force, specifically, a service that can support full-motion video at the current minimum speed of 1.5 megabits per second per individual user.[32] The problem with this is that it appears to encourage the delivery of current broadband service that does not meet even the contemporary International Telecommunications Union definition of broadband as a 10 megabit per second service.[33] In fact, the Task Force's own figures suggest that the 1.5 Mbps speed will not provide the bandwidth requirements for the applications, particularly health care and educational uses, that the Task Force cites to justify the subsidy plan.[34] According to the senior director for network projects at Canarie, the not-for-profit Canadian Internet research consortium, 'the task force was forced to define broadband as 1.5 Mbps service in order not to embarrass the telephone and cable companies on the task force that advertise their residential high-speed services as broadband services.'[35]

Criticism of the Task Force recommendations was so intense and vigorous that the critics won the day. There were few willing to defend the recommendations. Those on the Task Force representing the new entrants were silent, as were the consumer representatives. The president of the Canadian Association of Internet Providers, even though his was one of the official 'participating associations' in the work of the Task Force, expressed concern over the apparent favouritism shown to the incumbents, especially the cable companies, who, he argued, were not permitting competitors open third-party access to their cable systems, and were thereby able to continue to restrict consumer choice.[36]

Even Bell Canada's representative, sensing that the Report had died a quick death, quickly backed away from the recommendation that the foreign investment restrictions should be reviewed. The only two defenders of the Report were the Chairman of the Task Force, David Johnston, president of the University of Waterloo, and Brian Tobin, the minister of Industry Canada. Johnston wrote an op-ed piece accusing the critics of being 'urban-centric' and showing 'a limited understanding of the problems faced by rural and remote communities across Canada'.[37] Even Johnston appeared to acknowledge that his report had caused some of the problem by failing to distinguish effectively between the government's contribution of between $1.85 and $2.6 billion to connect the communities and the remainder of the cost, which would be used to connect businesses and residences, and of which the government share would be minimal.

For his part, Brian Tobin reluctantly conceded that the Task Force's recommendations were far too costly, and that he would fight only for a program to connect public institutions to high-speed broadband systems, a program, according to his estimate, that would cost $2 billion, to be shared with the private sector and provincial governments.[38] Nevertheless, he lashed out at the critics, stating that 'that kind of pompous, arrogant, misguided, short-sighted thinking has no place in a modern, contemporary Canada.' Given the overall very tepid performance by the defenders of the Task Force's recommendations, the issue immediately disappeared from the public agenda. This disappearance, however, was to be only temporary. Within a few months, the issue would re-emerge in a new form: as a competitive dance involving two aspiring leaders of the Liberal party.

'Pas de Deux': Martin and Tobin Resume the Dance

Despite Johnston's and Tobin's anger over what they clearly considered unjustified criticisms of the Task Force Report, the issue almost immediately disappeared from public discussion. Indeed, aside from his public comment, Tobin did not issue an official response to the Report. The assumption was that broadband access policy was a dead issue, and that the Task Force, much like a similar effort of a few years earlier, also chaired by Johnston, the Task Force on the Information Highway, had completely failed to have a policy impact. Four months later, however, the policy was resurrected and the ensuing conflict would play a significant role in a cabinet resignation and the apparent termination of one candidate's Liberal leadership ambitions. It may also have caused one of the combatants a promotion to the most senior position in the public service, Clerk of the Privy Council.

The issue was rejoined in October, when it was reported that Tobin, in a highly unusual manner, was publicly lobbying to have the forthcoming budget include a four-year commitment of $1.5 billion to provide broadband access to rural areas.[39] Both Paul Martin, as finance minister and as leadership rival for Tobin, and the Department of Finance were hostile to this demand. Martin did not want to support a high-level program that was so closely associated with his rival, especially one that would be popular with a potential source of major leadership campaign donations. In this the Minister was supported by his officials, albeit for different reasons. According to one source, Finance and Martin 'did little to disguise their contempt' for a progam that they regarded as suffering from 'obvious deficiencies'.[40] In particular, they did not want to send the mistaken signal to other ministers and departments with ambitious, ill-conceived spending projects that the attack on the deficit was over.

Tobin's claim in his recently published memoirs that he was only asking for $100 million for the next fiscal year in order to start the project probably reflected his retreat from the original request.[41] In part, this consolation amount was supposed to represent a compromise imposed on both parties by the Prime Minister.[42] In any event, even this amount was unacceptable to the Minister of Finance, who, in his budget on 11 December, would commit only $105 million in total and, more importantly, spread out over three years—and to rub it in even further, it would not begin until 2005, a year after the original promise to complete the project. Martin's explanation was that 'more planning is required to properly achieve our commitment, particularly given the rapidly changing technology and, as a consequence, we will shift our target to the end of 2005.' This stance may reflect more than political rival-ries. As Geoffrey Hale has noted, Paul Martin is not particularly sympathetic to large-scale government-directed industrial policies such as that originally called for by the Broadband Task Force, and he quotes Martin as stating in March 2001, pre-sumably with the pun intended, that 'innovation is by nature entrepreneurial, decentralized and highly dependent on a broad band of networks in communities right across the country.'[43]

Tobin states that he was 'surprised and disappointed' with the announcement, and claims that he had been promised by the Prime Minister prior to the budget 'that the broadband item would be in the budget, no ifs, or buts.' He also claims that when asked about it, 'the prime minister told me that his instructions had not been followed.'[44] Tobin states that he was so upset with Martin's action that it acted as a 'trigger' that led him to reassess his commitment to politics and his chances of win-ning the leadership, and ultimately to his resignation from the Chrétien cabinet and from the House of Commons. In a recent interview, Tobin contended that Chrétien, in an effort to talk him out of resigning, promised to advance the timetable for the broadband funding, but that he had already made up his mind.[45] According to one well-placed source, Tobin may not have been the only casualty of Martin's budget manoeuvre. Edward Greenspon of the *Globe and Mail* speculated that the Prime Minister's anger over the failure of the Privy Council Office to resolve the conflict cost the Clerk of the Privy Council his position and, because Finance did not respect the compromise he had ordered, excluded Kevin Lynch, the Deputy Minister of Finance, from the competition to replace the Clerk.[46]

Despite the resignation, the dance continued. Tobin has stated that one of the first things he did after resigning was to inform Alan Rock, his successor as Minis-ter of Industry Canada, of the Prime Minister's commitment to provide the funds in the current fiscal year and not after 2005. In spite of this commitment, the Finance Minister appears to have continued to stymie both the Prime Minister and Industry Canada, at least until he left the government in June 2002. Notwithstanding that res-ignation, and despite being lobbied to restore the commitment by a diverse group, including the Ontario Federation of Agriculture and the Canadian Advanced Tech-nology Alliance, the Prime Minister would only go so far, in June 202, as to state that an announcement by the Minister of Industry would be forthcoming on 'accel-erating our plan to improve broadband Internet access for rural communities.'[47] In mid-August, however, the Minister of Industry acknowledged he still 'doesn't know yet how much money set aside for the infrastructure program will go towards broadband.'[48]

That announcement came in early September 2002, when the Minister of Indus-try and the Secretary of State for Rural Development announced in Bracebridge, Ontario, without much fanfare, and despite the history of conflict, that the govern-ment was launching a $105 million Broadband for Rural and Northern Development Program. The program has two parts: first, funds would be available to assist com-munities that do not currently have access to develop a business plan; secondly, these communities would be eligible to enter a competition for funds to implement their plans.[49] According to the announcement, priority would be given to unserved First Nation, northern, remote, and rural communities. Eligible recipients are limited to 'community-based, legally-incorporated, not-for-profit Canadian organizations that will commit themselves to act as the "community champion" on behalf of the eligible community.' In other words, the 'public pipeline fund' so eagerly sought by the cable and telephone companies was an 'idea whose time never came'. Moreover, not only would the large-scale development envisioned earlier not materialize, but experiments using a wide range of technologies would be encouraged, so long as they were based in the individual communities.

CONCLUSIONS

And so the dance ended. In many respects this saga, in which a program was developed to fulfill the Liberal election commitment of 2000, is a perfect illustration of 'how Ottawa should not spend'. However laudable the commitment, the program was, as we have shown, highly debatable. Both the policy-making process and the substance of the original plan were fundamentally flawed. When one employs a task force comprised of widely conflicting and fundamentally self-seeking vested interests, served by a federal department in search of an expanded mission, it should not come as a surprise when the resulting product is a large, well-larded public trough. The Task Force obviously lacked effective direction: having been allowed to ignore its mandate, it produced a 'plan' effectively without details, and with grossly inflated costs. The avalanche of criticism that resulted, and the profound silence from would-be supporters, must have come as a great surprise to those hoping not to get caught with their hand in the public cookie-jar.

That the broadband access issue became entangled with the leadership and bureaucratic ambitions of two contenders to replace Jean Chrétien, and with their respective departments, was perhaps not surprising. The irony, of course, is that the ultimate product, the Broadband for Rural and Northern Development Pilot Program, is probably exactly the type of program that should have been created, given a technology whose form and applications are not yet predictable. It will be focused, not comprehensive; experimental, not an automatic extension of status quo technologies; and community- and entrepreneurially-designed and -driven, not an aid package for disabled corporate incumbents. However awkward and poorly choreographed, this first, albeit extended performance of the dance around the digital divide may ultimately prove to be an audience-pleaser.

NOTES

1 The quotation is from the Speech from the Throne, 30 Jan. 2001; the estimates are from the Report of the National Broadband Task Force, *The New National Dream: Networking the Nation for Broadband Access* (Ottawa: Industry Canada, June 2001)

(henceforth 'Task Force Report'). The program was announced on 5 Sept. 2002; the announcement and details can be found at www.broadband.gc.ca.

2 For interesting perspectives on these issues, some balanced, some less so, see, for example, Frances Cairncross, *The Death of Distance* (Cambridge, Mass.: Harvard University Press, 1997); George Gilder, *Telecosm: How Infinite Bandwidth Will Revolutionize Our World* (New York: The Free Press, 2000); Robert E. Litan and Alice M. Rivlin, *Beyond the Dot.coms: The Economic Promise of the Internet* (Washington: The Brookings Institution Press, 2001); and The BRIE-IGCC E-conomy Project, *Tracking a Transformation* (Washington: The Brookings Institution Press, 2001).

3 Cairncross, *The Death of Distance*, 2.

4 Ibid.

5 Peter K. Pitsch, *The Innovation Age: A New Perspective on the Telecom Revolution* (Washington: The Progress and Freedom Foundation, 1996), 5.

6 Stephen S. Cohen et al., 'Tools', in the BRIE-IGCC E-Conomy Project, *Tracking a Transformation*, 16. The reference is to Paul David, 'Computer and Dynamo: The Productivity Paradox in a Not-too-Distant Mirror', in *Technology and Productivity: The Challenge for Economic Policy* (Paris: OECD, 1991).

7 All of the figures in this paragraph are found in the Task Force Report.

8 Andrew Reddick, with Christian Boucher and Manon Groseilliers, 'The Dual Digital Divide: The Information Highway in Canada' (Ottawa: Public Interest Advocacy Centre, 2000), 7.

9 Ibid., 9. This was supported by an American study in 2000, which found that 'people earning $21,000 to $33,000 [US$], typically in blue-collar, farming or service fields, with a high school education at most, spend the most time online.' See 'Surprising Geography of America's Digital Divide', *The New York Times*, 25 Sept. 2000, C4.

10 Reddick, 'The Dual Digital Divide', 15–16.

11 Ibid., 9.

12 See Milton Mueller, *Universal Service: Competition, Interconnection and Monopoly in the Making of the American Telephone System* (Cambridge Mass.: MIT Press, 1997); Richard Schultz, 'Universal Service/Universal Subsidies: The Tangled Web', in David Conklin, ed., *Adapting to New Realities* (London, Ont.: Richard Ivey School of Business, the University of Western Ontario, 1998).

13 CRTC, 'Telephone Service to High-Cost Service Areas', Telecom Decision CRTC 99–16, 19 Oct. 1999, para. 24.

14 See Jitka Licenik, 'Canada's SchoolNet: Making a Difference', at www.connect.gc.ca April 2000, last updated 28 June 2002.

15 See Brad Latta, 'Community Access Program: It's All About Connections', at www.connect.gc.ca, April 2000, last updated 12 July 2002.

16 Reddick, 'The Dual Digital Divide', 20–1. This is supported by American survey data, which found that 57 per cent of Americans without Internet access were simply not interested in having it. See Julia Angwin, 'Internet Adoption Hits the Wall', *The Globe and Mail* [Toronto], 16 July 2001, B8.

17 See G. Bruce Doern, 'Regulating on the Run: The Transformation of the CRTC as a Regulatory Institution', *Canadian Public Administration* 40, 3, 516–38; Richard Schultz and G. Bruce Doern, 'No Longer "Governments in Miniature": Canadian Regulatory Institutions in a North American Context', in G. Bruce Doern and Stephen Wilks, eds, *Changing Regulatory Institutions in Britain and North America* (Toronto: University of Toronto Press, 1998); Richard Schultz, 'Still Standing: The CRTC

1976–1996', in G. Bruce Doern et al., eds, *Changing the Rules: Canadian Regulatory Regimes and Institutions* (Toronto: University of Toronto Press, 1999).

18 See 'The Great Crash' and 'The Telecoms Crisis', *The Economist*, 20 July 2002, 9 and 59 respectively.

19 See CRTC, 'Report to Governor in Council: Status of Competition in Canadian Telecommunications Markets' (Ottawa: CRTC, Sept. 2001).

20 See Geoffrey E. Hale, 'Innovation and Inclusion: Budgetary Policy, the Skills Agenda, and the Politics of the New Economy', in G. Bruce Doern, ed., *How Ottawa Spends 2002–2003: The Security Aftermath and National Priorities* (Don Mills, Ont.: Oxford University Press, 2002), 29.

21 Cited in Task Force Report, 54.

22 Jill Vardy, 'Foreign Restriction Bargaining Chip', *The Financial Post*, 2 June 2001, D5.

23 The wording is from Task Force Report, 84; the information is from confidential interviews and a review of relevant emails sent to participants.

24 Ibid., 71.

25 Ibid., 75.

26 For representative samples, see CBC, 'Liberal Internet Plan to Cost Billions: Panel', CBC.ca, 18 June 2001; Matthew Ingram, 'Ottawa's Broadband Plan Is Dumb and Expensive', *The Globe and Mail* [Toronto], 20 June 2001; Terrence Corcoran, 'Broadband Socialism', *The National Post*, 19 June 2001. A full listing of media coverage of the report is found at www.broadband.gc.ca.

27 Task Force Report, 55.

28 Ibid., 58.

29 The Reddick study is not included in the Task Force's list of studies, Task Force Report, 92.

30 Ibid., 46.

31 Ibid., 84.

32 Ibid., 60–1.

33 David Akin, 'Task Force Misses the Mark on Investment, Technological Issues', *The Financial Post*, 19 June 2001.

34 Task Force Report, 60.

35 Quoted in Akin, 'Task Force Misses the Mark'.

36 Quoted in Steven Bonisteel, 'Broadband for All: Canada's New National Dream', 18 June 2001, online at www.newsbytes.com. I am grateful to Michelle Henry, a student in Hudson Janisch's Internet Law and Governance course at the Faculty of Law, University of Toronto, whose course paper drew my attention to this source.

37 David Johnston, 'Broadband Critics Are Shortsighted', *The Globe and Mail* [Toronto], 27 June 2001.

38 Joan Bryden, 'Minister Defends Internet Access Plan', *The Ottawa Citizen*, 27 June 2001.

39 Heather Scoffield, 'Tobin to Seek $1.5-billion for Net', *The Globe and Mail* [Toronto], 13 Oct. 2001; Heather Scoffield, 'Tobin's Budget Tactics Criticized', *The Globe and Mail* [Toronto], 21 Nov. 2001.

40 Edward Greenspon, 'Did the Tobin Debacle Spark the Mandarin Shuffle?' *The Globe and Mail* [Toronto], 5 Feb. 2002.

41 Brian Tobin, *All in Good Time* (Toronto: Penguin Canada, 2002), 251.

42 Joan Bryden and Eric Beauchesne, 'PM Intervenes to Settle Martin, Tobin Tug of War', *The National Post*, 6 Dec. 2001.

43 Hale, 'Innovation and Inclusion', 30.

44 Tobin, *All in Good Time*, 252.

45 Brian Tobin interview with Don Newman on CBC Newsworld, 'Politics', 25 Nov. 2002.

46 Greenspon, 'Did the Tobin Debacle Spark the Mandarin Shuffle?'

47 On the lobbying activities see 'Farmers Want Access to High-speed Internet', CBC News Online, 14 Aug. 2002, and Ian and Lis Angus, 'Close the Digital Divide', in *Telemanagement*, Sept. 2002, 1. On the Prime Minister's announcement, see 'The New Agricultural Policy Framework', 20 June 2002, www.pm.gc.ca.

48 'Rural Canadians Hold Out Hope for Broadband Web Access', CBC News Online, 14 Aug. 2002.

49 'Alan Rock and Andy Mitchell Launch Broadband for Rural and Northern Development Pilot Program', 5 Sept. 2002, at www.ic.gc.ca Media Room.

13

The Doubling of Government Science and Canada's Innovation Strategy

JEFF KINDER

In its Innovation Strategy the Chrétien government has made a commitment to improve Canada's performance in research and development (R&D) so that by 2010 it will rank among the top five countries in the world in that policy area.[1] Given that R&D performance by the private sector accounts for over half of all R&D conducted in Canada, this goal, regardless of its merits, is not likely to be reached unless massive new investments are made by business and industry. On the other hand, another commitment made in the Innovation Strategy—to at least double the current federal investment in R&D by 2010—requires only the actions of government policy-makers in order for it to be realized. But what are the merits of this latter commitment and what does it mean for government science? Supporters are hopeful that government science, after suffering tight budgets and in some cases deep cuts during the 1990s, is now positioned to become a key player in federal policy-making. Indeed, many believe that the need for greater investment in government science has become critical.

Government science is evolving in the face of numerous contemporary pressures. The government must support important policy, risk-management, and stewardship objectives in order to protect the health and safety of Canadians and protect the environment. Government science supports the delivery of critical services such as weather forecasting, resource mapping, and the setting of measurement standards.

Government laboratories and research institutes, catalytic agents in national and local innovation systems, contribute to industrial innovation and regional economic development. At the same time, they are under pressure to adopt new institutional arrangements and management practices. The federal science community faces many challenges with respect to renewing its human resources and updating research infrastructures in order to grapple with emerging science-based issues. In this evolving context, a new understanding of the diverse and changing roles of government science and the imperatives for science policy is required.

This chapter contributes to such an understanding by reviewing the place of government science in Canada's innovation system. After providing an overview of the current context, I begin with a brief review of the history of Canadian science, and government's role in it. I then bring the story up to the present by examining in greater detail the evolution of science policy during the Chrétien era. This section focuses on the policy choices made during the first, deficit-fighting mandate and the second, budget-surplus mandate. Recent initiatives that attempt to reform the governance of government science are then examined, particularly the proposed Federal Innovation Networks of Excellence (FINE). Finally, I offer some conclusions as to the future direction of government science and its role in the overall Canadian innovation agenda.

GOVERNMENT SCIENCE WITHIN THE
NATIONAL INNOVATION SYSTEM

The notion that innovation could be fostered by a *national system of innovation* emerged during the last decade and has come to dominate science policy debates in Canada as well as in most other countries.[2] The *innovation system* is an institutional concept that focuses on the complex network of agents, policies, and institutions that support the process of technological change in the economy. While it is important to consider a wide range of institutions in order to fully characterize the whole innovation system, the focus in relation to the performance of R&D is typically on institutions within three sectors—universities, industry, and government.

Since the Second World War the government has invested heavily in building research capacity in the universities. This was accomplished initially through programs of the National Research Council (NRC), and later through the three granting councils (NSERC, MRC, and SSHRCC). More recently, the university research system has received large federal investments through the Canada Foundation for Innovation (over $3 billion to date), the three granting councils—including the recently formed Canadian Institutes of Health Research, which replaced the MRC—(up from about $770 million in 1994/5 to approximately $1.2 billion in 2001/2), the Networks of Centres of Excellence, made permanent in 1996 ($77 million), and the Canada Research Chairs ($900 million).[3] The federal government has further invested in academic research by contributing $200 million to cover a portion of the indirect costs associated with federally supported research. Indeed, columnist Jeffrey Simpson's contribution to the current debate about the outgoing Prime Minister's legacy rests on the argument that the increase in assistance to university research during the Chrétien years will prove one of his most constructive and enduring legacies.[4]

Similarly, the government has made extensive efforts to support R&D in industry. These efforts reflect the longstanding concern that R&D performance in Canadian industry has been persistently weak as compared to that of its international competitors. Government policy has historically looked to federal laboratories, particularly those of the NRC, to help compensate for these deficiencies, but it is arguable how much this approach actually has helped industrial R&D performance. 'Ultimately,' as one observer put it, 'it would seem that government laboratories can only go so far as engines of industrial technological growth.'[5]

More recently, government policy in relation to industrial R&D has emphasized tax incentives, technical assistance through the NRC's Industrial Research Assistance Program, and direct grants and subsidies in support of private sector research.[6] In particular, the Scientific Research and Experimental Development (SR&ED) program provides tax credits for business investments in R&D. In recent years, this program has represented over $1 billion in federal revenues forgone annually, which makes it in effect the government's largest science program.[7]

These investments in academic and industrial science, along with the strong growth in R&D expenditures made by those sectors, have led to a definite strengthening of the non-government sectors of the Canadian innovation system and a concomitant decrease in the relative contribution of the federal government. Indeed, the proportion of the nation's R&D performed in the federal government has declined in recent years to the point that government science now represents only about 10 per cent of the overall Canadian effort (see Figure 13.1).[8] This, in turn, has fostered a renewed debate on the appropriate roles for government science. In particular, the debate has centred on what, if any, ongoing role the government should have in *performing* scientific and technological research. Some have called for a reduction of government's role to that of a mere funder and facilitator, not a performer, of science.[9] Others argue that the federal government needs to maintain a robust in-house science capacity in order for the entire national innovation system to function effectively, and in order to conduct the science that supports public goods unlikely to be provided by the other sectors.[10]

The Chrétien government has not taken a clear position in this debate. It has indicated its intention to *at least double* the current federal investment in R&D by 2010. But much of the federal support for R&D passes to universities and the private sector through various granting and contracting mechanisms. Nevertheless, over half of federal R&D expenditures supports efforts conducted within government laboratories and research institutes (see Figure 13.2), and this does not include the government's major support of so-called related scientific activities (RSAs)—activities that reinforce R&D efforts by disseminating and applying scientific and technological knowledge (for example, statistical data collection, testing, S&T information services, museum services).

Figure 13.1

Intramural vs Extramural R&D by the Federal Government, 1996–2001

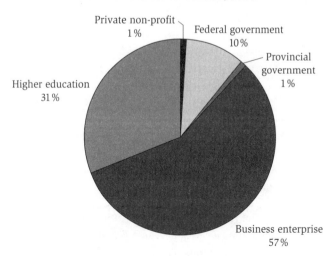

Note: For years, r means 'revised', p means 'preliminary', and e means 'estimated'.
Source: Statistics Canada, 2001, *Estimates of Canadian research and development expenditures (GERD) Canada, 1990 to 2001e, and by province, 1990 to 1999*, SIEID Working Paper Series, Cat. No. 88F0006XIE, No. 14.

Figure 13.2

R&D Performers in Canada, 2000

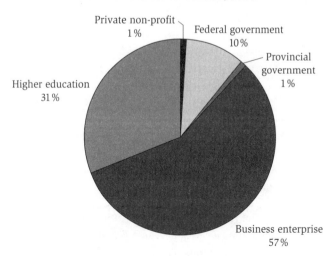

Source: Statistics Canada, 2001, *Estimates of Canadian research and development expenditures (GERD) Canada, 1990 to 2001e, and by province, 1990 to 1999*, SIEID Working Paper Series, Cat. No. 88F0006XIE, No. 14.

Thus it will be important to observe how the 'doubling' commitment is achieved. If the funding is distributed so as to maintain the current split between extramural and intramural support, it would represent an increase of government R&D from almost $2.0 billion in 2000 to $4.0 billion in 2010.[11] Even if new investment tends to favour extramural support, the federal science community is hopeful that government science will receive a critically needed injection of funding. However, government science faces many challenges, not all of them financial, and any such reinvestment is likely to come largely through new funding models rather than as increments to the core science budgets of the various line departments and agencies. These new funding models will emphasize new roles for government science and new ways to operate.

GOVERNMENT SCIENCE IN THE TWENTIETH CENTURY

The appropriate role for government science in the Canadian system of innovation has long been a subject of debate. In order to fully understand the current context for government science it is important to locate it within the history of science in Canada and the government's evolving role within that history. A quarter-century ago, J. Bruce Sinclair wrote that Canada does not have a coherent science policy because it is unconscious of its science history;[12] it can be argued that this remains true today. Many pieces of this story have been told by various scholars (though the definitive history of government science has perhaps not yet been written). A brief recounting here of the major milestones will trace the evolution of government science and the dynamics of its role within the national innovation system. For the sake of the narrative I have divided this history into various eras, which correspond to major shifts, although the most appropriate periodization of Canadian science policy history is open to debate.

Fits and Starts: Early History to the Second World War
The early history of Canadian government science overlaps extensively with the history of science in Canada generally, in that the government was the major patron and performer of science in the period prior to the Second World War. In his history of Canadian innovation, J.J. Brown reminds us that until the turn of the twentieth century Canada was a country of pioneers.[13] In such a harsh environment, the pursuit of scientific and technological activity was largely neglected in favour of the more immediate task of satisfying basic needs. To the extent that government in the nineteenth century supported science it was targeted at 'nation-building' activities to support the growth of a young country. Not surprisingly, the initial emphasis was on the inventory of natural resources and on their utilization. In particular, the Geological Survey of Canada, the Fisheries Research Board, and the experimental farms that grew up along the western railroads are usually cited as the key contributions of government science in this period.

In one of its earliest forays into science, the government appointed William Logan to make a comprehensive geological survey of the Dominion. Although the

Survey led to many fundamental advances, this early period of government science was characterized by pragmatic motives. As Logan relates, the Geological Survey was dominated by economic, not scientific objectives:

> The object of the Survey is to ascertain the mineral resources of the country, and this is kept steadily in view. Whatever new scientific facts have resulted from it have come out in the course of what I conceive to be economic researches, carried out in a scientific way.[14]

As the nation grew, so too did the amount of regulatory legislation and the organization of government departments to administer it. According to Gillis, 'forestry programs, irrigation work, regulation of water-power, wildlife conservation, and national parks all grew to be important aspects of Dominion policy during the first two decades of the twentieth century.'[15] The need for increasing numbers of civil servants with higher levels of technical expertise to administer these functions created a demand for scientifically trained personnel that helped stimulate the Canadian science system. Nevertheless, it is important not to overstate the role of government science in this period. Simply put, Canadian investment in science prior to the Second World War was minimal.[16]

The Great War of 1914–18 spurred the creation of the National Research Council, probably the single most important institution in the history of Canadian government science.[17] Initially created as the Honorary Advisory Council on Scientific and Industrial Research, the Council was given the role of advisor to the government on science matters related to the war effort. In fact, the NRC contributed little prior to the Armistice. At the time, this was attributed to Canada's serious shortage of scientific manpower and infrastructure, which led, in turn, to the NRC's early heavy emphasis on building science capacity, and some years later to the establishment of its own laboratories. As Doern and Levesque have reported, the beginnings of the NRC laboratories were quite modest, emerging as they did during the lean years of the Depression. Nevertheless, by 1939, on the eve of the Second World War, the NRC had about 300 employees and government science was positioned to take on a vastly expanded role.[18]

Expansion: The Second World War to the 1960s

For science in Canada the Second World War marked a major turning point, and it led to an era of expansion. The NRC's staff grew tenfold during the war, to reach almost 3000 employees in 1945. According to E.W.R. Steacie, who served as president of the NRC during the 1950s, 'In a real sense Canadian science came of age during the war.'[19] He attributes this maturation to two factors: 1) 'our traditional isolation was broken', and 2) 'the war provided facilities which had been sadly lacking, especially in the universities.'[20] Indeed, Steacie believed that 'it was only after World War II that the Canadian universities really came into their own as centres of research and graduate education.'[21]

Another factor that analysts have pointed to is the relationship between C.D. Howe, the wartime Minister of Industry, and C.J. Mackenzie, President of the NRC. It can be argued that their close personal relationship afforded the scientific community a privileged access to power that it had not enjoyed previously, nor, perhaps, has it since. Two decades later, when Dr Mackenzie was asked to report to Prime Minister Pearson on the organization of government science, he clearly sought to reproduce such an intimate advisory relationship through the creation of a science secretariat within the Prime Minister's Office.[22]

During the war, Allied science had demonstrated, through advancements in radar technology, atomic weapons, and penicillin, that it could make significant contributions. In the afterglow of victory, science was viewed with awe—as the source of new possibilities for achieving society's peacetime goals. To meet these new expectations, the government's science system expanded significantly through the 1950s and 1960s, and important new players emerged. The NRC's responsibilities for defence, atomic, and medical research were spun off to new agencies—the Defence Research Board, Atomic Energy of Canada Limited, and the Medical Research Council respectively. By 1961 the scientific workforce in the federal government had grown to include almost eighteen thousand people, working in a greatly expanded set of science-based departments and agencies with significant research portfolios. Throughout the period, federal scientists were internationally recognized, and government science remained the dominant actor in Canada's innovation system. Linkages between the various sectors of the system remained weak, with the government continuing to house the major proportion of Canada's research infrastructure and expertise.[23]

But What's the Policy? 1960s to 1970s

It would appear, however, that there was no general policy statement guiding the post-war period of expansion in Canada analogous to that by Vannevar Bush on the American context.[24] This may have been the expression of a 'hidden policy' of laissez-faire governance of the Canadian scientific enterprise.[25] Canada, like the United States, exhibited a Polanyian 'republic of science' style of policy paradigm, which held that government investments in science, if left in the control of scientists, would inevitably lead to economic prosperity and social benefit.[26] Dr. Steacie, a key science policy figure during this period, clearly exhibited an aversion to anything that smacked of 'planning' or 'coordination' of science:

> The problem is that those who are trying to make science efficient do not know what it is, and are trying to apply the normal criteria of cost accounting. This inevitably leads to enthusiastic attempts to 'plan' science, and I think that such planning is probably the greatest danger facing science today.[27]

His obvious preference for pure, academic-style science heavily influenced the direction of the NRC's work, and led to criticisms that the agency had drifted from its original mandate to support industrial research.

The 1960s and 1970s witnessed an increasing questioning of the laissez-faire approach to science policy. The Royal Commission on Government Organization (the 'Glassco Commission'), established in 1960, was charged with reporting on the organization and methods of operation of the Canadian government. As part of its broad examination the Commission undertook what many analysts agree was the first comprehensive overview of Canadian science policy.[28] The Commission's findings and recommendations addressed the government's high-level 'science policy machinery' and the need to reorganize federal science activities.

The Commission found that a whopping 82 per cent of federal S&T expenditures was spent intramurally, but that in-house S&T activity, for all its breadth, which might otherwise have been seen as a positive feature, was subject to no overall scrutiny or supervision. The Commission was concerned that the existing arrangements for central science policy-making were inadequate and virtually inoperative, and that consequently science policy decision-making was ad hoc. It followed that in the Commission's view Canadian science policy was merely the product of rapid post-war budget growth rather than of any well-considered policy design.

By challenging the state of Canadian science policy, the Glassco report initiated an active debate, as indicated by the numerous studies conducted in the ensuing decade, including those of the Science Council and Senator Lamontagne's committee.[29] In the years that followed, Canada experimented with various science policy and coordination mechanisms, including the Science Secretariat in the Privy Council Office and later the Ministry of State for Science and Technology (MOSST), but none of these institutions has survived. Interestingly, many of the issues examined by the Glassco Commission remain key concerns of government science to this day.

New Public Management: 1980s–1993

By the late 1970s and early 1980s, the policy agenda was being driven largely by energy crises and economic stagnation. With respect to government science, these problems translated into an increasing concern for its relevance to the process of improving Canada's economic competitiveness. As scholarly understanding of the innovation process evolved, the earlier exclusive emphasis on science and the policies associated with it gave way to a complementary interest in technology; the policy focus consequently changed, to the point that the policy area is now commonly referred to as *science and technology* (S&T). In the same period, administrative reforms associated with the so-called New Public Management (NPM) continued to gain prominence and were extended to the government science system. Partly an outgrowth of debates about the appropriate role of the state and the ills of bureaucratic governance, NPM is often correlated with the rise of the New Right political movement associated with the Thatcher, Reagan, and Mulroney governments and their emphasis on *privatizing, downsizing,* and *reinventing* government. Broadly speaking, NPM is an attempt to introduce management practices from the private sector into the public sector in order to improve efficiency and effectiveness.

Policy analyses in this period were highly critical of federal laboratory management, citing, for example, a 'growing atmosphere of irrelevance and an excessively bureaucratic management style'.[30] In general, government laboratories were under pressure both to become more market-oriented in their operations and to serve commercial innovation goals more directly. The National Advisory Board on Science and Technology (NABST), which reported to Prime Minister Mulroney, called for greater use of management boards, cost-recovery, contracting out, and other business-oriented approaches.[31] For those laboratories whose research had little market potential, the modus operandi was often to hunker down and hope to survive the excesses of the NPM reforms.

TRANSITION TO THE NEW CENTURY

In this section, we will highlight the major milestones of the Chrétien-era science policy, and thus bring the history down to the present. During the 1993 campaign the Liberals signalled in the Red Book their intention to place innovation at the centre of their agenda.[32] Once in power, however, the policy agenda quickly gave way to fiscal realities, and the ensuing cuts in program spending were particularly severe for many of the science-based departments and agencies.[33] The Liberals increased investment in R&D in their second mandate, with the return of a modicum of fiscal strength, although funding was primarily targeted to sectors other than government agencies, particularly to universities. Thus, for government science, Ottawa in the 1990s became 'a city of two tales'—one describing the Liberals' first 'deficit-fighting' mandate (the worst of times) and the second, the 'budget surplus' mandate that followed (better perhaps, but still not the best of times).

Deficit Era: Program Review and the Federal S&T Strategy

As part of its innovation agenda, the new government sought to re-examine the role and performance of government with respect to S&T.[34] A further impetus for a major S&T review was a 1994 report of the Auditor General of Canada that included a rather scathing assessment of federal S&T management.[35] The story of the S&T Review is well known,[36] and I will not dwell on it here. Launched in mid-1994, the comprehensive internal and external review was quickly overtaken by the fiscal imperative to reduce the federal budget deficits. Nevertheless, the consultation process proceeded, and in March 1996 the government released *Science and Technology for a New Century: A Federal Strategy*, along with a set of action plans outlining how each department would implement the strategy.

The outcome of the S&T Review may have been pre-empted by the Program Review cuts, but at least the resulting strategy seemed to change the tone of the debate with respect to government S&T. The strategy's overall message was that the government should evaluate and justify federal laboratory activities against strategic needs in order to determine whether others might better perform them. But to a greater extent than in the past, government science was viewed in the context of its role as a critical part of a 'national innovation system'—a concept that had become fashionable among scholars of innovation. Government science had something to offer, but rather than simply serving industrial clients, government laboratories would collaborate as partners with other sectors. The strategy emphasized that 'what matters most is the exchange of knowledge and information; cooperation among governments, business and universities; and the forging of partnerships for mutual benefit.'[37]

Clearly, however, the reductions in funding and personnel in this deficit-fighting period damaged the morale, if not the effectiveness, of government scientists and science managers. For many within the federal S&T community, the mid-1990s were the worst of times. And their outlook was not much improved when, after the return to budget surpluses, research spending resumed its flow, but through new channels, such as the Canada Foundation for Innovation—channels that were not directly accessible by most government laboratories.

Surplus Era: Re-investment but Through New Models
An important milestone in the recent history of government science was the 1999 publication of *Building Excellence in Science and Technology* by the Council of Science and Technology Advisors (CSTA). Called for in the 1996 federal S&T strategy, the CSTA was created in 1998 to provide external advice to Cabinet on internal federal S&T issues. In a climate of increasing expectations and decreasing resources, the CSTA was asked to advise on what roles, if any, the federal government should continue to play in S&T, and its capacity to deliver on those roles. The CSTA, after identifying a clear need for the federal government to be involved in S&T, determined that it should maintain the capacity to perform the following roles:

- support for decision making, policy development and regulations;
- development and management of standards;
- support for public health, safety, environmental and defence needs; and
- enabling economic and social development.[38]

Recognizing that the context for government science was changing, the CSTA also recommended that the government implement and fund new models for S&T, models that move away from a vertical approach to a more horizontal, competitive, and multi-stakeholder approach.

Indeed, the reduction of government investment in S&T made it necessary to find new ways of operating. Government laboratories came under greater pressure to leverage funds by collaborating with researchers in other sectors. At the same time the issues needing to be addressed, which were becoming increasingly complex, required multidisciplinary approaches. It was recognized that the organization of government S&T within vertical departments, focused on finding solutions to specific departmental missions, was not an appropriate means of addressing the complex challenges of such horizontal issues as climate change, sustainable development, and national security.

In recent years, the traditional hierarchical organization of government science has been complemented by a growing number of interdepartmental programs and resource funds, such as those highlighted in Box 13.1. Although typically managed by one or two lead departments, such programs seek to foster collaborations across government departments and with non-government researchers to focus on emerging issues not adequately addressed by existing research programs.

INTO THE TWENTY-FIRST CENTURY:
THE FUTURE LOOKS *FINE*, MAYBE

Out of the frustration of the late 1990s was born the initiative to create the Federal Innovation Networks of Excellence (FINE). This section will briefly describe the proposed FINE initiative and examine the prospects of its serving as a model for government science in the coming years. Whether or not the government decides to go forward with FINE networks, it has signalled its intention to adopt new approaches to science governance.

The Federal Innovation Networks of Excellence (FINE)

The purpose of the FINE initiative is, simply put, to increase the capacity of government laboratories to conduct public good science in support of national policy goals. Drawing on the lessons learned from previous and existing horizontal, collaborative science governance models, FINE would establish research networks that would integrate the resources and expertise of the various science-based departments and agencies, universities, and the private sector to address specifically identified priority themes. In essence, FINE networks led by government laboratories would represent a federal analog to the university-based Networks of Centres of Excellence. Following a competitive selection process based on expert peer review, FINE networks would be awarded funding for up to five years, with a possible renewal for an additional five years. Funding would support network administration and operations, investments in facilities and equipment, and the recruitment and development of S&T personnel. Even as the FINE initiative was being developed to enable government science to respond more adroitly to emerging, cross-cutting issues, circumstances converged that allowed the concept to be tested in practice.

A FINE Pilot

The terrorist attacks of 11 September 2001 and the subsequent anthrax scare raised concerns about Canada's preparedness and ability to respond to chemical, biological, radiological, and nuclear (CBRN) terrorism. In response, the government launched the CBRN Research and Technology Initiative, or CRTI, to coordinate the federal S&T community's efforts. The CRTI is an interdepartmental initiative led by the recently created Defense Research and Development Canada, and it involves fourteen other departments, agencies, and crown corporations. Funded at $170 million over five years, the CRTI announced an initial set of awards to 24 projects

Box 13.1
Examples of Horizontal S&T Programs

The governance and conduct of federal S&T is increasingly interdepartmental. Described here are just three examples of a growing number of horizontal S&T programs.

Climate Change Action Fund (CCAF)[1]
The Climate Change Action Fund (CCAF) was established in 1998 to help Canada meet its commitments under the Kyoto Protocol to reduce greenhouse gas emissions. Through the CCAF the federal government engages other governments, businesses, universities, communities, and individual Canadians to address climate change. The science component of CCAF is led by Environment Canada and Natural Resources Canada, with the involvement of seven other federal departments and agencies. CCAF was initially allocated $150 million over three years, of which $15 million was allocated for science and $56 million for technology measures. In 2000 the government extended funding for three more years (through 2003/4) at $50 million a year.

Program of Energy Research and Development (PERD)[2]
The Program of Energy Research and Development (PERD), which actually dates back to the 1980s, is operated by Natural Resources Canada (NRCan), but involves eleven other federal departments and agencies. PERD funds research and development designed to ensure a sustainable energy future for Canada and directly supports 40 per cent of all non-nuclear energy R&D conducted by the federal and provincial governments. PERD funding for approved projects ($57.6 million for fiscal year 2000/1) is provided under agreements between NRCan and the participating departments, which then provide support to their partners in the private sector, universities, provincial and municipal governments, and elsewhere.

Toxic Substances Research Initiative (TSRI)[3]
The purpose of the Toxic Substances Research Initiative (TSRI), established in 1998, was to promote collaborative research to enhance the knowledge base needed to manage risks associated with toxic substances and their effects on Canadians and the environment. The TSRI invested $40 million over four years (through 2001/2). The program was jointly managed by Health Canada and Environment Canada and overseen by a science management committee that included senior scientists from six federal departments, academe, industry, and the non-profit sector. Projects were awarded through a competitive peer review process in which the majority of reviewers came from outside government.

---

1 Refer to CCAF website < http://www.climatechange.gc.ca/ > .
2 Refer to PERD website < http://www2.nrcan.gc.ca/es/oerd/english/
   View.asp?x = 659 > .
3 Refer to TSRI website < http://www.hc-sc.gc.ca/ehp/ehd/tsri/ > .

totalling $46 million in September 2002. These projects reflect priorities that were established in consultation with the scientific community and with those entities that first responded. According to a recent press release,

> Through CRTI, clusters of federal science laboratories are working together for the first time to take a coordinated approach to CBRN emergencies. Through the project structure, they will partner with private-sector organizations and academic laboratories to increase the national science and technology capability to respond to CBRN threats.[39]

This first round of projects that received awards involves eleven industry partners and twelve university partners. Although FINE is not yet an approved program, the CRTI is being referred to as a 'pilot' of the FINE principles.

FINE: A Model for the Future?

By late 2002, the FINE concept appeared to have garnered substantial support both politically and within the bureaucracy. This was demonstrated by supportive references in the Innovation Strategy and in the Speech from the Throne, and by the activities of the federal S&T community. After a number of unsuccessful attempts to 'make the case' for government science in the late 1990s, the federal S&T community seemed confident it had found a winner.

The Innovation Strategy recognizes the need to renew government science capacity and to create new approaches, in order to respond to emerging public policy, stewardship, and economic challenges and opportunities. It states,

> In addition to providing traditional support for government science, the Government of Canada will consider a new approach to investing in research in order to focus federal capacity on priority, emerging science-based issues. New investments in scientific research would ensure that sound science-based policies are adopted to support environment, health and safety objectives. The government would build collaborative networks across government departments, universities, non-government organizations and the private sector. This approach would integrate, mobilize and build on recent government investments in universities and the private sector. Funding would be competitive, based on government priorities and informed by expert advice.[40]

Although this passage is not referring specifically to FINE, it clearly espouses the program's principles of new investments, collaborative networks, and competitive funding.

Similarly, the Speech from the Throne, delivered in September 2002, contained the following reference: '[The Government] will strengthen government science, integrating its efforts across departments and disciplines, and focusing on the priorities of Canadians.'[41] Supporters of the FINE initiative chose to interpret this as a positive reference to their proposed program. There were other positive signs. At a forum of the federal S&T community held in October 2002, the FINE initiative was held up as a guiding light for the future. In CRTI, the FINE initiative had a pilot program that was funded and operating. Finally, two scientific foresight exercises were being conducted under the FINE banner. In short, the future of government S&T was looking FINE.

Then, in early November, the program's future suddenly became somewhat murkier. According to one observer of government science, the FINE proposal was being withdrawn, just weeks before it was to be submitted to Cabinet for approval.[42] What happened? At the time of writing, it is not at all clear. Reports are that 'a more fundamental change is being considered',[43] but details of this alternative vision for reforming government science have not been made public.

In light of this latest development, it is possible that FINE proponents may have overestimated the depth of support for the program. The references in the Innovation Strategy and the Throne Speech, while consistent with the themes of FINE, did not mention the program by name, and thereby left wiggle room for an alternative model to emerge as the debate about government science progressed. Although supporters may have hoped that FINE could become a source of new money—that is, funding beyond the regular A-base allocations to science-based departments—it is not clear that the political masters have signed up to that. Indeed, the language in the Throne Speech suggests an intention to work within existing resources.[44]

In an era of heightened security concerns, and given the political desirability of demonstrating Canada's commitment to the war against terrorism, the fact that CRTI received $170 million in new money was not surprising. But FINE supporters should not misinterpret it as an indication of a broader commitment to new resources for government science that may not in fact exist. In addition, it is not clear that the main issue is one of resistance from 'the centre'—it may in fact be a failure of government departments to develop consensus on how to move the government science agenda forward. Hoping to see 'new money' for government science, departments have been reluctant to support FINE if it is to be funded through reallocations from their core budgets. We will have to wait and see whether FINE will become an on-ramp to the road to a revitalized government science or the latest in a long list of aborted initiatives.

CONCLUSIONS

Throughout Canada's history, the federal government has been a key player in the areas of science, technology, and innovation. For much of this history, policy analysts and decision-makers have focused to a large extent on the roles government science can play in fostering a competitive economy. Given the persistent weakness of Canadian industry's support for research and development, science policy has emphasized how government laboratories and research facilities could be used to support industrial innovation. Enhancing the competitiveness of its industries through innovation is clearly an important function of the federal government, and the current Innovation Strategy is the latest attempt to create the conditions that drive economic growth in a knowledge-based society.[45]

Partnerships between government and the private sector can yield many benefits, by bringing more expertise and resources to bear on science and technology projects, and by expediting knowledge transfer and the commercialization of research results. On the other hand, the increase in linkages with the private sector can challenge the public's confidence in the independence of government science and the protection of the public interest. An emphasis on support for industrial innovation can create tension with other public good roles of government science.

As has been discussed, government science plays a variety of roles. With so much attention being given to the part government can play in supporting an 'innovation agenda', it would be wise to consider the role government science must play in supporting policy and regulatory decision-making and the delivery of science-based services. In the wake of controversies over water contamination, security of the blood supply, genetically modified organisms, and 'mad cow' disease, it is important that government take the necessary steps to regain and enhance public confidence in its ability to address such science-based issues and to protect the public interest. After suffering nearly a decade or more of tight budgets and a bruised morale, government science may require substantial new investment.

This is not to say that government science should simply be reconstructed along historical lines. As the CSTA has argued, the debate over the 'rust-out' of the infrastructure for government science too often centres on 'restoring' or 'replacing' federal S&T facilities that may in fact no longer be required. Rather, resources need to be reallocated to focus government science capacity on meeting significant new demands and emerging issues. Most government science will probably continue to target the specific, often legislated mandates of individual departments. However, responses to the complex policy issues to which government science must contribute will increasingly require more horizontal approaches. Whether or not the FINE initiative prevails in its current form, government science needs to embrace the competitive, horizontal funding models it represents. While the government seems to have embraced the notion of horizontal governance of its science, it continues to face many challenges in making the concept work in practice.

NOTES

1 Government of Canada, *Achieving Excellence: Investing in People, Knowledge and Opportunity–Canada's Innovation Strategy* (Ottawa: Industry Canada, 2002), 84.

2 Bengt-Ake Lundvall, ed., *National Systems of Innovation: Towards a Theory of Innovation and Interactive Learning* (London: Pinter Publications, 1992); Richard R. Nelson, ed., *National Innovation Systems: A Comparative Analysis* (Oxford: Oxford University Press, 1993); John de la Mothe, 'Canada and National Innovation Systems', in J.A.D. Holbrook, ed., *Science and Technology Resource Handbook* (Ottawa: Government of Canada, 1994); Jorge Niosi, *Canada's National Innovation System* (Montreal and Kingston: McGill-Queen's University Press, 2000).

3 'The Changing Face of Public Good Science', *Canada Research Horizons* 1, 1 (Ottawa: The Impact Group, 2001-2), 8; Jeffrey Simpson, 'There's at Least One Chrétien Legacy: Universities', *The Globe and Mail* [Toronto], 9 Nov. 2002, A17; Government of Canada, *Science and Technology Data–2001* (Ottawa: Industry Canada, 2002), 15.

4 Simpson, 'There's at Least One Chrétien Legacy: Universities'.

5 M.E. Smith, 'The Role of Federal Laboratories in the Technological Development of Canadian Industry', *Journal of Canadian Studies* 17, 4 (1982/3), 14.

6 CSTA, *Building Excellence in Science and Technology (BEST): The Federal Roles in Performing Science and Technology* (Ottawa: Industry Canada, 1999), 8.

7 Finance Department, *Tax Expenditures and Evaluations 2002*, report at < http://www.fin.gc.ca/toce/2002/taxexp02_e.html >.

8 Government of Canada, *Investing in Excellence, 1996–2001: A Report on Federal Science and Technology* (Ottawa: Industry Canada, 2002), 55.

9 William Leiss, 'Between Expertise and Bureaucracy: Risk Management Trapped at the Science-Policy Interface', in G. Bruce Doern and Ted Reed, eds, *Risky Business: Canada's Changing Science-based Regulatory Regime* (Toronto: University of Toronto Press, 2000), 49–74.

10 CSTA, *Building Excellence in Science and Technology*; John de la Mothe, 'Government Science and the Public Interest', in Doern and Reed, *Risky Business*, 31–48.

11 Government of Canada, *Science and Technology Data: 2001* (Ottawa: Industry Canada, 2002), 10.

12 Bruce Sinclair, 'Foreword', in Richard Jarrell and Norman Ball, eds, *Science, Technology, and Canadian History* (Waterloo: Wilfrid Laurier Press, 1980), xiii.

13 J.J. Brown, *Ideas in Exile: A History of Canadian Invention* (Toronto: McClelland and Steward Ltd., 1967).

14 Quoted by Frank Dawson Adams, 'The History of Geology in Canada', in H.M. Tory, ed., *A History of Science in Canada* (Toronto: The Ryerson Press, 1939), 15–16.

15 Peter Gillis, 'Early Federal Regulatory Records as Potential Sources for the History of Science and Technology in Canada', in Jarrell and Ball, *Science, Technology, and Canadian History*, 60–1.

16 Trevor Levere, 'What Is Canadian About Science in Canadian History?' in Jarrell and Ball, *Science, Technology, and Canadian*, 15.

17 Although the NRC's importance is clear, it is possible that the amount of attention it has received by academic scholars and historians has led to an under-appreciation by science policy-makers of other elements of government science, particularly the roles and functions of laboratories within the various line departments.

18 G. Bruce Doern and Richard Levesque, *The National Research Council in the Innovation Policy Era* (Toronto: University of Toronto Press, 2002), 38, 46–7.

19 E.W.R. Steacie, quoted in J.D. Babbitt, ed., *Science in Canada: Selections from the Speeches of E.W.R. Steacie* (Toronto: University of Toronto Press, 1965), 126.

20 Ibid., 126.

21 Ibid., 163.

22 G. Bruce Doern, *Science and Politics in Canada* (Montreal and London: McGill-Queen's University Press, 1972), 8–10.

23 CSTA, *Building Excellence in Science and Technology*, 8.

24 Bush's 1945 report, *Science: The Endless Frontier* (Washington: United States Government Printing Office, 1945), is widely regarded to be the single most influential document shaping US science policy in the second half of the twentieth century. Bush offers an image of science as an 'endless frontier', which could replace the

physical frontier of the American West as a driving force for economic growth, improved standards of living, and positive social change.

25 Senate of Canada, *A Science Policy for Canada: Report of the Senate Special Committee on Science Policy* (Ottawa: Queen's Printer, 1970).

26 Michael Polanyi, *The Republic of Science: Its Political and Economic Theory* (Chicago: Roosevelt University, 1962).

27 Quoted in Babbitt, *Science in Canada*, 178–9.

28 Royal Commission on Government Organization, *Report No. 23: Scientific Research and Development* (Ottawa: Queen's Printer, 1963).

29 Science Council of Canada, *Towards a National Science Policy for Canada* (Ottawa: Queen's Printer, 1968); Senate of Canada, *A Science Policy for Canada, Report of the Senate Special Committee on Science Policy* (Ottawa: Queen's Printer, 1970).

30 Report of the Task Force on Federal Policies and Programs for Technology Development (Ottawa: Minister of Supply and Services Canada, 1984).

31 See, for example, *Government Committee Report* (Ottawa: NABST, 1988); *Industry Committee Report* (Ottawa: NABST, 1988); *Revitalizing Science and Technology in the Government of Canada* (Ottawa: NABST, 1990); *Spending Smarter: Committee on Federal Science and Technology Priorities* (Ottawa: NABST, 1993).

32 The Liberal Party of Canada, *Creating Opportunity: The Liberal Plan for Canada* (Ottawa, 1993).

33 David Wolfe, 'Innovation Policy for the Knowledge-Based Economy: From the Red Book to the White Paper,' in G. Bruce Doern, ed., *How Ottawa Spends 2002–2003: The Security Aftermath and National Priorities* (Don Mills: Oxford University Press, 2002), 140.

34 J. Meisel, 'Caesar and the Savants: Some Socio-Political Contexts of Science and Technology in Canada', in A.M. Herzberg and I. Krupka, eds, *Statistics, Science and Public Policy* (Kingston: Queen's University, 1998), 158.

35 Office of the Auditor General, *Report of the Auditor General of Canada to the House of Commons*, vol. 6 (Ottawa: Supply and Services Canada, 1994).

36 John de la Mothe, 'One Small Step in an Uncertain Direction: The Science and Technology Review and Public Administration in Canada', *Canadian Public Administration* 39, 3, 403–17; J. Meisel, 'Caesar and the Savants', 153–77.

37 Government of Canada, *Science and Technology for the New Century: A Federal Strategy* (Ottawa: Industry Canada, 1996), 4.

38 CSTA, *Building Excellence in Science and Technology*, 2–3.

39 'CRTI Announces $46 Million for Counter-Terrorism Research Projects', Department of National Defence News Release, 16 Sept. 2002.

40 Government of Canada, *Achieving Excellence: Canada's Innovation Strategy* (Ottawa: Industry Canada, 2002), 52–3.

41 Governor General of Canada, Speech from the Throne, 30 Sept. 2002, available at < http://www.sft-ddt.gc.ca/sft.htm >

42 Re$earch Money, 'Latest Proposal to Boost Federal Science Capacity Suffers Setback', *Re$earch Money* 16, 17 (4 Nov. 2002).

43 Ibid., quoting Dr William Doubleday.

44 For example, 'The government will reallocate resources to the highest priorities and transform old spending to new purposes.' Governor General of Canada, Speech from the Throne, 30 Sept. 2002.

45 For more discussion of the Innovation Strategy see John de la Mothe's chapter in this volume and Wolfe, 'Innovation Policy for the Knowledge-Based Economy'.

Appendix A

CANADIAN POLITICAL FACTS AND TRENDS

2002

22 January: Federal Ethics Counsellor Howard Wilson is under fire for privately advising high-priced lobbyists on how to avoid the 'traps' in government lobbying laws.

25 January: Premiers agree to create a health care council charged with finding ways to sustain Canada's medicare system. They give the federal government a three-month ultimatum to finalize a system for resolving disputes under the Canada Health Act.

4 February: The updated Young Offenders Act is passed by Parliament.

4 February: The federal government adopts Bill C-38, an Act to amend the Air Canada Public Participation Act. This legislation removes the ownership limits, by which one individual was not allowed to own more than 15 per cent of the shares in the airline.

5 February: The federal Liberals, reversing a plan outlined in the December budget, put the $2 billion Strategic Infrastructure Foundation under the control of Deputy Prime Minister John Manley.

6 February: The federal government approves the creation of an expanded, elite military team to respond to biological, nuclear, and chemical attacks on Canada.

12 February: Industry Minister Allan Rock and Human Resources Minister Jane Stewart introduce two strategy papers detailing the federal government's innovation agenda.

21 February: Minister of the Environment David Anderson says that Ottawa is prepared to ratify the Kyoto Protocol over objections by the provinces.

4 March: The Canadian Institutes of Health Research unveils its guidelines on stem cell research; they include a ban on public funding that could lead to cloning, and a ban on the creation of embryos simply for research purposes.

13 March: The Ontario Court of Appeal rules that disabled veterans have the right to file a class action lawsuit against the federal government for interest owed to them.

20 March: Stephen Harper is elected leader of the Canadian Alliance party.

21 March: Ethics Counsellor Howard Wilson develops a series of rules for federal cabinet ministers who are organizing to be candidates in the next Liberal leadership campaign.

22 March: The US Commerce Department imposes duties averaging 29 per cent on Canadian softwood lumber imports.

22 March: Fishing vessels from the Faroe Islands are banned from Canadian ports for the remainder of the year by the federal government.

25 March: The Canada Customs and Revenue Agency announces that it will impose provisional duties of up to 71 per cent on imports of fresh American tomatoes.

2 April: Heritage Minister Sheila Copps announces that her department will undertake a review of the Canadian content rules as they apply to film and television productions. She launches a two-month consultation to bring the 30-year-old regulations up to date.

3 April: Health Canada creates a new branch, the Marketed Health Products Directorate, to effectively monitor drugs and medical devices.

6 April: Paul DeVillers, federal minister responsible for amateur sports, announces that federal, provincial, and territorial governments have endorsed Canada's first-ever policy on sport in an effort to create a healthier sports community.

16 April: Auditor General Sheila Fraser issues her second report on the federal government's spending.

18 April: The federal government announces that Air Canada will receive only $60 million in compensation for the effects of the 11 September terrorist attacks, significantly less than $100 million, the airline's assessment of its losses.

19 April: The federal government launches a board of inquiry into the Afghanistan bombing that took the lives of four Canadian soldiers.

22 April: Agriculture Minister Lyle Vanclief announces that the federal government will spend $21 million over five years to help farmers improve their farming methods so as to reduce greenhouse gas emissions.

22 April: The federal government tightens the SIN system after a probe reveals widespread abuse.

29 April: The federal government tables the new Public Safety Act, which greatly limits the powers of cabinet ministers to invoke executive decrees that could threaten civil liberties, but which expands the powers of authorities to scan airline manifests.

30 April: As part of a shuffle of his senior mandarins, Prime Minister Jean Chrétien appoints Alex Himelfarb Clerk of the Privy Council.

8 May: Auditor General Sheila Fraser recommends that the RCMP investigate contracts worth $1.6 million that were awarded to a Montreal ad agency.

9 May: Health Minister Anne McLellan introduces a new bill governing reproductive technology.

13 May: The federal Liberals lose ridings in Newfoundland and Windsor in by-elections.

15 May: Lucienne Robillard, President of the Treasury Board of Canada, announces the adoption of a new Policy for Continuous Learning in the Public Service of Canada.

15 May: Justice Minister Martin Cauchon launches a sweeping review of the justice system.

17 May: Joe Clark, leader of the Conservative party, accuses Public Works Minister Don Boudria of breaching the ethics code by taking a ski holiday at the Quebec country estate of one of the largest recipients of federal government advertising contracts.

24 May: Ethics Counsellor Howard Wilson rules that Defence Minister Art Eggleton violated conflict of interest guidelines when he awarded an untendered $36,500 contract to Maggie Maier, an Ottawa consultant and former girlfriend.

24 May: The RCMP decides to conduct a full criminal investigation into $1.6 million worth of contracts the federal government awarded to Groupaction Marketing Inc. of Montreal.

26 May: Prime Minister Jean Chrétien fires Art Eggleton as defence minister and shifts Don Boudria out of the controversial post of public works minister in the face of opposition allegations of corruption in the federal government.

2 June: Paul Martin announces that he is stepping down as minister of finance but that he will stay on as an MP from Quebec.

5 June: Alexa McDonough resigns as leader of the New Democratic party after seven years at the helm.

11 June: Prime Minister Jean Chrétien introduces new rules governing Cabinet ministers' dealings with crown corporations and with people who finance their leadership campaigns.

11 June: The federal government decides to stockpile enough smallpox vaccine to inoculate every Canadian in the event of a bioterrorist attack with the deadly virus.

11 June: The Species at Risk Act passes in the House of Commons.

11 June: Minister of Citizenship and Immigration Denis Coderre unveils the federal government's proposed final amendments to its Immigration and Refugee Protection bill.

13 June: Indian Affairs Minister Robert Nault introduces a bill that sets up a new tribunal to try to settle aboriginal land claims.

19 June: Agriculture Minister Lyle Vanclief announces a farm aid plan of more than $1 billion a year to help offset new US subsidies.

21 June: Minister of Veterans Affairs Rey Pagtakhan announces that the federal government will offer native veterans up to $20,000 in compensation for benefits they were denied after returning from war.

27 June: Former finance minister Paul Martin makes his first campaign promises: he vows that should he be elected prime minister he would strike a new deal for ailing cities, and he calls for tougher punishments for white-collar criminals who deceive shareholders.

10 July: The House of Commons public accounts committee's hearings into federal contracts begin.

11 July: Federal Ethics Counsellor Howard Wilson is set to disclose the amounts of Liberal leadership campaign contributions under new conflict of interest rules.

11 July: The Supreme Court rules that the federal Cabinet does not have absolute power to keep its inner workings secret from the public.

29 July: Justice Minister Martin Cauchon announces that in order to have the laws clarified, his department will appeal an Ontario court decision in favour of same-sex marriages.

8 August: Prime Minister Jean Chrétien appoints Quebec Court of Appeal Justice Marie Deschamps to the Supreme Court of Canada.

14 August: Justice Minister Martin Cauchon announces $57.5 million in funding to renew the national Aboriginal Justice Strategy for five years.

21 August: Prime Minister Jean Chrétien announces he will step down from the Liberal party leadership in February 2004.

26 August: Health Minister Anne McLellan says that the federal government is not backing away from its plan to supply patients with medical marijuana.

2 September: Prime Minister Jean Chretien announces at the Johannesburg Summit on Sustainable Development that Canada will ratify the Kyoto Protocol by the end of the year.

13 September: Justice Minister Martin Cauchon announces he will attempt to overhaul the criminal law system.

14 September: The federal government launches another challenge of US softwood lumber duties at the World Trade Organization, this time targeting the final anti-dumping duties imposed on Canadian lumber exports in May.

23 September: Minister of Health Anne McLellan vetoes the plan to supply marijuana for medical purposes.

23 September: All four opposition leaders sign a statement saying they will not accept any candidates for the position of Ethics Commissioner proposed by the prime minister unless he amends the job description to make the incumbent report only to the House of Commons.

26 September: The Finance Department proposes changes to the disability tax credit that will make it more difficult for people to qualify.

26 September: Public Works Minister Ralph Goodale says that five more government contracts have been sent to the RCMP since June, raising the number of contracts to 13, worth $6 million, being investigated by police for overbilling.

30 September: Governor-General Adrienne Clarkson delivers the Speech from the Throne.

8 October: Prime Minister Jean Chrétien announces that he has appointed Minister of Canadian Heritage Sheila Copps to lead the government of Canada's efforts to strengthen its relationship with the voluntary sector.

9 October: Prime Minister Jean Chrétien warns cabinet ministers to stop taking 'cheap shots' at each other and chastises his troops for leaking details of their weekly closed-door sessions to the news media.

11 October: Solicitor-General Lawrence MacAulay is questioned in the House of Commons after a Tory MP charges that a company owned by a political ally of Mr MacAulay 'raked in' government grants worth more than $2.5 million.

15 October: Finance Minister John Manley announces that the federal government has posted a surplus of almost $9 billion for the most recent fiscal year.

31 October: In the House of Commons, the federal government introduces the Public Safety Act, an improved package of public safety initiatives in support of its Anti-Terrorism Plan.

3 November: Finance Minister John Manley announces that he would oppose any attempt to raise taxes for extra health care funding.

4 November: Finance Minister John Manley says that Ottawa's transfer payments to the provinces will likely rise this year.

5 November: Prime Minister Jean Chrétien rejects a call by premiers to hold a first ministers meeting before Canada ratifies the Kyoto Protocol, as planned, by the end of the year.

5 November: Fifty-six Liberal MPs, including Mr Martin, stand with opposition parties to vote against Prime Minister Jean Chrétien on the issue of electing committee chairs by secret ballot. The Canadian Alliance motion passes by a margin of 174–87.

6 November: Solicitor-General Wayne Easter announces that provincial and territorial justice ministers have agreed to establish a federal sex-offender registry.

7 November: Minister of Justice and Attorney General of Canada Martin Cauchon announces that he intends to bring forward a series of legislative and other measures that will improve efficiency, modernize the law, and clarify existing Criminal Code provisions that govern the mentally disordered accused.

20 November: The RCMP lays 32 charges in the tainted blood case.

20 November: Ralph Goodale, Minister responsible for status Indians and Métis, announces a cost-sharing agreement in principle with the Anglican Church. The move came after an Alberta court decision found that the national church body could not be considered legally responsible for the operation of the schools.

28 November: Roy Romanow delivers the Final Report of the Royal Commission on the Future of Health Care in Canada.

4 December: Justice Minister Martin Cauchon says that major spending on the database of gun owners has been frozen until he obtains the results of an independent audit.

5 December: Minister of Canadian Heritage and Minister Responsible for the Voluntary Sector Sheila Copps announces the establishment of three new national centres to support volunteerism across Canada.

9 December: Public Works Minister Ralph Goodale announces the death of a $27-million tourism promotion project that duplicated the work of another government agency.

10 December: Minister of Justice and Attorney General of Canada Martin Cauchon announces the Child-centred Family Justice Strategy.

10 December: Parliament approves the resolution regarding the ratification of the Kyoto Protocol.

11 December: Solicitor-General Wayne Easter introduces a national sex-offender registry, and changes to the Divorce Act that attempt to make negotiations between parents less controversial.

12 December: Justice Minister Martin Cauchon indicates that he will find funding for the gun registry within existing Justice Department programs.

12 December: The Senate approves the Kyoto Protocol resolution.

16 December: Prime Minister Jean Chrétien signs the Kyoto Protocol in his Parliament Hill office.

17 December: Provincial and territorial governments call on Ottawa to boost its health care spending immediately by a combined $24.7 billion over the next four years.

17 December: In response to allegations of mismanagement and of patronage that favoured Liberal-friendly firms, Public Works Minister Ralph Goodale and Treasury Board President Lucienne Robillard announce that the federal government will overhaul its advertising system.

17 December: Public Works Minister Ralph Goodale introduces changes to the federal government's sponsorship program.

18 December: Finance Minister John Manley says that he cannot commit Ottawa to more funding for the provinces until he receives final economic estimates from his department in January—but he doubts it will be the $5.1-billion the provinces are requesting for the current fiscal year.

21 December: Liberal MPs and officials predict major divisions in the Liberal caucus and party as a result of strong opposition to Prime Minister Jean Chrétien's announced plan to ban corporate donations to political parties.

21 December: Public Works Minister Ralph Goodale announces that the federal government has earmarked $1.7 billion to settle up to 18,000 native residential school lawsuits over seven years.

27 December: A Liberal party poll finds that a majority of Canadians want the Liberal government to direct significant surplus funds to medicare and to increased spending for the military in the upcoming federal budget.

2 January (2003): Environment Minister David Anderson announces that he has finalized tougher emission standards for 2004 and later model Canadian vehicles and engines.

3 January: Government sources reveal that automakers have been dropped from the list of industries whose factory emissions it proposes to regulate under the Kyoto Protocol.

7 January: US President George W. Bush unveils a massive $647-billion growth and jobs plan to stimulate the American economy. The plan consists mainly of tax reductions, including the proposed abolition of personal income taxes on dividends. The plan will increase the US deficit and will likely put pressure on Canada to make further tax cuts in order to remain competitive with the United States.

7 January: Justice ministers from all but two provinces call on Ottawa to halt operations with respect to the national gun registry. The registry has been the subject of a highly critical report by the Auditor General of Canada regarding over-spending, which revived the strong opposition to the gun registration policy, especially in western Canada and among Canadian Alliance MPs.

8 January: Grant Aldonas of the US Commerce Department announces a plan regarding softwood lumber. Presented as way of solving the longstanding trade dispute between Canada and the United States, the plan would see the provinces of

Canada adopt market-based timber-pricing practices and end long-established provincially administered practices in Canada.

9 January: Defence Minister John McCallum states that Canada may contribute to the war on Iraq without a supporting resolution from the United Nations Security Council.

10 January: A group of Canadian business leaders indicate that they intend to help fund and support Finance Minister John Manley in the race for the Liberal leadership. Their support is cast partly in terms of the need to have a 'generational shift' in leadership.

13 January: Canada's big business lobby, the Canadian Council of Chief Executives, announces that it is seeking the creation of a jointly managed North American perimeter with a common approach to borders, trade, immigration, security, and defence.

15 January: Industry Minister Allan Rock announces that he will not be running in the Liberal leadership race to succeed Jean Chrétien.

Appendix B

FISCAL FACTS AND TRENDS

This appendix presents an overview of the federal government's fiscal position, and includes certain major economic policy indicators for 1990-2002, as well as some international comparisons.

Facts and trends are presented for federal revenue sources, federal expenditures by ministry and by type of payment, the government's share of the economy, interest and inflation rates, Canadian balance of payments in total and with the United States in particular, and other national economic growth indicators. In addition, international comparisons on real growth, unemployment, inflation, and productivity are reported for Canada, the United States, Japan, Germany, and the United Kingdom.

The figures and time series are updated each year, providing readers with an ongoing current record of major budgetary and economic variables.

Table B.1

Federal Revenue by Source

1992–3 to 2001–2

As a Percentage of Total

Fiscal Year	Personal Tax[a]	Corporate Tax	Indirect Taxes[b]	Other Revenue[c]	Total Revenue	Annual Change
1992–3	63.0	6.0	21.7	9.4	100.1	−1.4
1993–4	60.1	8.1	23.0	8.8	100.0	−3.8
1994–5	61.0	9.4	22.0	7.6	100.0	6.0
1995–6	60.4	12.2	20.4	7.0	100.0	5.4
1996–7	59.0	12.1	20.7	8.3	100.0	7.5
1997–8	58.6	14.7	20.1	6.7	100.0	8.2
1998–9	59.1	13.8	20.1	7.0	100.0	1.5
1999–00	59.2	13.9	19.8	7.1	100.0	6.2
2000–1	56.8	15.7	20.1	7.4	100.0	7.5
2001–2	58.7	13.9	21.1	6.3	100.0	−3.6

Revenue by Source is on a net basis.

(a) Employment Insurance contributions are included in the total.

(b) Consists of total excise taxes and duties.

(c) Consists of non-tax and other tax revenues.

Source: Department of Finance, *Fiscal Reference Tables*, October 2002, Table 3.

Figure B.1

Sources of Federal Revenue as a Percentage of Total, 2001–2

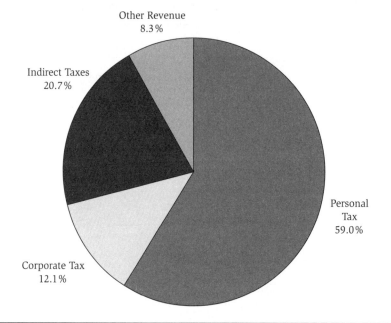

Source: Department of Finance, *Fiscal Reference Tables*, October 2002, Table 3.

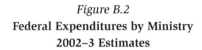

Figure B.2
Federal Expenditures by Ministry
2002–3 Estimates

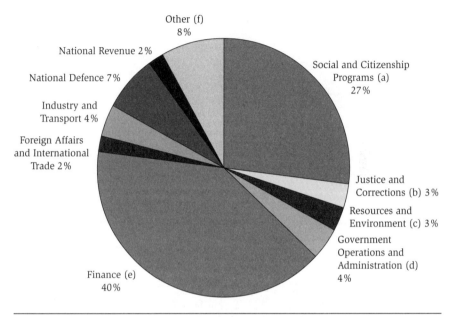

(a) Social Citizenship programs include departmental spending from Canadian Heritage, Citizenship and Immigration, Human Resources Development, Veterans Affairs, Health, and Indian Affairs and Northern Development.
(b) Justice and Corrections includes spending from the Department of Justice and the Solicitor General.
(c) Resources and Environment includes departmental spending from Agriculture and AgriFood, Environment, Fisheries and Oceans, and Natural Resources.
(d) Government Operations and Administration Spending includes that from Public Works and Government Services, the Governor General, Parliament, the Privy Council, and the Treasury Board.
(e) Finance expenditures include, but are not limited to, spending on public interest charges and many major social transfers to the provinces.
(f) Other includes the consolidated specified purposes account (Employment Insurance).

Source: Department of Finance, *Main Estimates, Budgetary Main Estimates by Standard Object of Expenditure*, Part II, 2002–2003, 1–29 to 1–36.

Figure B.3

Federal Expenditures by Type of Payment
1997–8 to 2003–4

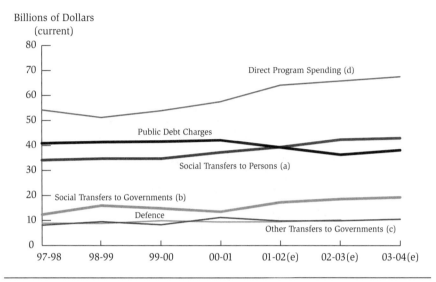

(a) Includes elderly benefits, Employment Insurance benefits, and relief for heating expenses.

(b) Consists of the Canada Health and Social Transfer (CHST). Prior to the CHST, two separate social transfers existed: Established Program Financing for health and post-secondary education expenditures, and the Canada Assistance Plan for welfare and welfare services. The CHST figures include cash transfers to the provinces, and do not include the value of the tax point transfer.

(c) Includes fiscal equalization and transfers to Territories, statutory subsidies, and recoveries under the Youth Allowance program.

(d) Includes all operating and capital expenditures, including defence.

(e) Figures for these years are budgetary estimates.

Source: Department of Finance, *Budget Plan 2001*, Table 1.4 and Table 7.7; Public Accounts of Canada, Vol. I, External Expenditures by Type, various years.

Figure B.4

Federal Revenues, Program Spending, and Deficit/Surplus as Percentage of GDP 1993–4 to 2003–4

Percentage of GDP

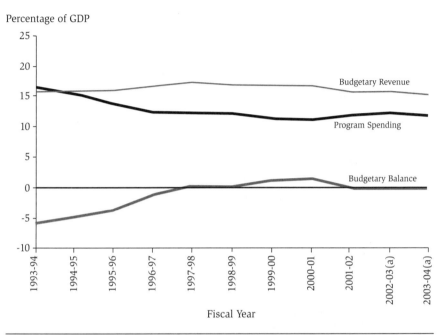

Fiscal Year

(a) Figures for these years are estimates.

Note: Budgetary revenue and program spending are based on fiscal years, while GDP is based on the calendar year. Revenues, program spending, and the deficit/surplus are on a net basis. Program spending does not include public interest charges. GDP is nominal GDP.
    Beginning in 1997–8, the budget deficit trend line changes to indicate a budgetary surplus as a percentage of the GDP.

Source: Department of Finance, *Fiscal Reference Tables*, October 2002, Table 2; Department of Finance, *Budget Plan 2001*, Table 1.4.

Table B.2
Federal Deficit/Surplus
1993–4 to 2004–05

Billions of Dollars (current)

Fiscal Year	Budgetary Revenue	Total Expenditures	Budgetary Deficit/Surplus	As % of GDP
1993–4	116.0	158.0	–42.0	–5.8
1994–5	123.3	160.8	–37.5	–4.9
1995–6	130.3	158.9	–28.6	–3.5
1996–7	140.9	149.8	–8.9	–1.1
1997–8	153.5	149.7	3.8	0.4
1998–9	155.9	152.8	3.1	0.3
1999–00	166.1	153.4	12.7	1.3
2000–1	179.6	161.4	18.1	1.7
2001–2	173.3	164.4	8.9	0.8
2002–3[a]	173.9	169.9	4.0	0.4
2003–4[a]	184.1	177.0	7.1	0.6
2004–5[a]	191.9	183.3	8.5	0.7

(a) Figures for these years are estimates.

Note: While revenue, expenditures, and deficit categories refer to fiscal years, nominal GDP is based upon a calendar year. Total expenditures include program spending and public debt charges.

Source: Department of Finance, *Fiscal Reference Tables*, October 2002, Tables 1 and 2; Department of Finance, *The Economic and Fiscal Update 2002*, 30 October 2002, Table 3.3.

Figure B.5
**Federal Revenue, Expenditures, and the Deficit
1995–6 to 2004–5**

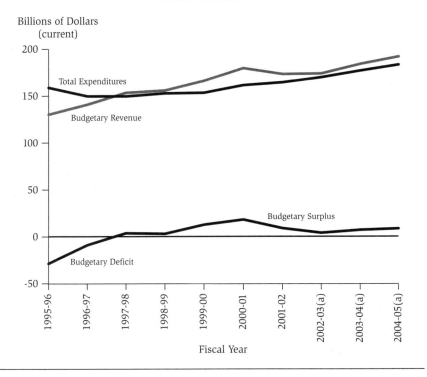

(a) Figures for these years are estimates.

Note: Expenditures include program spending and public interest charges on the debt.

Source: Department of Finance, *Fiscal Reference Tables*, October 2002, Tables 1 and 2;
Department of Finance, *Budget Plan 2001*, Table 1.4; *Public Accounts of Canada*, Statement
of Revenues and Expenditures, various years.

Figure B.6
Growth in Real GDP
1993–2002

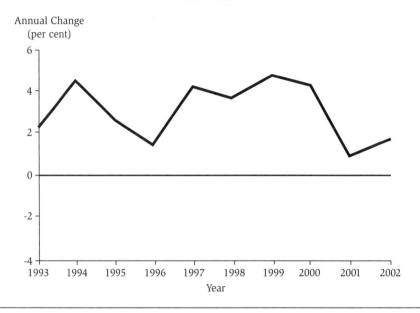

Source: Statistics Canada, *The Daily*, cat. # 13-001, various years.

Figure B.7

**Rates of Unemployment and Employment Growth
1993–2002**

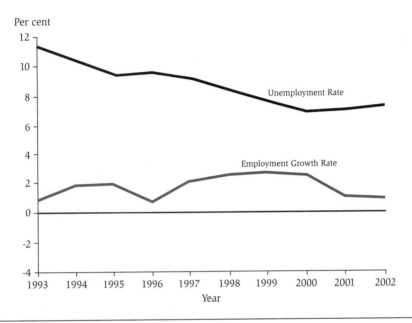

Note: Employment growth rates and the unemployment rate apply to both sexes, 15 years and older, and are seasonally adjusted.

Source: *Historical Labour Force Statistics* (71-201), Statistics Canada, various years.

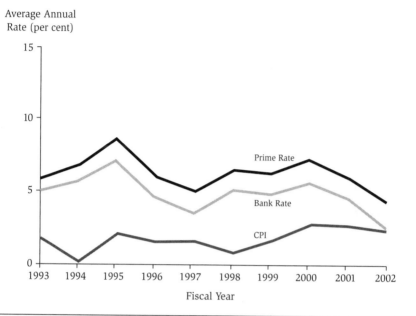

Figure B.8
Interest Rates and the Consumer Price Index (CPI)
1993–2002

Note: The CPI is not seasonally adjusted. The Prime Rate refers to the prime business inter-est rate charged by the chartered banks, and the Bank Rate refers to the rate charged by the Bank of Canada on any loans to commercial banks.

Source: *Bank of Canada Review*, Table F1, various years; Statistics Canada, *The Consumer Price Index*, cat. # 62-001, various years.

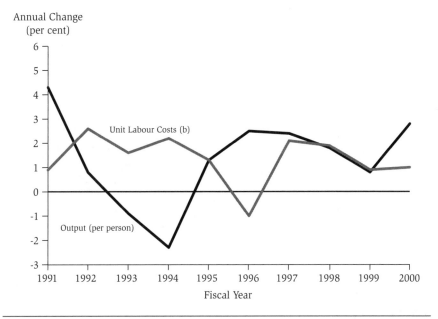

Figure B.9
Productivity and Costs
1991–2000

(a) Output per person hour is the real GDP per person hour worked in the business sector, and is a measure of productivity. This trend shows the annual percentage change of this indicator. Real GDP is based on constant 1986 prices.

(b) Unit Labour cost in the business sector is based on the real GDP, in constant 1986 prices. This trend shows the annual percentage change in this indicator.

Source: Statistics Canada, cat. # 15-204, various years.

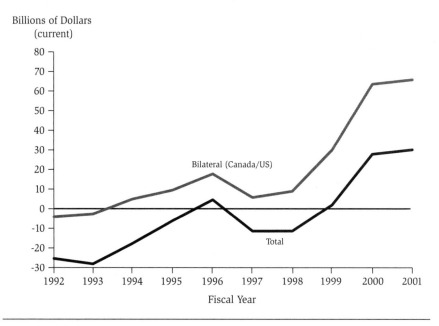

Figure B.10
Balance of Payments
1992 to 2001

Source: Statistics Canada, cat. # 67-001, various years.

Figure B.11
Growth in Real GDP
Canada and Selected Countries
1992–2001

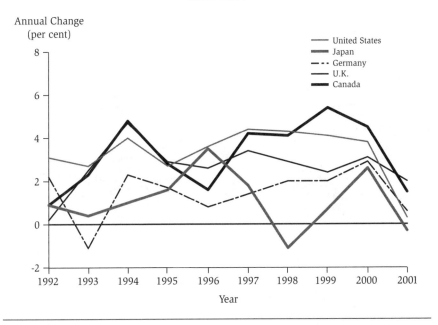

Source: Organization for Economic Cooperation and Development (OECD), *Economic Outlook*, no. 72, Dec. 2002, Annex Table 1.

Figure B.12
Standardized Unemployment Rates
Canada and Selected Countries
1992–2001

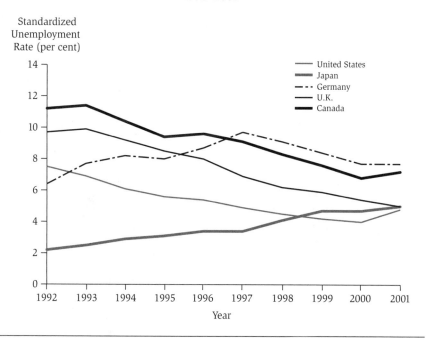

Source: *OECD Economic Outlook*, no. 72, Dec. 2002, Annex Table 15.

Figure B.13
Annual Inflation Rates
Canada and Selected Countries
1992–2001

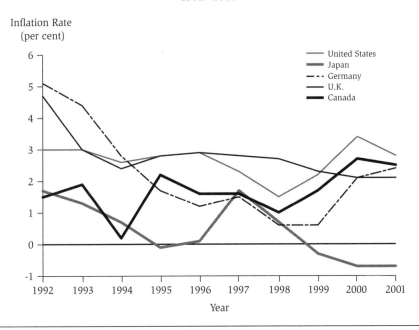

Source: *OECD Economic Outlook*, no. 72, Dec. 2002, Annex Table 19.

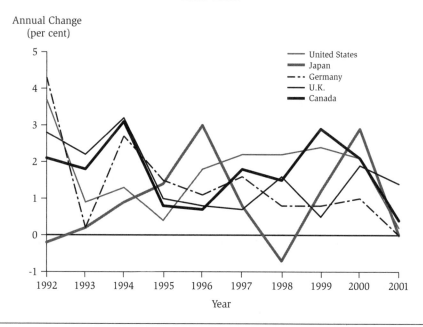

Figure B.14
Labour Productivity
Canada and Selected Countries
1992–2001

Note: Labour productivity is defined as output per unit of labour input. The data is for labour productivity growth in the business sector. The series on total economy unit labour cost was dropped because inclusion of the public sector was thought to be a distorting influence.

Source: *OECD Economic Outlook*, no. 72, Dec. 2002, Annex Table 13.

Table B.3
International Comparisons
1992–2001

Percentage Change from Previous Year

Growth in Real GDP

	1992	1993	1994	1995	1996	1997	1998	1999	2000	2001
Canada	0.9	2.3	4.8	2.8	1.6	4.2	4.1	5.4	4.5	1.5
US	3.1	2.7	4.0	2.7	3.6	4.4	4.3	4.1	3.8	0.3
Japan	0.9	0.4	1.0	1.6	3.5	1.8	-1.1	0.7	2.6	-0.3
Germany	2.2	-1.1	2.3	1.7	0.8	1.4	2.0	2.0	2.9	0.6
UK	0.2	2.5	4.7	2.9	2.6	3.4	2.9	2.4	3.1	2.0

Unemployment Rates

	1992	1993	1994	1995	1996	1997	1998	1999	2000	2001
Canada	11.2	11.4	10.4	9.4	9.6	9.1	8.3	7.6	6.8	7.2
US	7.5	6.9	6.1	5.6	5.4	4.9	4.5	4.2	4.0	4.8
Japan	2.2	2.5	2.9	3.1	3.4	3.4	4.1	4.7	4.7	5.0
Germany	6.4	7.7	8.2	8.0	8.7	9.7	9.1	8.4	7.7	7.7
UK	9.7	9.9	9.2	8.5	8.0	6.9	6.2	5.9	5.4	5.0

Labour productivity

	1992	1993	1994	1995	1996	1997	1998	1999	2000	2001
Canada	2.1	1.8	3.1	0.8	0.7	1.8	1.5	2.9	2.1	0.4
US	3.7	0.9	1.3	0.4	1.8	2.2	2.2	2.4	2.1	0.2
Japan	-0.2	0.2	0.9	1.4	3.0	0.8	-0.7	1.2	2.9	0.0
Germany	4.3	0.2	2.7	1.5	1.1	1.6	0.8	0.8	1.0	0.0
UK	2.8	2.2	3.2	1.0	0.8	0.7	1.6	0.5	1.9	1.4

Source: *OECD Economic Outlook*, No. 72, December 2002, Annex Tables 1, 13, 15.

ABSTRACTS / RÉSUMÉS

Geoffrey Hale

The Unfinished Legacy: Liberal Policy on North America

This chapter assesses the legacy of the Chrétien government in Canada–US relations, contrasting its relatively coherent approach to domestic priorities with its drifting, reactive responses to developments on cross-border policy issues. The federal government's traditional balancing act between the accommodation of closer economic relations with the United States and the pursuit of a 'distinctly Canadian' foreign policy has become increasingly tenuous since September 2001. The challenge this presents is reinforced by the segmentation and decentralization of policy-development on cross-border issues arising from the traditional federal avoidance of linkage between the management of cross-border disputes and internal debates over the most effective means of promoting Canadian sovereignty and identity. The chapter reviews tentative efforts by federal politicians to frame the continuing debate over Canada–US relations in ways that balance different concepts of sovereignty and political choice, thus setting the terms for debate during the upcoming Liberal leadership contest.

Ce chapitre évalue l'héritage Chrétien dans les relations canado-américaines et contraste l'approche relativement cohérente du gouvernement en matière de priorités internes avec les réponses réactives et peu constantes de celui-ci dans le domaine des questions transfrontalières. La tradition qui consiste à assurer un équilibre entre l'accommodement de relations économiques plus serrées avec les États-Unis d'une part, et la poursuite d'une politique étrangère "nettement canadienne" d'autre part, est devenue de plus en plus fragile depuis septembre 2001. Le problème est aggravé par la segmentation et la décentralisation de l'élaboration des politiques transfrontalières provenant de la tendance fédérale à éviter de lier les différents conflits transfrontaliers ainsi que des débats internes sur les moyens les plus efficaces de promouvoir la souveraineté et l'identité canadiennes. Ce chapitre examine les premiers efforts des politiciens fédéraux pour donner un cadre au débat continu sur les relations canado-américaines qui assure un équilibre entre les différents concepts de souveraineté et de choix politiques, donnant le ton aux débats de la course imminente à la direction du parti libéral.

Reg Whitaker

More or Less Than Meets the Eye? The New National Security Agenda

The terrorist attacks of 11 September 2001 were a relatively rare example of the sudden reprioritization of the policy agenda in Ottawa as the result of an external event. Although domestic concerns about security—supported by particular interests and advocates—were important, the most pressing factors shaping the new agenda were, first, the expectations of the United States with regard to the common standards and practices of coalition participants in the US-declared war on terrorism, and secondly, the implications for Canadian economic security of Canada–US border restrictions, post-11 September. In this chapter the Canadian response in terms of administrative arrangements and with respect to civil liberties and due process is contrasted to the US response. Attention is paid to the legal response (the Anti-Terrorism act, the Public Safety bill); budgetary reallocations to security; the reorganization of security and intelligence functions; military contributions to the war on terrorism; initiatives on border security and refugee policy; and the management of the impact of ethnic risk profiling on multicultural relations. Canada's responses are assessed as more damage limitation with respect to Canadian economic security than as positive anti-terrorist initiatives. Nor is the impact very durable: within less than a year, priorities had largely reverted to the old, pre-11 September policy agenda.

Les attaques terroristes du 11 septembre 2001 constituent un exemple plutôt rare d'un événement externe qui a soudain donné de nouvelles priorités au programme d'élaboration des politiques d'Ottawa. Malgré l'importance des préoccupations internes relatives à la sécurité (soutenue par certains groupes d'intérêt), il n'en reste pas moins que le facteur le plus pressant dans la formulation des politiques était constitué premièrement par les attentes américaines quant à l'établissement de normes et pratiques communes chez les membres de la coalition dans la guerre au terrorisme déclarée par les États-Unis, et deuxièmement par les implications pour la sécurité économique canadienne des restrictions frontalières à la suite du 11 septembre. Ce chapitre contraste les réponses des deux pays en ce qui concerne les arrangements administratifs ainsi que les libertés civiles et la procédure équitable. Nous examinons la réponse juridique (la Loi antiterroriste, la Loi sur la sécurité publique), les réaffectations budgétaires au profit de la sécurité ; la réorganisation des fonctions de sécurité et de renseignement ; les contributions militaires à la guerre contre le terrorisme ; les initiatives en matière de sécurité à la frontière et de politique à l'égard des réfugiés ; la gestion de l'impact du profilage ethnique sur les relations multiculturelles. On estime que les réponses canadiennes visent à limiter les dégâts en matière de sécurité économique plutôt qu'à prendre des initiatives antiterroristes positives. L'impact n'est pas durable non plus : en moins d'un an, les priorités étaient redevenues en grande partie ce qu'elles étaient avant le 11 septembre.

Jonathan Malloy
The House of Commons Under the Chrétien Government
This chapter examines the status of the House of Commons under the Chrétien government, particularly since the 2000 election. It argues that the House has seen significant but not transformative changes under Jean Chrétien. Looking at four different dimensions of parliamentary activity—policy ideas, accountability, the passage of bills, and leadership struggles—the chapter shows that MPs have become more assertive and influential, even to the point of undermining their own party leaders. However, it is not clear whether these developments represent permanent changes to the institution.

The chapter suggests that a major reason for Members' assertiveness is the unusually high number of seasoned MPs in the current 37th Parliament. The relatively low turnover of MPs in the 1990s means that the large group of government backbenchers elected in 1993 have become thoroughly familiar with parliamentary institutions and policy issues. They also realize that their hopes of cabinet promotion are increasingly slim, and these factors have prompted them to develop more assertive and influential identities as backbench MPs. However, conflicting expectations and assumptions remain about the role of Members in a parliamentary system of government such as Canada's.

Ce chapitre examine le statut de la Chambre des communes sous le gouvernement Chrétien, en particulier depuis les élections de 2000. Nous soutenons que la Chambre a vu des changements significatifs, mais non transformateurs, sous Jean Chrétien. En regardant quatre dimensions différentes de l'activité parlementaire - les idées en matière de politiques, la responsabilité, l'adoption des lois et la course à la direction - ce chapitre montre que les députés se sont affirmés et ont acquis plus de poids, au point même de miner le pouvoir de leur propre chef. Il n'est cependant pas évident qu'il s'agisse de changements permanents à l'institution.

Ce chapitre suggère que cette nouvelle assurance remonte en grande partie au nombre exceptionnellement élevé de députés expérimentés siégeant au trente-septième parlement. Le faible roulement des députés au cours des années 90 a fait que les députés élus en 1993 connaissent à fond les institutions parlementaires et les questions en matière de politiques. Conscients de leurs chances de plus en plus faibles d'une promotion au Cabinet, ils se sont fait une identité plus assurée et plus influente de députés d'arrière-ban. Des attentes et des hypothèses conflictuelles persistent, cependant, quant au rôle des députés dans un système parlementaire tel que celui du Canada.

Debora VanNijnatten and Douglas MacDonald
Reconciling Energy and Climate Change Policies: How Ottawa Blends
Three policy options are currently being considered by the Chrétien government as it attempts both to meet an international Kyoto commitment and to continue to use energy policy as a major element of economic development. These options are: moving to a lower-carbon economy; developing technology to reduce the carbon intensity of manufacturing and transport; and gaining credit for carbon sinks and clean energy exports. The contradiction between the Chrétien government's energy objective and its climate objective could be resolved by a combination of these three measures, but only if the Prime Minister and cabinet provide leadership far more clear and consistent than any seen to date. Moreover, the lack of a coherent strategy at the political level is replicated at the administrative level. Although there has been greater coordination of energy and climate policy objectives and programs over the past few years, the development of climate policy continues to rest with Environment Canada, whose raison d'être is environmental protection, while imple-

mentation rests largely with Natural Resources Canada, the premier energy depart-ment. This division of responsibilities, the authors argue, must give way to more organizational and program coherence.

Le gouvernement Chrétien considère actuellement trois possibilités de politiques dans la tentative de tenir un engagement international relatif au protocole de Kyoto et en même temps de continuer à utiliser la politique énergétique comme élément majeur du développement économique : la transition vers une économie à plus faible car-bone ; le développement d'une technologie permettant de réduire l'intensité en car-bone des usines et de l'industrie des transports ; et le mérite des puits de carbone et des exportations d'énergie propre. Une combinaison de ces trois mesures pourrait résoudre la contradiction entre les objectifs du gouvernement Chrétien en matière d'énergie et ceux en matière de climat, mais il faudrait un niveau de leadership de la part du premier ministre et de son cabinet qui soit beaucoup plus clair et plus cohérent. De plus, le manque d'une stratégie cohérente au niveau politique se repro-duit au niveau administratif. S'il y a eu une plus grande coordination d'objectifs et de programmes en ce qui concerne l'énergie et le climat au cours des dernières années, il n'en reste pas moins que l'élaboration de politiques climatiques continue de résider chez Environnement Canada, qui a comme raison d'être la protection de l'environnement, alors que la mise en oeuvre de celles-ci réside en grande partie chez Ressources naturelles Canada, ministère de l'énergie par excellence. Nous soutenons que cette division des responsabilités doit être remplacée par une cohérence accrue au niveau de l'organisation et des programmes.

Gerard W. Boychuk
The Federal Role in Health Care Reform: Legacy or Limbo?
Over the past year the federal political context has shifted dramatically, and the challenges to the successful achievement of major health care reform now seem sig-nificantly more daunting. Internal leadership challenges have undermined the Chré-tien government's ability to deal forcefully with the provinces, and the latter appear well positioned to demand large financial concessions from the federal government. At the same time, internal leadership politics are likely to constrain the commitment of federal funds. In the wake of the Kirby Committee and Romanow Commission reports, the federal government will undoubtedly undertake a major health care reform initiative. However, given these changing political dynamics, it will take con-siderable skill for the Prime Minister to successfully deliver major health care reform. In examining these issues, this chapter first provides an overview of the main substantive issues confronting the federal government in health care. It then considers how the federal role in health care reform has been affected by the politics of both the Chrétien legacy agenda and the federal Liberal leadership. Finally, it briefly overviews the Kirby Committee and Romanow Commission reports and con-siders whether they seem likely to provide a promising blueprint for federal health care reform in the final period of Jean Chrétien's tenure as prime minister.

Au cours de cette dernière année, le contexte politique fédéral a changé de façon dramatique et les défis que devra relever une réforme majeure des soins de santé semblent encore plus grands. Les conflits internes quant à la direction du parti ont miné la capacité du gouvernement Chrétien de traiter avec les provinces de pied ferme et celles-ci paraissent bien placées pour exiger des concessions financières importantes de la part du gouvernement fédéral. En même temps, la lutte au sein du parti va probablement restreindre l'engagement de fonds fédéraux. À la suite des rapports du comité Kirby et de la commission Romanow, le gouvernement fédéral entreprendra sans aucun doute une initiative majeure en matière de réforme des soins de santé. Cependant, vu la dynamique politique changeante, le premier ministre devra être très habile pour mener à bien cette réforme. En examinant ces questions, ce chapitre donne premièrement un aperçu des grandes questions de fond auxquelles le gouvernement doit faire face dans le domaine de la santé. Nous traitons ensuite des façons dont le rôle joué par le fédéral dans la réforme des soins de santé a été influencé par la politique de l'héritage Chrétien ainsi que la lutte à la direction. Nous examinons finalement les rapports Kirby et Romanow et nous nous demandons si ceux-ci vont fournir un plan directeur prometteur pour la réforme des soins de santé dans cette période finale du mandat du premier ministre.

Allan Tupper

The Chrétien Governments and Higher Education: A Quiet Revolution in Canadian Public Policy

The governments of Prime Minister Jean Chrétien have launched major programs for research at Canadian universities. Such programs have substantially strengthened the research capacity of universities. Major federal initiatives include the Canada Foundation for Innovation, the Canada Research Chairs, the Canadian Institutes for Health Research, and the Millennium Scholarship Foundation. These programs are the driving forces in Canadian universities. They are strongly supported by universities, even though they have altered university priorities.

The government of Canada sees university research as a crucial determinant of Canada's economic future. Its overall program for universities is to attract outstanding researchers to Canada, to promote greater commercialization of university research, and to provide incentives for interdisciplinary research. These themes are emphasized in the Innovation Strategy, unveiled in 2002 by Industry Canada and Human Resources Development Canada. Another major federal program for universities—this time for the 'indirect costs' of federal research—is likely to be funded very soon.

The chapter shows that in 2003 Canadian universities look to Ottawa, not to provincial capitals, for leadership. Anxieties have been expressed about the possibility that the role of smaller universities, where research is a lesser priority, will be diminished, and about the impact of federal policy on humanities and social science. A major question is whether universities can meet Ottawa's high expectations for a substantial economic payoff from university research.

Les gouvernements de Jean Chrétien ont lancé des programmes majeurs favorisant les recherches au sein des universités canadiennes. De tels programmes ont renforcé de façon importante la capacité en recherches de celles-ci. Parmi ces initiatives, on compte la Fondation canadienne pour l'innovation, le Programme des chaires de recherche du Canada, les Instituts de recherche en santé du Canada ainsi que les Bourses d'études canadiennes du millénaire. Ces programmes constituent des élé-ments moteurs dans les universités canadiennes. Ils jouissent d'un appui solide de la part des universités même s'ils ont modifié les priorités de celles-ci.

Le gouvernement du Canada voit la recherche comme déterminante dans l'avenir économique du Canada. Le programme global dans le domaine des universités vise à attirer des chercheurs exceptionnels vers le Canada, à favoriser une commercialisation accrue de la recherche dans les universités et à inciter la recherche interdisciplinaire. Ces thèmes sont soulignés dans la Stratégie d'innovation lancée en 2002 par Industrie Canada et Développement des ressources humaines Canada. On prévoit l'inauguration prochaine d'un autre programme fédéral majeur à l'intention des universités, cette fois-ci pour les "coûts indirects" de la recherche fédérale.

Ce chapitre montre qu'en 2003 les universités canadiennes en quête de leadership se tournent vers Ottawa, plutôt que vers les capitales provinciales. Certains ont exprimé des inquiétudes sur le rôle diminué que joueront peut-être les petites universités où la recherche est moins prioritaire ainsi que sur l'impact de la politique fédérale sur les humanités et les sciences sociales. Il reste à savoir si les universités pourront répondre à l'attente d'Ottawa en assurant l'importance des retombées économiques de leurs recherches.

Joanne Kelly

The Pursuit of an Elusive Ideal: Spending Review and Reallocation Under the Chrétien Government

The Chrétien government's efforts to reform the expenditure management system in Ottawa provide some important lessons about the usefulness of review and reallocation in public expenditure management. First, review and reallocation have been used on various occasions by the government, but to pursue three distinct budgetary objectives: fiscal restraint, reprioritization, and the encouragement of better program management. As the budgetary environment shifted—deficit turned to surplus or the government moved to implement new policy initiatives—new budget tools were developed that adapted the practices of review and reallocation to address specific budgetary problems. No single model was able to achieve all three objectives equally well. This reminds us that while review and reallocation are useful tools in expenditure management, they are not ends in themselves. A second and related point is that any view or assumption that review and reallocation are inextricably linked is not supported by recent experience.

A review of government programs can provide useful information for budget decision-makers, but it will not necessarily provide evidence that leads incontrovertibly to the support of reallocation. Nor will it replace the need for the government to make political choices. Finally, review and reallocation will often under-mine one of the fundamental—if often forgotten—objectives of government budget-ing: conflict resolution. Incorporating reallocation and review into the expenditure management system is politically and technically difficult. Governments will only tolerate the political turmoil associated with review and reallocation if they believe that the pain is unavoidable, or that it will be counterbalanced by rewards in other areas. Under these circumstances it is difficult to envisage any technical solution that would provide the 'best way' to encourage review and achieve reallocation, despite the rhetoric of some.

Les efforts du gouvernement Chrétien pour réformer le système de gestion des dépenses d'Ottawa fournit des leçons intéressantes sur l'utilité de l'examen et de la réaffectation dans la gestion des dépenses publiques. Premièrement, l'examen et la réaffectation ont été utilisés à plusieurs reprises par le gouvernement afin d'atteindre trois objectifs budgétaires distincts : les restrictions budgétaires, l'établissement de nouvelles priorités, et l'encouragement à une meilleure gestion des programmes. À mesure que l'environnement budgétaire changeait - le déficit devenant un excédent ou le gouvernement cherchant à mettre en oeuvre de nouvelles initiatives - de nou-veaux outils budgétaires ont été développés qui adaptaient les pratiques d'examen et de réaffectation pour s'attaquer à des problèmes budgétaires spécifiques. Aucun mod-èle unique n'a pu atteindre également bien ces trois objectifs. Cela nous rappelle que l'examen et la réaffectation sont utiles dans la gestion des dépenses mais que ceux-ci ne constituent pas des fins en soi. Ensuite, il faut retenir que l'idée qu'il existe un lien inextricable entre examen et réaffectation n'est pas appuyée par les expériences récentes. Si l'examen des programmes peut fournir des renseignements utiles aux décideurs budgétaires, celui-ci n'apporte pas nécessairement des arguments irréfuta-bles en faveur de la réaffectation. L'examen n'enlève pas non plus aux gouverne-ments la nécessité de faire des choix politiques. Finalement, l'examen et la réaffectation minent souvent l'un des objectifs fondamentaux - souvent oubliés - de l'élaboration des budgets : la résolution des conflits. Il est difficile sur le plan poli-tique et technique d'incorporer la réaffectation et l'examen dans le système de gestion des dépenses. Les gouvernements ne sont prêts à tolérer le trouble politique relié à l'examen et à la réaffectation que s'ils croient la douleur inévitable, ou si celle-ci est contrebalancée par des récompenses dans d'autres domaines. Dans les circonstances, il est difficile d'envisager une solution technique quelconque qui puisse fournir la "meilleure façon" d'encourager l'examen et de réussir la réaffectation, malgré la rhé-torique de certains.

Michael Prince

Taking Stock: Governance Practices and Portfolio Performance of the Canada Pension Plan Investment Board

Established in 1998 by the federal government and participating provincial govern-ments, the Canada Pension Plan (CPP) Investment Board is a Crown corporation with a mandate to invest CPP savings in capital markets. This chapter examines the political origins of the Board, its corporate governance, organizational culture, and investment policy framework, and the performance of the assets it manages. The Board's governance requirements and ethical practices are exemplary for pension plans and for government organizations. While definitely an instrument of federal and provincial policy, on matters of management or investment the Board is largely independent of governments. The Board, striving to be a virtual corporation, keeps its staff small by relying on the contracting of investment, legal, and other services with external partners. The Board is also guided by policies of transparency to the public and strong policies on conflict of interest. The author concludes that with assets likely to approach $150 billion within a decade, the Board's long-term achievements may facilitate the expansion of CPP retirement benefits. Whereas executive federalism in the past may have restrained the liberalization of pension benefits, the equity capitalism of the Investment Board may well give confidence in the future, and promote the expansion of CPP benefits.

Établi en 1998 par le gouvernement fédéral et les gouvernements provinciaux participants, l'Office d'investissement du régime de pensions du Canada (RPC) est une société de la Couronne ayant comme mandat d'investir les économies du RPC dans les marchés financiers. Ce chapitre examine les origines politiques de l'Office, son gouvernement d'entreprise, sa culture organisationnelle, le cadre de sa politique de placement ainsi que le rendement des actifs gérés par l'Office. L'Office a des exigences en matière de gouvernance pour les régimes de pensions et pour les organisations gouvernementales. Tout en étant un instrument de politique fédérale et provinciale, l'Office est en grande partie indépendante des gouvernements en ce qui concerne la gestion ou le placement. L'Office cherche à être une société virtuelle, conservant un personnel restreint et faisant appel à la sous-traitance de services juridiques et de placement auprès de partenaires externes. L'Office est guidé aussi par des politiques de transparence devant le public et par des politiques fortes relatives aux conflits d'intérêt. L'Office ayant des actifs susceptibles d'atteindre les 150 milliards $ d'ici dix ans, nous concluons que les réussites à long terme de l'Office pourront bien faciliter l'expansion des prestations de retraite du RPC. Alors que le fédéralisme exécutif a pu restreindre la libéralisation des prestations de retraite, le capitalisme boursier de l'Office pourra à l'avenir assurer la confiance et promouvoir l'expansion des prestations de retraite du RPC.

Ross Finnie, Saul Schwartz, and Eric Lascelles
'Smart Money'? Government Spending on Student Financial Aid in Canada
The last decade was a tumultuous one for student financial aid programs in Canada. As tuition fees rose substantially, provincial governments replaced many of their grant programs with loans; a few years later loan remission programs were introduced. The structure of the Canada Student Loans Program (CSLP) changed twice. Loan limits and other program parameters were adjusted, and interest relief pro-

grams for those experiencing repayment difficulties were expanded. Education-related tax credits were ramped up and a new credit for interest on student loans was put in place. The Canada Millennium Scholarship Foundation was created and began disbursing funds. This chapter estimates the amount of government spending on the various student financial aid programs in the 2000/1 fiscal year. It includes not only the standard types of aid, such as loans and grants, but also some less obvious ones, such as tax credits. The interesting and, in some cases, surprising results include a finding that spending is increasingly geared to supporting the middle classes rather than low-income students and families. The estimates create an empirical basis for future discussions regarding the structure of government spending on student financial assistance, how resources could perhaps be spent differently, and whether overall spending levels should be adjusted.

La dernière décennie a été mouvementée en ce qui concerne les programmes d'aide financière aux étudiants du Canada. Alors que les frais de scolarité augmentaient de façon importante, les gouvernements provinciaux ont remplacé plusieurs de leurs programmes de bourses par des programmes de prêts ; des programmes de remises des dettes ont été introduits quelques années plus tard. La structure du Programme canadien de prêts aux étudiants (PCPE) a changé deux fois. Les limites de prêts et d'autres paramètres de programmes ont été ajustés, et les programmes d'exemption de paiement d'intérêts pour ceux qui avaient des difficultés à rembourser ont été étendus. Les crédits d'impôt relatifs à l'éducation ont été majorés et un nouveau crédit pour l'intérêt des prêts aux étudiants a été mis en place. La Fondation canadienne des bourses du millénaire a été créée et a commencé à verser des fonds. Ce chapitre évalue le montant de dépenses gouvernementales, dans l'année fiscale 2000-01, sur les différents programmes d'aide financière aux étudiants. Nous tenons compte non seulement des types standard d'aide, tels que les prêts et bourses, mais également des types moins évidents, tels que les crédits d'impôt. Les résultats sont intéressants, y compris la constatation que les dépenses sont de plus en plus axées sur le soutien des classes moyennes plutôt que des étudiants et des familles à faible revenu. Ces évaluations fournissent une base empirique pour des discussions futures sur la structure des dépenses gouvernementales relatives à l'aide financière aux étudiants, la possibilité de distribuer autrement les ressources ainsi que l'opportunité d'ajuster les niveaux globaux de niveaux de dépenses.

John de la Mothe
Ottawa's Imaginary Innovation Strategy: Progress or Drift?
The chapter reviews the Chrétien Liberals' February 2002 Innovation Strategy against the backdrop of both leadership politics and the longer track record of the government since 1993. The chapter concludes that innovation is centrally important to the future of Canada, that many parts of government are being innovative, thoughtful, and entrepreneurial, and that many are attentive to what has been done already (and why). However, the Liberals' 2002 Innovation Strategy exercise was

fraught with flaws. Most importantly, it lacked content, and as an exercise was fraught with confusion.

The chapter shows that the Innovation Strategy demonstrated a remarkable discontinuity with more progressive science, technology, and innovation policy documents produced by Chrétien governments between 1993 and 2000. To a much greater extent than the Innovation Srategy, these were informed by a framework. The author concludes that the entire process has resulted in nothing resembling a strategy, an agenda, or a consultation. Whereas the 1993 to 2000 period could reasonably be labelled a period of progress in the area of science, technology, and innovation policy, this most recent exercise must be characterized as a soon-to-be-forgotten period of mere 'drift' in the midst of a sea of innovation-based activities, both within and outside government.

Ce chapitre traite de la Stratégie d'innovation de février 2002 lancée par les libéraux et examine celle-ci dans le contexte de la course à la direction du parti et dans celui du dossier du gouvernement depuis 1993. Nous concluons que l'innovation joue un rôle central pour l'avenir du Canada et que plusieurs secteurs de gouvernement font preuve d'innovation, de réflexion et d'esprit d'entreprise et que plusieurs accordent une attention à ce qui a déjà été fait (et pourquoi). Cependant, l'exercice de la stratégie d'innovation de 2002 était plein de défauts. Ce qui est encore plus grave, cette stratégie manquait de contenu et était désordonné. Ce chapitre démontre que la stratégie d'innovation montrait une discontinuité par rapport aux documents politiques plus progressifs en matière de science, technologie et innovation produits par les gouvernements Chrétien entre 1993 et 2000. Ceux-ci étaient beaucoup plus informés par un cadre politique que ce n'est le cas pour la stratégie d'innovation. Nous concluons que le processus dans l'ensemble n'a produit ni stratégie, ni programme ni consultation. Si la période 1993–2000 a pu raisonnablement être étiquetée comme une période de progrès dans le domaine de la politique en matière de science, technologie et innovation, ce tout dernier exercice doit être caractérisé comme une période qui sera bientôt oubliée, une simple vague dans toute une mer d'activités axées sur l'innovation à l'intérieur et à l'extérieur du gouvernement.

Richard Schultz

Dancing Around the Digital Divide: The Fight for a Federal Broadband Access Policy

Ever since the 2000 election and the subsequent Speech from the Throne in 2001, the federal government has placed a high priority on a program to provide all Canadian communities with high-speed broadband access to the Internet. This chapter analyses the political, bureaucratic, and interest group processes that resulted in a very different program—a much more modest one in terms of both funds and focus. The chapter begins with a discussion of two of the most important background issues that should have informed the policy development process but for the most part did not: the perils of designing policy at a time of technological turmoil, and the confusion that exists over the very concept of a 'digital divide'. The next section reviews and assesses the results of, and reaction to, the National Broadband Task Force, which was dominated by corporate and bureaucratic interests that would be among the primary beneficiaries of a generous, largely federally-funded broadband 'pipeline' policy. The analysis then shows how the proposed policy became caught up in the political competition not only between the then ministers of finance and industry but also between their departments. The chapter concludes with commentary on the program that was announced in September 2002.

Depuis les élections de 2000 et le discours du Trône de 2001, le gouvernement fédéral a accordé une haute priorité au programme visant à rendre les services Internet à large bande et à haute vitesse accessibles aux citoyens de toutes les collectivités du Canada. Ce chapitre analyse les processus impliquant des groupes d'intérêt, la politique et la bureaucratie qui ont abouti à un programme très différent - beaucoup plus modeste quant à son financement et son envergure. Ce chapitre commence par une discussion de deux des plus grandes questions de fond qui auraient dû informer le processus d'élaboration des programmes mais qui, pour la plupart, ne l'ont pas fait, à savoir le danger qu'il y a de formuler une politique à un moment de trouble technologique ainsi que la confusion qui existe autour du concept même de "fossé numérique". La section suivante examine et évalue les résultats du Groupe de travail national sur les services à large bande ainsi que la réaction à celui-ci. Le Groupe était dominé par les entreprises et la bureaucratie qui devaient être parmi les premiers à tirer profit d'une politique généreuse, financée en grande partie par le fédéral, visant à généraliser l'accès à l'Internet. Cette analyse montre ensuite la façon dont cette politique s'est fait prendre dans la concurrence politique entre le ministre des Finances et le ministre de l'Industrie ainsi que celle entre leurs ministères respectifs. Ce chapitre conclut par un commentaire final sur le programme qui a été annoncé en septembre 2002.

Jeff Kinder
The Doubling of Government Science and Canada's Innovation Strategy
The Chrétien government has announced its intention to double the federal investment in research and development by 2010. Much of this investment, if it materializes, will likely pass through the federal government to universities and the private sector. But supporters of science performed within the federal government are hopeful that, after sustaining tight budgets and in some cases deep cuts during the 1990s, government laboratories and research institutes will receive new investments to deal with the diverse and complex challenges they are expected to address. While new investment may be tied to the promotion of an 'innovation agenda', there are other 'public good' roles supported by government science that make calls for new funding compelling. But any such reinvestment will likely come through new funding models that stress national priority issues, horizontal collaboration, and competitive selection. This chapter traces the historical evolution of government science

and its diverse roles within the national innovation system. It then explores recent initiatives, including the proposed Federal Innovation Networks of Excellence (FINE), to reform the governance of government science. Finally, the chapter offers some conclusions as to the future direction of government science and its role in Canada's overall innovation agenda.

Le gouvernement Chrétien a annoncé son intention de doubler l'investissement en recherche et développement d'ici 2010. Une bonne partie de cet investissement, si celui-ci se matérialise, ira sans doute du gouvernement fédéral aux universités et au secteur privé. Mais ceux qui appuient la science au sein du gouvernement espèrent bien qu'après les budgets serrés et certaines compressions importantes au cours des années 1990, les laboratoires et les instituts de recherche du gouvernement recevront de nouveaux investissements pour les aider à relever les défis divers et complexes auxquels ils devront faire face. Si le nouvel investissement peut bien être lié à la promotion d'un "programme d'innovation", il y a d'autres rôles favorisant le "bien public" soutenus par la science au sein du gouvernement qui rendent convaincantes les demandes d'un nouveau financement. Mais un tel réinvestissement viendra probablement par l'entremise de nouveaux modèles de financement qui mettent l'accent sur les questions de priorités nationales, de collaboration horizontale, et de sélection compétitive. Ce chapitre retrace l'évolution historique de la science au sein du gouvernement et les différents rôles de celle-ci à l'intérieur de système national d'innovation. Nous explorons ensuite des initiatives récentes, dont les réseaux fédéraux d'excellence en innovation visant à réformer la gouvernance de la science gouvernementale. Nous terminons par quelques conclusions sur la direction future de la science au sein du gouvernement ainsi que son rôle dans la stratégie globale d'innovation du Canada.

CONTRIBUTORS

Gerard W. Boychuk is an Assistant Professor of Political Science at the University of Waterloo.

John de la Mothe is a Professor in the Faculty of Administration at the University of Ottawa.

G. Bruce Doern is a Professor in the School of Public Policy and Administration at Carleton University and holds a joint Research Chair in Public Policy in the Politics Department at the University of Exeter.

Ross Finnie is a Research Fellow and Adjunct Professor in the School of Policy Studies at Queen's University.

Geoffrey E. Hale is an Assistant Professor of Political Science at the University of Lethbridge.

Joanne Kelly is an Assistant Professor of Political Science at Griffith University in Australia.

Jeffrey Kinder is a Ph.D. student in the School of Public Policy and Administration at Carleton University.

Eric Lascelles is a graduate student in the Department of Economics at Queen's University.

Douglas MacDonald is a Lecturer in the Environmental Studies Program at Innis College, the University of Toronto.

Jonathan Malloy is an Assistant Professor in the Department of Political Science at Carleton University.

Michael Prince is the Lansdowne Professor of Social Policy and an Associate Dean in Social Development at the University of Victoria.

Richard J. Schultz is a Professor in the Department of Political Science at McGill University.

Saul Schwartz is a Professor in the School of Public Policy and Administration at Carleton University.

Allan Tupper is a Professor in the Department of Political Science at the University of British Columbia.

Debora L. VanNijnatten is an Assistant Professor in the Department of Political Science at Wilfrid Laurier University.

Reg Whitaker is a Visiting Professor in the Department of Political Science at the University of Victoria.

THE SCHOOL OF PUBLIC POLICY AND ADMINISTRATION
at Carleton University is a national centre for the study of public
policy and public management.

The School's Centre for Policy and Program Assessment provides research services and courses in the evaluation of public policies, programs, and activities to interest groups, businesses, unions, and governments.

The *How Ottawa Spends* Series

How Ottawa Spends 2002–2003: The Security Aftermath and National Priorities
edited by G. Bruce Doern

How Ottawa Spends 2001–2002: Power in Transition
edited by Leslie A. Pal

How Ottawa Spends 2000–2001: Past Imperfect, Future Tense
edited by Leslie A. Pal

How Ottawa Spends 1999–2000: Shape Shifting: Canadian Governance Toward the 21st Century
edited by Leslie A. Pal

How Ottawa Spends 1998–99: Balancing Act: The Post-Deficit Mandate
edited by Leslie A. Pal

How Ottawa Spends 1997–98: Seeing Red: A Liberal Report Card
edited by Gene Swimmer

How Ottawa Spends 1996–97: Life Under the Knife
edited by Gene Swimmer

How Ottawa Spends 1995–96: Mid-Life Crises
edited by Susan D. Phillips

How Ottawa Spends 1994–95: Making Change
edited by Susan D. Phillips

How Ottawa Spends 1993–94: A More Democratic Canada . . . ?
edited by Susan D. Phillips

How Ottawa Spends 1992–93: The Politics of Competitiveness
edited by Frances Abele

How Ottawa Spends 1991–92: The Politics of Fragmentation
edited by Frances Abele

How Ottawa Spends 1990–91: Tracking the Second Agenda
edited by Katherine A. Graham

How Ottawa Spends 1989–90: The Buck Stops Where?
edited by Katherine A. Graham

How Ottawa Spends 1988–89: The Conservatives Heading into the Stretch
edited by Katherine A. Graham

How Ottawa Spends 1987–88: Restraining the State
edited by Michael J. Prince

How Ottawa Spends 1986–87: Tracking the Tories
edited by Michael J. Prince

How Ottawa Spends 1985: Sharing the Pie
edited by Allan M. Maslove

How Ottawa Spends 1984: The New Agenda
edited by Allan M. Maslove

How Ottawa Spends 1983: The Liberals, The Opposition & Federal Priorities
edited by G. Bruce Doern

How Ottawa Spends Your Tax Dollars: National Policy and Economic Development 1982
edited by G. Bruce Doern

How Ottawa Spends Your Tax Dollars: Federal Priorities 1981
edited by G. Bruce Doern

Spending Tax Dollars: Federal Expenditures, 1980–81
edited by G. Bruce Doern